Developmental Discipline

Developmental Discipline

KEVIN WALSH AND MILLY COWLES

with special chapters by
JAMES MICHAEL LEE
and
JALAN AUFDERHEIDE

Religious Education Press
Birmingham, Alabama

Library of Congress Cataloging in Publication Data

Walsh, Kevin, 1946–
  Developmental discipline.

  Includes bibliographical references and index.
  1. School discipline.   2. Educational sociology.
3. Discipline of children.   4. Discipline.   5. Conduct
of life.   I. Cowles, Milly.   II. Lee, James Michael.
III. Aufderheide, JAlan.   IV. Title.
LB3012.W34   1982   371.5   82-13305
ISBN 0-89135-032-2

Religious Education Press, Inc.
1531 Wellington Road
Birmingham, Alabama 35209
10   9   8   7   6   5   4   3   2

Contents

Preface

The aim of this book is to consider critically and constructively the intimate relationship between American society and the discipline process by which its young will develop the essentials of their culture. *Developmental Discipline* is expressly designed for use by students of education, teachers, school administrators, parents, leaders of youth groups, and all others who are concerned with the healthy development of society's young people.

This volume reflects an attempt at relating developmental theory and practice to the task of discipline. It is the fruit both of research on the development of children and of personal first-hand practical experiences with children. *Developmental Discipline* should be viewed by those who read it as a beginning of the solution to the difficult problem of discipline for social education rather than as an end to the problem.

It is a pleasure to acknowledge those scholars and practitioners whose works and ideas are used in this book and who have influenced the position of the authors. I would like to thank Shirley Foster and Bette Vos for their helpful research, and their stylistic and typewriting assistance. I am particularly grateful to Janet Crocker who painstakingly supervised and skillfully coordinated all phases of the editorial work involved in the preparation of this book.

I am most especially indebted to my wife, Donna Linn Walsh, for her wonderful patience and unflagging support during the many months of writing.

Kevin Walsh

CHAPTER 1

Cultural Crisis and Discipline

The Roots of the Crisis

A serious, objective examination shows clearly that the American culture has certain morals and values which are vital to its existence. The present generation is living in a time in which major decisions must be made concerning the directions of the future culture. There is the ominous responsibility to reconstruct lost morals and values in the society, or perhaps face the steady disintegration of the "American way of life." The present time is pregnant with possibilities for leading the way to a better society. But the present time is also filled with dangerous trends and nihilistic apathy. Traditional values are being questioned and violated. Nearly a century of advances in technology and science has generated radically changed forms of the economic and industrial nature of the society with little reformulation of the social processes taking place. We have indeed become, as George Counts stated, "so enraptured by technological advance that we have tended to conceive human progress largely in its terms. We are learning today, to our sorrow, that this advance, when not accompanied by equally profound reconstruction in the realms of understanding and value, of customs and institutions, of attitudes and loyalties, can bring trouble and disaster."[1]

John Dewey put it well when he wrote: "A culture which

permits science to destroy traditional values but which distrusts its powers to create new ones is a culture which is destroying itself."[2]

Societies must sustain themselves through a planned educational process (both formal and informal; in the school and the home) by which the young and immature acquire the insights, beliefs, morals, values, and desires of the older, more mature members of society. For culture is the "social inheritance" from preceding generations in a society as complex as that of the United States, and it is absurd to think that this process can be left to chance, hoping that somehow children will gain the beliefs of the culture. It is equally difficult to believe that children can be brought into the totality of their culture merely by hammering in or training them in desired beliefs. A democratic society demands that its citizens possess their beliefs as a result of thought, not merely as reflex habits of action. They can only gain the desired aspects of the culture by living them. Thus, the overall environment that children experience is of utmost importance to the development of thinking, responsible adults.

Certainly there is a great difference between people in the home or school who are aware of the importance of the total environment on the emerging child and those who are not. When one is aware, he or she models beliefs, knows the needs of children, and interacts with children in selected ways in order to bring them to direct experience. The intelligent parent or teacher envisions his home or classroom environment as a medium that consciously and unconsciously influences the total development of the child and therefore is constantly directing and arranging it as a master conductor works with the orchestra.

The contemporary crisis in discipline, real or imagined, affects all segments of the society. Obviously, the effect of this crisis can be either positive or negative. Positively, it can become the means by which the society realizes it has a serious moral dilemma. Negatively, it can be taken as a separate issue from the overall cultural problems and can therefore be dealt with as a behavior problem and not as an integral part of a serious moral dilemma.

Today's moral dilemma in the American culture initially developed in the radical changes that took place during the turn of the twentieth century, and it has continued to grow in scope and intensity. The fundamental structure of the American social order was changing from a rural, agrarian society comprised largely of small towns and small businesses to an industrial society of large cities and large corporations. The drastic changes in communication, transportation, housing patterns, and service functions are obvious to the casual observer. Just as radical but not as apparent, a transformation has occurred in the morals, values, beliefs, attitudes, tastes, habits, and powers of the American people. The person who is responsible for putting a bolt on the wheel of an automobile is not the same worker as the person who made the entire wagon or at the very least, the wheel for that wagon. The person who only digs the foundation for the house is not the same craftsman who was responsible for the entire construction of the house. Indeed, as Dewey warned, men and women are acquiescing to the demands of machines. The social order has become such that at most an individual perceives himself as having little more responsibility than to put his hours into the monotonous routine he calls work. On his return home he enters an apartment, a condominium, or a house knowing few of his neighbors and having relatively little interest in them or in his neighborhood. He has become what Dewey predicted he would: an anonymous, alienated, and undeveloped organism.[3] He is a victim of a social and economic system that has separated him from the traditional sources of community life and responsibility, leaving him with feelings of isolation, often cleverly disguised and labeled as individualism. It is a misguided and misconceived individualism which looks upon man as a freely precipitated atom, unconnected and unresponsive to the thoughts and needs of the overall society.[4]

Likewise, the child who is reared in a family with two working parents, who is often at home alone after school for several hours each day, or who is left at an after-school care program has a vastly different environment than the child who was greeted by his mother or grandparents when he arrived home from school. The child who sits and watches television with little or no responsibility in the home is not the same as the child who had essential responsibilities on the farm, in his father's small business, or in some neighborhood store. The child who is paid for every chore does not develop in the same way as the child who had to contribute energy to the family in order for that family to prosper.

The point to be made is not that the great advances which the American culture has achieved in technology and science should be somehow forfeited or that the present generation should return, even if it could, to agrarian America. Rather, the basic point is that such changes ultimately affect the entire culture. Hence, they dictate the necessity for a basic change in the social structure, most specifically in rearing the children in the nature of their schooling. To think of technology and science only in terms of their products, leisure time, and convenience, with little regard for their impact on the essential morality of the American culture, is to condemn the culture to a state of social crisis, as is the case today.

It is common for people living in cultures in crisis to believe or at least to hope that their present state of degeneration is the result of current symptoms rather than the result of more obscure causes. People tend to recall the serenity and security of the past and enact reactionary plans. With blind faith they typically believe that a previously existing social climate can be retrieved with little more than superficial changes to present life. Alas, degeneration continues and cultural chaos evolves from cultural crisis.

The Role of Education

There exists only one means by which people in a culture can avoid the blind process of returning to the past to solve problems and to cope successfully with changes which naturally occur within their culture. This means is education. Fortunately, throughout its history some perceptive leaders within the American culture have realized this fact and have emphasized the need for education. Since the passage of the Old Deluder Satan Act of 1647, American culture has held that education of its young would solve the problems the culture would face. Since the time of Thomas Jefferson, Americans have generally believed that education is the means for both social and technological growth within the culture. To quote George Counts: "Faced with any difficult problem of life we set our minds at rest sooner or later by the appeal to the school. We are convinced that education is the one unfailing remedy for every ill to which man is subject, whether it be vice, crime, war, poverty, riches, injustice, racketeering, political corruption, race hatred, class conflict, or just plain original sin. We even speak glibly and often about the general reconstruction of society through the school."[5]

Today, however, many people in American society have not only lost their belief that education can solve its social ills but have in fact become hostile toward the school because of its failure to solve the innumerable social problems it has been given during the past two decades. For example, many people blame the school for not satisfactorily solving immediate pressing problems such as racial integration, moral decay, sexual promiscuity, and so on. In short, today's schools have become a scapegoat for the failure of American society as a whole—a failure occasioned by the three or more centuries of unwarranted sublime faith placed in education by the American people.

This antagonism between school and society merely accentuates and nurtures a warped, pessimistic individuality within society at the cost of beneficial social evolution. Without the belief that education can help to remedy the problems that exist in a society, cultural disaster is inevitable. This is especially true for the American culture, for as the French political philosopher Alexis de Tocqueville noted early in the nineteenth century, "the universal and sincere faith that they (the Americans) profess here in the efficaciousness of education seems to be one of the most remarkable features of America."[6] Indeed, for America it is now truly a "race between education and catastrophe," to quote H. G. Wells. If education does not regain the respect it must have, cultural catastrophe is a certainty.

At first glance there appear to be two problems facing formal education today. First, how can it gain the respect and confidence of society once again? Second, what procedures can schools employ to deal with our cultural problems? However, this dualistic interpretation of the current crisis is in itself a contributing factor to the crisis. The schools cannot overcome the American public's loss of faith in education by trying to appeal to every faction in society, to every vested interest group, to every political clientele. Since the early 1970s educators have tried to have schools reflect the desires and needs of the public by having "open curricula" committees, parent advisory councils, and citizen participation groups. This "open door" policy has not only failed but in truth has been disastrous to the education system as a whole. The curricula and methods that, according to the premise of this "open door" movement, would be supported by the public have in reality never been supported by them because of personal involvement and compromises to the various factions that participated.

The schools cannot respond *carte blanche* to every individual need and demand of every citizen in the society, for not only are these needs and demands too numerous, but they are in many instances contradictory to one another. Consequently, the function of the school is not and can never be to address itself to all sorts of spontaneous needs, but rather to assist society in understanding its needs and developing a means to meet those needs. Very simply, it is the educator's job to read the overall condition of society and to develop curricular and instructional practices to meet the needs of this condition. The school is basically an institution established by society to maintain the life of the culture and advance the welfare of its people.

The cultural crisis in America today constitutes a mandate to the schools to begin to see education in its broader social view, "otherwise, changes in the school institution and tradition will be looked at as the arbitrary inventions of particular teachers; at the worst transitory fads, and at the best merely improvements in certain details—and this is the plan upon which it is too customary to consider school changes."[7]

Professionals conducting schools must come to realize that the present condition of the culture demands that educators develop those kinds of basic changes within their process that will accommodate to the need of the culture. Therefore, the schools must set about the task of solving the social crisis of lost morals and values by devising a process of education which will develop within the children of the society those morals and values that are vital to its existence. In this way the schools will perform the function for which they exist and will simultaneously solve the present social-educational antagonism.

It is no coincidence that in this time of cultural crisis, discipline problems with children are the number one concern with both parents and educators. As society unravels morally, it quite naturally becomes more difficult to rear a child who will possess the morals and values of the culture. When a culture passes through nearly a century of technological change without corresponding social adjustments, the problem of properly rearing children follows.

Prior to the turn of the century, when American society was comprised basically of small towns, the morals and values of the

American culture were transmitted to the inheritors of the culture by the lifestyle itself. Many children gained the work ethic, perseverance, constructive self-criticism, cooperation, and responsibility toward family, primarily in their experiences of home, church, and community living. However, when the great urban-technological shift took place at the turn of the century these experiences, and their corresponding social influences upon developing children, changed drastically. The morals, attitudes, beliefs, and discipline developed in the young through the social experiences of life before the technological shift were radically altered because the texture of the social experiences themselves also changed drastically. As already indicated, a child who has little concrete responsibility to the family is vastly different from the child who had essential responsibilities around the farm. Furthermore, the person who had these essential responsibilities in his childhood experiences and who entered an occupation which further nurtured these morals and values as was the case in nineteenth-century America, was a different parent than the person who never encountered these morally educative experiences and entered an occupation that neither developed nor nurtured them.

Social Change

As a result of political and economic events (World War I, the Great Depression, World War II) the moral problems in the culture which were created by the dramatic technological changes at the turn of the century did not manifest themselves for approximately fifty years. Children and workers continued to develop the morals of the culture not by the social experience of agrarian America but by means of a radically different process, i.e., because of living the turmoil of national emergencies. During this time period, many people developed the work ethic, perseverance, constructive self-criticism, cooperation, and responsibility toward family primarily due to the need for social and economic survival, which also provided experiences by which these moral aspects are developed.

By the middle of the twentieth century the United States had not only succeeded in dealing effectively with its national emergencies but also had emerged as the most productive, powerful nation on earth. In retrospect, this powerful emergence of the United States from its earlier years of national emergencies produced two major cultural consequences.

First, the drastic technological changes that had taken place early in the century, and that in truth had changed the social experience by which the morals of the culture were developed and nurtured in its young, began to take effect. The tremendous technology began to nurture a different set of morals and values, namely that of pervasive materialism.

As Robert Hutchins so eloquently stated near mid-century, "at the root of the present troubles of the world we must find a pervasive materialism, a devastating desire for material goods, which sweeps everything before it, up to, and perhaps over, the verge of abyss. Since the desire for material goods is unlimited, it cannot possibly be satisfied. Everybody cannot possibly have everything he wants."[8]

Furthermore, Hutchins observed that we are living by a doctrine whereby material goods are an end in themselves. Therefore, all activities are judged by the profits they bring. In essence, the American culture has replaced its initial moral criteria of life with economic criteria.

No doubt man needs material goods to survive. However, he does not need them without limit and at the cost of his true being. Man can be a moral, rational, spiritual being. Therefore, the excessive preoccupation with material goods will deter him from his true goal, which is the fullest development of what he can become. The law of human beings is wisdom and goodness, not unlimited acquisition. The economic rationalization of life proceeds in the face of the basic law of human nature. That law would suggest to us the idea of sufficiency rather than the idea of unbounded material possessions.[9]

The second cultural consequence resulting from the series of national emergencies is that of "permissive parenting." Because of nearly two generations of national crisis, the parents of the early fifties entered parenthood with an overly permissive attitude, expressed by such statements as "my children will never have to go through what I went through" and "my children will have everything I never had." Consequently, the age of permissiveness in parenting was born. Contradictory to current beliefs, child experts such as Dr. Benjamin Spock in his best-selling book *Baby and Child Care* stressed that "a child, like an adult, knows when he is getting away with too much naughtiness or rudeness even when his mother is trying to close her eyes to it. He feels guilty inside. He would like to be stopped. But if he isn't corrected, he's likely to behave worse and worse. It's as if he were saying 'How bad do I have to be before somebody stops me?'"[10] Spock added: "The way we avoid irritation the rest of the time, whether we realize it or not, is by keeping our children under reasonable control and by being extra firm or sufficiently disapproving when things first threaten to go wrong. Such firmness is one aspect of parental love. Firmness, by keeping children on the right track, keeps them lovable. And they love us for keeping them out of trouble."[11] However, the parents of the age of permissiveness only believed or wanted to believe Spock's more romantic notions, such as ". . . your baby is born to be a reasonable, friendly human being"[12] and "goodhearted parents. . . can get good results with either moderate strictness or moderate permissiveness."[13] In short, it was not that Spock and others caused parents to go astray from "proven" parenting practices, but rather that historical influences developed within them an attitude or mind-set toward permissiveness.

Today's moral crisis in America was not caused by permissive parenting but merely facilitated by it. Therefore, by simply doing away with permissive parenting the culture will not regain its fundamental moral structure, as so many naively would have us believe. In effect to attack permissive parenting in isolation is merely attacking a symptom rather than the root cause. A stance against (or for) permissive parenting is a stance ultimately based upon the idea of fixed morals with little thought to social experience. As John Dewey stated, "When we observe that morals is at home wherever considerations of the worse and better are involved, we are committed to noting that morality is a continuing process not a fixed achievement. 'Morals' means growth of conduct in meaning; at least it means that kind of expansion in meaning which is consequent upon observations of the conditions and outcome of conduct."[14]

Furthermore, Dewey has written: "Present activity is not a sharp-narrow-knife-blade-in-time. The present is complex, containing within itself a multitude of habits and impulses. It is enduring, a course of action, a process including memory, observation, and foresight, a pressure forward, a glance backward, and a look outward."[15] Certainly it is a moral moment because it marks a transition in direction of breadth and clarity of action or of triviality and confusion.

Quite obviously in this time of tremendous moral confusion the efforts of most persons in education, counseling, child psychology, social work, and parenting are foolishly being spent jousting with the minor windmill of parent permissiveness while the true and latent problems of a radically changed social order and inherited social experiences go unnoticed. The moral, social problems are far greater and deeper than ineffective parenting practices. To quote William J. Byron, "I think the U.S. is now in a state of national emergency. It is not a military emergency. I do not define it in terms of the presence of an external enemy. The enemy resides within. Specifically, it lies within the youth of the nation. There is a crisis of purposelessness. It is evident on inner-city street corners, in the youth unemployment rates, in the problems of drug abuse, vandalism, violence, and crime. It [the general malaise] resides in the suburbs as well, and populates our college campuses too. The affluent young are not immune to drift. Alienation from their families and themselves may run deeper in the privileged young than does purposelessness in the poor who are trying to climb higher on the economic ladder."[16]

This purposelessness of which Byron speaks is the result of the moral changes brought about by the industrial, technological changes in the society since the turn of the century. That is to say, the youth of the culture lack basic purpose in that they have not acquired a fundamental moral purpose during their developing years. Therefore, they lack basic beliefs which provide the foundation that guides positive actions and desires. Their inadequate belief systems almost inevitably generate a pervasive mindless materialism. Their aimlessness is both mentally and verbally justified and defended by a warped perception of the words freedom and individuality. They have fallen victim to erroneous beliefs that freedom has no responsibility. They have in their desire to escape all external control jumped out of the frying-pan into the fire. They have in essence replaced the external controls of parents and schools (society) with the most dangerous form of external control: impulses and desires not ordered by intelligence. It is indeed a "loss rather than a gain to escape from the control of another person only to find one's conduct dictated by immediate whim and caprice; that is, at the mercy of impulses into whose formation intelligent judgment has not entered. A person whose conduct is controlled in this way has at most only the illusion of freedom. Actually he is directed by forces over which he has no command."[17] True freedom is born in the arena of self-fulfillment through responsible self and social awareness. In this way, freedom is no longer something to long for but rather something to rely upon and to use responsibly. To do one's own thing at the cost of responsibility and social consequences leads only to frustration, social pessimism, and purposelessness.

As Robert Hutchins said, ". . . the mind cannot be free if it is a slave to what is bad. It is free if it is enslaved to what is good. To determine the good and the order of goods is the prime object of all moral and political education. We cannot hope that one who has never confronted these issues can be either a good citizen or a good man."[18]

Conclusion

In summary, American culture is in a moral and social crisis. The cause of this crisis is little understood. Consequently, present plans and programs to correct such symptoms as permissive parenting practices, permissive sexual practices, and excessive television viewing are doomed to failure. One result of this failure is that the culture will continue to deteriorate. It will do little good to attempt to return to the serenity of the past and attempt to solve today's present problems by using parenting practices from the past. It is absurd to try to construct a new generation with old beliefs and practices. We must look beyond the simple-minded solutions given to us by reactionaries. We must understand the present through the past and construct a process for developing within the children of society the most essential morals and values that will make a culture of a higher order.

Although the discipline of children today may be perceived as the major problem both in home and school, nevertheless discipline also remains one of the major hopes for tomorrow. Discipline is the process through which the children of today will develop the morals, values, and attitudes by which they will live tomorrow. It is the process by which the youth of the culture will confront the issues of being a good citizen and a good person. The time for acquiring individual creativity and dynamic social interaction occurs when children are growing and developing. The discipline process by which children are guided makes the difference in what they will become and provides them with a mode for understanding their social order. At this point in the history of the American culture we must practice a discipline process which will lead to the development of a social consciousness within the inheritors of the culture. Discipline practices which result in better behavior but do not lead to the necessary moral development within the youth of society will not abate the cultural destruction.

Surely, then, now is the time for revolution in parenting and educational practices. Now is a time that calls for wise individuals to construct homes and classrooms which will develop a social conscience within the young.

According to Hutchins, those who are called to this reconstruction process are the people of this society who understand the seriousness of the situation. All of us must begin to reconstruct the social, political, and economic life of the country by reconstructing our own lives. This means that we must revitalize and indeed reconstruct educational activity to deal effectively with the moral and social problems we now face. To accomplish this task, we must look upon economic activity not as an end unto itself but as a means of sustaining and improving the quality of life for all.[19] In short, we must reconstruct the most essential morals of the American culture in order to overcome successfully the social, economic, and political problems which threaten our very existence.

Notes

1. George Counts, *Education and American Civilization* (Westport, Ct.: Greenwood, 1952), p. 130.
2. John Dewey, *Freedom and Culture* (New York: Putnam's, 1939), p. 154.

3. John Dewey, *Individualism Old and New* (New York: Balch, 1930), pp. 51–72.

4. John Dewey, *The Public and Its Problems* (New York: Holt, Rinehart, and Winston, 1927), pp. 156–157.

5. George S. Counts, *Dare the Schools Build a New Social Order?* (New York: Arno, 1969), p. 3.

6. George Wilson Pierson, *Tocqueville and Beaumont in America* (New York: Oxford University Press, 1938), p. 452.

7. Martin Dworkin, *Dewey on Education* (New York: Teachers College Press, 1959), p. 34.

8. Robert Maynard Hutchins, *Education for Freedom* (Baton Rouge, La.: Louisiana State University Press, 1943), pp. 39–40.

9. Ibid., pp. 41–43.

10. Benjamin Spock, *Baby and Child Care* (New York: Pocket Books, 1946), p. 330.

11. Ibid., pp. 22–23.

12. Ibid., p. 4.

13. Ibid., p. 7.

14. John Dewey, *Human Nature and Conduct* (New York: The Modern Library, 1930), p. 280.

15. Ibid., p. 281.

16. William J. Byron, "Of Drift and Draft," *The Scranton Journal* II (Winter, 1981), p. 8.

17. John Dewey, *Experience and Education* (New York: Collier, 1963), pp. 64–65.

18. Paul Hanna, in Arthur Cohen, *Humanistic Education and Western Civilization: Essays from Robert M. Hutchins* (New York: Holt, Rinehart, and Winston, 1964), p. 16.

19. Hutchins, *Education for Freedom*, pp. 47–48.

CHAPTER 2

Human Development and Culture

The Upward Progression of Life

Discipline is the primary process by which the children of all cultures develop the vital morals, values, and attitudes of the culture they inherit. Nevertheless, discipline is merely one aspect of the overall plan of Nature that provides people in all cultures throughout time with a way to continue to renew and improve themselves through their young. The process of culture is then *the* process of life itself. This cultural life-process does not occur through mere chance evolution but rather, as was expressed by Plato and inherited by Aristotle, is conceptualized as a single hierarchy of stages wherein each stage is related to its former stage as a more developed version of it.[1] The process, however, is not necessarily and automatically a more perfected version, for although it is an aspect of what Friedrich Hegel called Absolute Spirit (Being in itself and Subject for itself), "Truth is the ontological consciousness of Being in us, the One becoming aware of itself in many beings."[2] For Hegel, culture and life are not processes of purifying ascent toward the Absolute, as Plato saw it, for each level of these processes is in itself an appearing phase of the Absolute: "In all seemingly fixed or one-sided positions, the Absolute's own negations must be recognized."[3]

The culture-life process is best explained by Pierre Teilhard de

Chardin when he expresses the successive stages of the development of life. In Teilhard's view, life is a grand progression upward from the fluid contours of the early earth to humanity. Beneath the pulsations of geochemistry, of geotectonics and of geobiology, he detected one and the same fundamental process always recognizable—the one which was given material form in the first cells and was continued in the construction of the nervous system. He saw geogenesis evolving to biogenesis, which in turn evolved into psychogenesis, which has erupted into the human person.[4]

Teilhard potently wrote, "Now it effaces itself, relieved or absorbed by another and a higher function—the engendering and subsequent development of the mind, in one word of noogenesis. When for the first time in a living creature instinct perceived itself in its own mirror, the whole world took a pace forward."[5]

Teilhard bridges the naively perceived gap between man and biology, and between Nature and culture.

As a matter of intellectual routine and because of the positive difficulty of mastering a process in which we are ourselves swept along, the constantly increasing auto-organization of the human myriad upon itself is still regarded more often than not as juridical or accidental process only superficially, "extrinsically," comparable with those of biology. Naturally, it is admitted, mankind has always been increasing, which forces it to make more and more complex arrangements for its members. But those modus vivendi must not be confused with genuine ontological progress. From an evolutionary point of view, man has stopped moving, if he ever did move.[6]

To Teilhard, common sense—the same common sense which has over and over been corrected beyond all question by physics—tells us that man's biological evolution has reached its ceiling: "In reflecting upon itself, life has become stationary. Should we not rather say that it leaps forward? Look at the way in which, as mankind technically patterns its multitudes, *pari-passu* the psychic tension within it increases with the consciousness of time and space and the taste for, and power of, discovery."[7] This is what Teilhard calls "knowledge for power." This knowledge is not power for dominance over the world or over others, but rather increased power for increased human action. Obviously and indubitably, this power is in the direction of the understanding of matter put to the service of the mind. In essence, increased power for increased action leads to increased being.[8]

Therefore, he wonders why we often fail to recognize the "revealing association of technical organisation [mastery over environment] and inward spiritual concentration as the work of the same great force (though in proportions and with a depth hitherto never attained), the very force which brought us into being?"[9]

Further, Teilhard believes that it is through human socialization that the very axis of the cosmic vortex of interiorization is pursuing its course.[10] However, Teilhard asserts that when man realizes that he carries the world's fortunes in himself and that a limitless future stretches before him, he often tends to fall victim to trying to find fulfillment in isolation and blind egotism.[11] Man wrongly believes that progress is by isolation which in essence is the selection and election of races.[12] For Teilhard, whether it is the extreme doctrine of individualism, as found in existentialism, or the belief of isolation and superiority of a group, it is a subtle deformation of the great truth of life and culture.

To Teilhard, "what matters at the moment is to see clearly that those in both groups deceive themselves, and us too, inasmuch as, ignoring an essential phenomenon—the natural confluence of grains of thought—they disfigure or hide from our eyes the veritable contours of the noosphere and render biologically impossible the formation of a veritable spirit of the earth."[13]

In essence, the evolution of life is the evolution of culture and vice versa. Above the elementary process that culminates in each individual, more importantly there is developing a collective of the whole culture and of the human race as a whole. Since life's transition to the noosphere, the true evolution of humanity can be found only as the material and spiritual energies of man are envisioned as one in the same which are merely divided into two distinct components: a tangential energy which links the element (mankind) with all others of the same complexity and centricity (that is, the same order) as itself in the universe and a radical energy which draws it toward ever-greater complexity and centricity, in other words, forward in closer harmony.[14] "Without the slightest doubt there is something through which material and spiritual energy hold together and are complementary. In the last analysis, somehow or other, there must be a single energy operating in the world. And the first idea that occurs to us is that the 'soul' must be as it were a focal point of transformation at which, from all the points of nature, the forces of bodies converge, to become interiorised and sublimated in beauty and truth."[15]

Cultures which do not show the relationship among people are cultures which are in the process of being destroyed. Their end result must always be a moral structure based on materialism and a social order grounded in a pessimistic individualism or segregationism. So, too, is it for the American culture. Thus, the thesis in Chapter 1 that the American culture is in serious trouble is reiterated and reinforced in Teilhard's illuminating analysis of the process of life itself.

The American Culture

Before any analysis of Nature's plan can be attempted, it is essential to examine the unique characteristics of the American culture. Of the innumerable characteristics, the face of uniqueness can be found in two distinct but interrelated elements, the combination of which provides the potential for the greatness or failure of the culture. First, it is a culture that reflects the true ideals of democracy, a culture whose beliefs are that all people are created equal and, as such, are entitled to human dignity and rights. Second, it is a culture that has a fundamentally pluralistic foundation. The very life and breath of the culture are found in the strength and dignity extended to each contributing people and, in turn, given back to the overall culture.

The element of democracy is for the American much more than a political system or a form of government. Primarily it is a mode of associated living, of conjoint, communicated experience. Democracy signifies not only numerous and varied points of shared interest, but greater reliance upon the recognition of mutual interests as a primary factor in the social order. Furthermore, a democratically constituted society means not only freer interaction between and among individuals and social groups, but changes in social habits and a continuous readjustment through meeting the new situations that are produced by varied interactions of socially diverse individuals and groups. [16]

A democratic society is by its very nature the highest value cultivated by human intelligence. However, because of the democracy's essential aspects of freedom and individualism, there exists the danger of an overdramatization of the meaning of each of these aspects. The eventual result of such overdramatization is a cancerous effect upon the organism as a whole. Unless freedom of action is based upon intelligence and informed resolve, its manifestation will most often result in individual confusion and social disorder. The idea of freedom within democracy is not the right of each individual to "do his own thing," even if it is qualified by the cliché "as long as it does not interfere with the freedom of others." The true meaning of freedom within the democratic ideal is that of freedom of mind, freedom of intelligence. Freedom of belief, of conscience, of expression of opinion, of assembly for discussion and conference, of the press, of religion are guaranteed because without them true freedom of intelligence cannot exist. [17] "They are guaranteed because without them individuals are not free to develop and society is deprived of what they [in their highest intellectual action] might contribute."[18] True individual freedom is found in self-fulfillment through responsibility and contributions to society by all of the functioning members.

The element of cultural pluralism as an essential aspect of the American culture was developed at the turn of the twentieth century. Until this time the factors of an expanding frontier, the common challenges to the American people, and the controlled number and stature of immigrants served as means for by-passing the fundamental philosophical and social issues involved with a culture being influenced and developed by people from different cultural backgrounds.

In 1916 John Dewey, speaking to the National Educational Association, best stated what was to become the fundamental concept of pluralism. In that speech Dewey stated that all Americans are "hyphenated" and that to be an American is automatically to be international and interracial. Dewey correctly observed that American nationalism was a unique form of internationalism because of its fundamental cultural pluralism.[19]

In essence, cultural pluralism is the concept of democracy for the American culture. It is each individual culture maintaining itself in harmony with all others to produce a stronger, richer sameness of character. Cultural pluralism is the concept of mutual adjustments for the overall good of the whole society.

Cultural pluralism, like individualism, does not exist as an end in itself. When cultural pluralism becomes an end in itself, as it has in the American culture since the late 1960s, there emerges cultural antagonism. This kind of antagonism is directed not only against other cultures but also against society as a whole. As with over-individualism, meaning is lost; for, as we have seen in Nature through Teilhard's eyes, life and progress occur not in the isolationism of racial selection and election but rather in confluence, in the developing collective homogeneity or likeness.

Anything less than this kind of confluence results in a deformation of the "great truth" of life, whether such truth be envisioned in nature or in social order. The greatest danger facing the American culture is not the rights of individuals and the recognition of each multiculture, but rather the antagonism which can result from our recent overtures to lost individualism and cultural heritage. The peril and challenge of our time are found in our ability to achieve beneficial mutuality between multiculturalism and individualism; "where there is no mutuality there may be 'law and order,' but there cannot be peace."[20] Where there is no mutuality there is a multiculturalism and an individualism which inevitably go against the best interests of society as a whole.

The characteristics of democracy and cultural pluralism within the American culture hold great importance for education and for the discipline process by which the young are brought into the culture. Although Nature provides an overall plan by which the young inherit their culture, quite obviously each particular culture has its own characteristics which mandate individual educational processes unique to that culture. This is precisely the case for the American culture. The education (formal and informal) by which our young develop must contain and maintain the ideals of democracy and cultural pluralism. The educational system and educational practices of a culture clearly embody that which a culture wants and that which a culture will become. After all, the process of culture and education is one of complete reciprocity. In other words, society creates education and education creates society.

Thought Process and Education

Since the purpose of education (formal and informal) is to improve people in and for the American culture, it naturally follows that the purpose of American education entails the im-

provement of people's thinking processes. In essence, true freedom is, as has been stated, freedom of mind, not action. As
Hutchins stated: "Any opinion that a man holds simply because
it has been pumped or pounded into him is no good, because it
cannot last. Children should be brought up in good habits; but
those habits cannot endure the stress and strain of circumstances
unless they have some foundation in the convictions of the person who has them. Durable conviction about the affairs of this
world is a matter of reason. It is easy to show by reason that
Marxism is a fallacious doctrine. But what if the person with
whom you are discussing it has never learned to reason? Since we
cannot hope to insulate our young people from access to the false
doctrines in the world, the thing to do is to train them so that they
can see the falsity in them. This means helping them learn to
think for themselves."[21] We emphasize *for* themselves, not only
about themselves. Education for the American culture must be
founded upon the improvement of its people by the development
of morals, values, and attitudes which will produce a stronger,
richer sameness of character. For people in the American culture to believe that they must improve themselves through education, but that education is only to clarify each cultural group's
values (values clarification), is a total contradiction.

Essential Elements of Morality

There are five essential elements of morality that are absolutely
vital to the American culture: (1) the work ethic, (2) perseverance, (3) constructive self-criticism, (4) cooperation, and (5)
responsibility toward family. To many people these do not constitute elements of morality. However, as Dewey said, "Morals
are as broad as acts which concern our relationships with others . . . Morals concern nothing less than the whole character,
and the whole character is identical with the man in all his
concrete make-up and manifestations. To possess virtue does not

signify to have cultivated a few nameable and exclusive traits; it means to be fully and adequately what one is capable of becoming through association with others in all the offices of life."[22]

To restate an old phrase, it is not enough for a person to be good; he must be good for "something." The "something" for which he must be good is his ability to be a positive, contributing member of the society. That is, what an individual gets from living with others must balance with what he contributes. "Discipline, natural development, culture, social efficiency, are moral traits—marks of a person who is a worthy member of that society which it is the business of education to further."[23]

There are, of course, other morals which the young need to develop—for example, truthfulness, honesty, respect for life, and amiability, among others. However, our intention is to direct the attention of all those who work with the young (parents and teachers) to the five hidden elements of morality that are essential to the culture. They are the means of shared interest by which the sameness of character is developed within the culture. A process of discipline can be developed in which children become acculturated soundly and positively; however, home, school, and community have to work together.

The work ethic has two chief components. First, the work ethic involves taking personal pride in what one does. One's work is a measure of his ability to contribute toward the improvement of society and the ability to become himself. Second, the work ethic means that an individual works for what he gets. That is, an individual balances what he gets from society with what he contributes. ("An honest day's work for an honest day's wages.")

Perseverance is that element of morality which enables a person to overcome the problems he faces as an individual-in-society and which provides a foundation for the understanding that it is the responsibility of every member of society to work toward the betterment of the overall social order. Perseverance is the power which develops the belief that the problems of society can be solved by harmonious resolve and dedication.

Constructive self-criticism is that element of morality which stresses the need for all individuals within the culture to rigorously examine themselves and their contributions to the society in order to determine how their contributions can be improved. Constructive self-criticism is absolutely necessary if a people and their culture are to evolve to higher social and technological stages.

Cooperation is that element of morality which entails working jointly with others. Since cultures came into being through mutuality of interests and the process of cooperation, this element is vital for advancement. As a culture evolves and becomes more complex both socially and technologically, the essential aspect of cooperation must also evolve to keep pace with the changes within the culture. Quite obviously, because the unique characteristics of democracy, cultural pluralism, and advanced technology call for high levels of cooperation, the evolution of the aspect of cooperation for the American culture is magnified more. The culture's very existence depends upon it.

Responsibility toward family and others provides the backbone and foundation for the underlying structure of the normal processes in the social order. Both the foundation for looking beyond extreme individualism and the vehicle by which the present generation considers future generations are derived from responsible actions toward family and others. The basic relationship between the individual and society, then, is largely determined by the degree to which responsibility is shown. Patriotism is founded in the moral aspect of responsibility toward the family and the extended family.

The development of the five basic aspects of morality that build a sound American culture, when viewed holistically, constitutes social consciousness: the responsibility of the individual within a democratic, pluralistic society and a society composed of individuals. Therefore, education and discipline of the young must have as their basic goal that children develop the essential quality of a social conscience.

Notes

1. Plato, *The Sophist*, translated by A. E. Taylor (New York: Barnes and Noble, 1971), pp. 110–114.

2. Warren E. Steinkraus, *New Studies in Hegel's Philosophy* (New York: Holt, Rinehart, and Winston, 1971), p. 24.

3. Ibid.

4. Pierre Teilhard de Chardin, *The Phenomenon of Man*, translated by Bernard Wall et al. (New York: Harper & Row, 1959), p. 181.

5. Ibid.

6. Ibid., p. 305.

7. Ibid.

8. Ibid., p. 249.

9. Ibid., p. 304.

10. Ibid.

11. Ibid., p. 237.

12. Ibid., p. 238.

13. Ibid., pp. 238–239.

14. Ibid., pp. 64–65.

15. Ibid., p. 63.

16. John Dewey, *Democracy and Education* (New York: Free Press, 1916), pp. 86–87.

17. John Dewey, *Intelligence in the Modern World* (New York: Modern Library, 1939), p. 404.

18. Ibid.

19. John Dewey, "Nationalizing Education," in Horace Kallen, *Culture and Democracy in the United States* (New York: Liveright, 1924), pp. 131–133.

20. Ibid., pp. 178–179.

21. Robert M. Hutchins, *The Conflict in Education in a Democratic Society* (Westport, Ct.: Greenwood, 1953), pp. 10–11.

22. Dewey, *Democracy and Education*, pp. 357–358.

23. Ibid., p. 359.

CHAPTER 3

Nature and Discipline

The rhythm, harmony, and beauty of "Nature's plan" of human development sheds helpful light on the discipline process.

Every child is born basically helpless. He possesses capacities to grow and develop physically, mentally, and socially. At birth these are simply capacities. It takes the rest of his life to develop and maximize these capacities. It is through the intricate and interacting relationships among heredity, experience, and environmental nurturance that the young child gradually grows and develops. Each component in human development is inextricable, each is vital, each is of tremendous importance. For example, in physical development it can readily be observed that the child grows steadily and regularly toward maturity, but over a period of sixteen to nineteen years. Not as easily observed is the concomitant intellectual and social development which takes at least as long a period of time. Each aspect of human development is intimately tied to the others and thus develops as part of a whole, nonfragmented process.

As a result of Jean Piaget's research on cognitive development we are able to understand two basic underlying structures of "Nature's plan." First, development as a part of life is not a collection of separate processes or a series of unrelated encounters but rather is the total integrated functioning of all aspects of the developing person. Piaget's research illumines the intimate, inseparable relationship of heredity, environment, experience, and disequilibration in the development of cognition. Also, he has explained thoroughly that superior levels of intelligence and thinking evolve from elementary forms of behavior. [1]

At birth, the child possesses two interrelated characteristics which are vitally necessary for authentic human development. First, the child is egocentric. Second, he is extremely aggressive. In normal growth, these two characteristics are extremely useful and powerful.

The child's egocentrism is beyond self-centeredness. It is a natural state in the developmental process. Sigmund Freud developed the notion that a newborn child's mental structure is comprised primarily of the id, which he described as the primordial or initial principle of life (the pleasure principle). The function of the id is to rid the individual of tension and discomfort or, if this is impossible, to reduce the tension to as low a level of discomfort as possible. The basic aspect of life found in the pleasure principle consists of the child's making every attempt to avoid pain and seek pleasure. Thus the newborn's thinking process also is tied to sensorimotor processes and is primarily egocentric. The helpless state of the newborn child demands that he be egocentric in order to solve his basic problems of discomfort. It is by means of his interaction with the environment that the child is driven to higher levels of thinking, for in spite of the solicitude of parents, the child soon experiences degrees of frustration and discomfort which the simple trial-and-error and wish-fulfillment discharges of the id can not deal with satisfactorily. Hence, Freud states that the ego or reality principle of personality is developed as a secondary process which postpones the impulsive discharge of energy until the actual object which will satisfy the need has been discovered or produced. In other words, the ego is the process of thinking that is used to solve problems which the child encounters in his life.

This is the time-frame which Piaget refers to as the *sensorimotor* period (birth to age two). During this time-frame, the child, through sensorimotor activities, establishes the roots of his intellectual development. The child is born capable of performing only simple reflexive behaviors. In a few years he can, as a result of environmental interaction, obtain objects he wants; he can use one object to retrieve another; he can mentally "invent" means that permit him to do things he wishes; and he can use these inventions to attain desired ends.

In Freud's theory of personality development through maturation and interaction and Piaget's theory of intellectual development, development comes about by virtue of the inherent desire in the person to maintain balance within his being together with his constant interaction with an indifferent environment. In other words, an individual's intelligence and personality come to fruition as he attempts to successfully negotiate his problems of existence.

When Erik Erikson developed his theories on the psychosocial development of human beings, he too, in addition to maturation, found the interaction of the organism and the environment to be the fundamental process which affected the development of personality. From the basic maturational and interactional process of life, Erikson believes people go through eight successive stages of personality evolution. During the first year of life the child moves toward either a sense of basic *trust* or *mistrust* about the world. This sense of basic trust or mistrust flows from the qualitative relationship between his primary caretaker and himself. Thus, as the helpless child experiences frustrations in the form of needs and has them relieved or not, he comes to realize the world is a place he can depend upon or a place which is consistent and totally indifferent to him.

As the child matures and experiences life through interaction with the environment, his intelligence and personality develop somewhat simultaneously. The child is a total being and not simply a bundle or even a series of dimensions. For example, Piaget believes that by two years old the child cognitively develops object permanence; that is, he comes to realize that things exist which are not presently within his range of sight. In Erikson's stages this is the time the child develops, through maturation and interaction within his personality, either *autonomy* or *doubt*. Autonomy consists in the child realizing that he is an independent person, one separate and distinct from his primary caretaker. His doubt, on the other hand, occurs when the child has severe shadows on his abilities to be independent. Thus, at birth the child grasps everything to himself—or more precisely, to his body—whereas at the termination of this period when more advanced thought begins, he realizes that he is but one element or entity among others in a universe which he has gradually constructed himself, and which hereafter he will experience as external to himself.[2] When he arrives at this point he now is ready to begin to be an individual unto himself, a person separate and autonomous.

From the age of two until about seven years, the child is in a stage Piaget terms *preoperational*. Although the descriptions of this stage have many other aspects, a primary one is that the child is prelogical. The child's thinking is dominated by perception, and he goes from the particular—to the particular (transductive thinking). Therefore, he is unable mentally or cognitively to perform three basic functions which are necessary for logical thinking. First, the child cannot transform. For example, when material changes shape he believes that it has more or less than it had in its original form. Second, the child does not possess reversibility of thinking; he cannot follow a line of reasoning back to where it started. Third, the child is unable to decenter. When presented with a visual stimulus the child places his attention on a limited perceptual aspect of that stimulus, e.g. its height.

In one of his many classical experiments, Piaget presented preoperational children with two glasses which held the same amount of liquid. One of the glasses was short and round and the other one tall and slim. When preoperational children poured the same amount of liquid into the different glasses, they were perceptually bound and attended only to one dimension—height or width. They could not attend to both simultaneously and make more than a transductive judgment. They either thought there was more or less liquid. They could not see both dimensions.

During the preoperational period as defined by Piaget, Erikson believes that a child is developing either the positive aspect of *initiative* (the confidence to initiate himself in his environment) or moving more toward the negative aspect of *guilt* about himself and his ability to deal with his world. Although the child initiates himself in many ways, this developmental period is especially marked by his asking innumerable questions, such as "Why?" "How come?" "When?" He has an insatiable desire to experiment with ideas and with things.

Obviously there is method to his actions. The child who is busy pouring water, playing in the mud, stacking blocks and knocking them down is both initiating himself in his environment and finding out how the world operates. By pouring water and mixing sand, he develops a greater understanding of cause and effect—he learns to reverse, decentrate, and transform. Through his desire to understand his world, the child initiates himself into it by questions and actions and furthers the development of his intelligence and personality. Through activities of construction, the child grows and expands.

Between the ages of six or seven and twelve years, the child is in what Piaget names the *concrete operations* stage of cognitive development. During this time, the child's reasoning processes become more logical. The child has mastered the problems of transformation, centration, and reversibility. When he encounters a discrepancy between thought and perception, as when one glass appears to have more because it is taller, he is no longer dominated by perception but rather can make cognitive and logical decisions. Furthermore, he now evolves to the initial phase of the social aspects of cooperation and nonegocentric communication. The concrete operational child possesses the ability to assume the viewpoint of others and realizes that others can reach conclusions that are different from his, and as a consequence comes to seek validation of his thoughts through meaningful interaction with others. In short, the concrete operational child is free from many of the characteristics that dominated preoperational thought.

During the same age period, Erikson believes the child reaches the age he labels *industry versus inferiority*.[3] The inner stage is all set for entrance into life outside the home. A large portion of the time is spent in school. Since the child has his newly developed ability to perform deductive reasoning and thinking, he is able to learn and live. This time represents a stage which is a most decisive one socially. "Industry" means working for oneself and with others, and it also represents a first sense of understanding the division of labor and differential opportunity. A sense of the technological ethos of the culture develops during this stage of development.[4] The child begins to prepare to be a worker and becomes a potential provider for self and others. A sense of industry develops and the child becomes eager about and absorbed in productive situations. Bringing a productive situation to completion is an aim which gradually supersedes the whims and wishes of nondirected and no-goal-oriented play. The child's ego boundaries include his tools and skills and the work ethic teaches him the pleasure derived from the completion of work by steady attention and persevering diligence.[5] The danger during this stage lies in the child's meeting failure in his industrial endeavors, resulting in a sense of inadequacy and inferiority. When this happens the child rejects the world of work and remains in a stage of immature isolation from behaviors that enable growth toward the next stage to take place.

Once again, the harmony and rhythm of "Nature's plan" is clearly shown. The child is now cognitively capable of thinking logically, at least in a deductive manner, when given proper activities with concrete materials and opportunities for verbal analysis about his activities. In addition, the child becomes more social, for he is mentally capable of understanding that others can have different opinions. He therefore leaves the world of ego-centric play and immature communication with others and enters a world of social living. For example, the child is driven to play games with peers that have rules and regulations. He talks, argues, and reports on others. Furthermore, his desire to be industrious helps him to behave as a worker among other workers. He likes to construct club-houses, bunks, models, and puzzles. Through these activities even his physical need to develop fine motor skills is met. Indeed, by now in his development the child is a whole being who, through experience, is moving ever onward toward becoming an individual who is aware that he has a place in society. Although it is possible to see that a great deal is happening to the child's development during this time period, Freud was not totally wrong in terming it the "latency" period. When compared to the tremendous growth, intellectual undertakings, and social problems of both stages which surround this stage, there is a relatively latent period of turmoil in the developmental process.

Quite often the most difficult period for parents, teachers, and the developing individual is adolescence. However, when it is understood, this period is a necessary and natural time for development, and like other stages, it contains rewards as well as difficulties for those involved.

For Piaget, adolescence is the time of the *formal operations* stage of intellectual development. When it is reached, the individual's cognitive processes reach a maturity necessary to perform logical-operational thinking. This new power means that the adolescent has reached a point in his development (around twelve to fifteen years) when he has the ability to do thinking as logically as an adult can. However, we should not construe the ability to reason as meaning that he, the adolescent, necessarily thinks as maturely as a well-developed adult. He lacks the quantitative aspects of cognition, maturity, and experience which form the content and function (use of thought) of intelligence. Since the adolescent lacks these elements, there exist classic differences between adolescent thought and adult thought.

In formal thinking, the individual is no longer fettered by solving tangible problems of the present or past. He can deal with problems in the present and the past and can project the future. He can perform hypothetical verbal problems with more than one variable. In other words, the formal-operational child can "think about thought," and with this new power, the individual develops very different ways of looking at the world. For example, the adolescent can think of many possibilities at one time; therefore, he gets bored very easily. He can see injustice for the first time; he becomes extremely idealistic, for he can think about the perfection of life. He can think about hypocrisy for the very first time. In short, the adolescent is very much like the young child who is discovering through his own physical activity, for the adolescent is now experiencing new mental activities and many new realities.

Although many theorists have tried to explain the unique period of adolescence, none has contributed more toward our understanding of it than Erikson. According to him the adolescent period is a time of *identity versus role confusion*. Erikson believes that with the establishment of a relationship to the world of industry and the advent of the physical changes of puberty, many aspects of childhood come to a close. Therefore, the individual is, at least initially, half-child/half-youth. During this stage all continuities and samenesses relied on during the previous stages are more or less questioned again. Faced with drastic physiological changes (rapid growth and the advent of puberty) and the oncoming tasks and responsibility of adulthood, the adolescent now primarily becomes concerned with what he appears to be to others as compared with what he feels he really is as an individual. Erikson states that, "In their search for a new sense of continuity and sameness, adolescents have to refight many battles of earlier years, even though to do so they must artificially appoint perfectly well-meaning people to play the roles of adversaries; and they are ever ready to install lasting idols and ideals as guardians of a final identity."[6]

The adolescent must question the sameness he has acquired (what he has learned during his previous years of experience) in order to transform it to inner continuity. He must, in essence, question what he has learned as an individual (because of the structure of his thinking) and compare and contrast it with and to attitudes and habits of others. Initially this process is dominated by a desire to measure personal attitudes, values, and tastes by group norms. Therefore, the adolescent tries very hard to fit into the group. As a consequence, adopting group norms can lead to caustic attitudes and behaviors toward those who are not part of the group and its standards. Furthermore, it can cause the individual to "demand" of those authorities in his life that he be allowed to perform behaviors which everyone else is doing or to have the latest fashion that is "in" with the group. Of course, this desire also drives him to try what others are trying and to mimic what adults do as a demonstration of his own maturity and independence.

When an adolescent cannot attain identity because of either an experientially poor childhood or a present social existence to which it is difficult for him to relate mentally or socially, he suffers a severe role confusion, a sense of not knowing who he is or where he belongs. He is lost and is in his own being neither fish nor fowl. It is therefore quite common for the adolescent to desire even a "negative" identity in contrast to having "no identity." He may even join gangs or "counter culture" groups largely in an attempt to deal with his total disenchantment with people in a culture which has not prepared him to cope with the process of moving toward a positive identity.

In summary, adolescence is a time when the child passes rapidly toward adulthood and when he tries out what he has been taught by parents, teachers, and significant other adults. Also, it is a time when the formerly egocentrically thinking child can become truly aware of the thinking of others and as a consequence become overly concerned with what others think about him. Indeed, it is a time of emotional turbulence as the individual experiences, due to advanced thinking power, injustice, idealism, boredom, and hypocrisy. Furthermore, the adolescent undergoes physiological changes which produce extreme moodiness. He also senses social changes through the pressures of finding himself in relationship to the group and members of the opposite sex. He wants to assume the responsibility of adulthood and longs to escape the former controls of parents and teachers but also is still very much in need of controls and help.

Once during a conversation with a mature twelve-year-old girl we gained invaluable insight with regard to the adolescent's demand for freedom and for limits at the same time.

"Jean, why do you always end up fighting with your mother?"

"'Cause she always tries to control me."

"How does she control you?"

"Lots of ways."

"For example?"

"She always makes me be in at ten on weekends."

"That doesn't seem to be unfair. What time would you choose to come in if she didn't make you be in at ten?"

"Probably one or two, even though I know I would just get in trouble."

"Then you really think you do need a curfew?"

"Yes."

"What time would you say the curfew should be?"

"Uh, ten o'clock."

"Ten! That's your mother's time."

"I know, but don't you tell her I said that."

As irrational and paradoxical as this conversation seems to be, it merely exemplifies how the adolescent is thinking. Normally, children in this age group will try to fool parents and teachers if they can, but are better off, even in their opinion, if they cannot. Parents and teachers should be patient with the individual. They should be understanding and at the same time give every appearance of being aware of all the "happenings" in their adolescent's life.

Identity in Today's Society

Presently in the American culture there exist three major identity problems found in today's adolescents. This is due in part to a lack of their developing the five aspects of basic morality which we have presented as being essential to people in a highly developed culture. As we have stated, many of the present generation of young people are filled with a sense of purposelessness. Many are, to use their own term, "lost."

First, there are those adolescents who have what can best be described as a poor social identity. Because of being ignored, misguided, or not treated fairly by home and school they have developed mistrust, doubt, guilt, and feelings of inferiority during their childhood years. As a result, they have no doubts in their mind as to what the world is about. These youths are not "lost" but rather desperately believe that the only way for one to survive is "to get what one can, when one can." Thus, they tend to join youth gangs and quite often take the path that leads directly to juvenile deliquency. There is an attempt on their part to exert power over a society in which they find very little meaning. There seems to be an impossible search and a drive to seek meaning and value in the form of the false power of monetary gain.

The second outcome resulting from a failure to develop the morals of the culture is the identity of pessimistic individualism. This is the false belief that one should do whatever he desires, when he desires. Catchwords such as freedom and individualism become guides to the socially destructive practices of taking without giving and only doing what is perceived to benefit oneself. The sixties and seventies were witness to generations that identified themselves by pessimistic individualism. It was also a time of social chaos, economic recession, and psychological turmoil, for the emerging members of the culture did not acquire and understand the aspects of morality which would have given them a truer identity, purpose, and social meaning. As a result, even the foundations of social order have become victims of the false identity associated with individualism. As an example, in the name of individual rights criminals are being freed on technicalities and victims are left to suffer. Because of a misguided understanding of the individual and the society, the judicial system is allowing the social order to unravel. The erroneously perceived individual good is taking precedence over the collective good. Indeed, in the fruitless search for selfish individualism, people have often gone beyond the best interests of the society-at-large and are systematically contributing to the erosion of a sound social order.

Pervasive materialism is the third and final identity outcome and may be the identity process of future generations. What one owns, how much one possesses, and getting whatever one can are the principles on which a pervasive materialistic identity will be based. The eighties likely will show an overall "backing away" by the majority of the population from pessimistic individualism, and an attraction to the false identity of pervasive materialism.

This identity too can contribute to the destructive direction of a culture in chaos.

As the generations of the sixties and seventies experience the failure of pessimistic individualism to fill their loss of identity, they will replace that failing process with the false process of pervasive materialism. Individuals who during the sixties and seventies denounced materialism will believe it to be the only way to find meaning in their lives as adults. It also will fail them in their search for identity, but it will be too late. They will have spent a lifetime searching for meaning which can only come through the realization that "meaning" is not doing what one pleases, nor is how much one possesses important; rather, it is what one does to contribute to the meaning and advancement of society that provides meaning to life. In addition, they will pass on to their children the belief in pervasive materialism rather than a morality which provides personal and social identity. These children in turn will find materialism to be vacuous and as adults will long for individualism until eventually the culture cannot be sustained. Thus, there is exigency for a social-discipline process by which parents and teachers can rear their children in order that they acquire the morals which will provide them with identity, purpose, and social meaning.

Morals and Development

Studies in moral development provide an understanding of "Nature's plan" and what it means for the individual as he grows toward maturity. As early as 1908, John Dewey, in *Theory of the Moral Life*, first expressed this belief. For Dewey, the developing individual should become more rational, more social, and finally more moral. He greatly emphasized the importance of communication and also the necessity for the development of a social-self through experiences the individual has with participation, cooperation, and shared social processes with others in the home, community, and school. He believed that rational and social conduct should itself be valued as being good. Therefore, such conduct should be developed, chosen, and sought; and "in terms of control. . . the law which society or reason prescribes should be consciously thought of as right, used as a standard, and respected as binding."[7]

Dewey wrote:

> As a standard it is rather a cautionary direction, saying that when we judge an act, accomplished or proposed, with reference to approval or disapproval, we should first consider its consequences in general, and then its special consequences with respect to whatever affects the well-being of others. As a standard it provides a consistent point of view to be taken in all deliberation, but it does not pretend to determine in advance precisely what constitutes the general welfare or common good.[8]

For Dewey, there existed a moral trinity: social intelligence, social power, and social interests.[9] Through the three processes, the individual comes to understand the meanings of life; that is, the morals that sustain a sound society must be developed *within* the children in order for them to reach the necessary understanding of themselves and their responsibility in society.

Dewey stated that there are three levels of behavior and conduct: "(1) behavior which is motivated by various biological, economic, or other nonmoral impulses or needs (e.g. family, life, work), and which yet has important results for morals; (2) behavior or conduct in which the individual accepts with relatively little critical reflection the standards and ways of his group as these are embodied in customs or mores; (3) conduct in which the individual thinks and judges for himself, considers whether a purpose is good or right, decides and chooses, and does not accept the standards of his group without reflection."[10]

The moral theory that has gained the most recent interest and support in education was developed by Lawrence Kohlberg and is based on the tenets of cognitive developmental psychology. However, Kohlberg himself has said that the cognitive developmental approach to moral development was fully stated for the first time by John Dewey. Furthermore, Kohlberg states that Dewey's three levels of moral development do in fact correspond to the three levels he describes[11] (see appendix). Unlike Dewey, Kohlberg dismisses the influence and importance of all underlying experience. According to Kohlberg, "a person whose logical stage is only concrete operational is limited to the preconventional moral stages."[12] Thus, children from birth until approximately ten to twelve years of age are only capable of preconventional (the lowest level) moral thinking. Kohlberg denies the impact of the experience the child has during his first eleven years. Even if a person reaches the level of formal operations intellectually, that does not mean he will necessarily leave the preconventional moral thinking level.

Indeed, there is a major difference in Dewey's conception of moral education and Kohlberg's conception. For Dewey, "education itself is precisely the work of supplying the conditions which will enable the physical functions, as they successfully arise, to mature and pass into higher functions in the freest and fullest manner."[13] Therefore, Dewey, for two reasons, would never agree that education should be based upon a formalist moral philosophy, as Kohlberg's is, whereby students who have reached the cognitive level of formal operations would learn by means of prepared hypothetical moral dilemmas, structured to focus upon conflicts between moral principles. First, Dewey believed that all education must be grounded in meaningful experience, that is, in the students' having a sincere interest in their own activity. Kohlberg's structured dilemmas, for Dewey, would have little more meaning and power than lessons "about morals." Second, Dewey explicated profoundly the importance of early experience and the subtle and pervasive unconscious influence of the environment.[14] According to him, "Example is notoriously more potent that percept. Good manners come, as we say, from good breeding—or rather are good breeding; and breeding is acquired by habitual action, in response to habitual stimuli, not by conveying information. Despite the never-ending play of conscious correction and instruction, the surrounding atmosphere and spirit is, in the end, the chief agent in forming manners. And manners are but minor morals. Moreover, in major morals conscious instruction is likely to be efficacious only to the degree in which it falls in with the general walk and conversation of those who constitute the child's social environment."[15]

In his attempt to avoid all aspects of indoctrination, Kohlberg has failed to understand Dewey and Piaget. For example, Dewey said, "We never educate directly but indirectly by means of the environment. Whether we permit chance to do the work, or whether we design environments for the purpose makes a great difference. And any environment is a chance environment, so far as its educative influence is concerned; unless it has been deliberately regulated with reference to its educative effect."[16] Further, Dewey believed that there was a vast difference between an intelligent home and an unintelligent one, in that the habits and interaction which took place were planned and chosen for the best development of the children.[17]

Therefore, it follows that "Nature's plan" dictates that adults not wait until the child reaches total cognitive development for moral education to begin. Indeed, studies have shown that many people will never reach the stage of formal operations, thus rendering them to chance moral development. The approach, then, that obviously must be advocated is that of a contextual, deliberately planned moral development-discipline program. Furthermore, it must be designed to be totally consistent with the aims of developmental, moral education which includes the child's movement through stages. There must be a heavy emphasis on the importance of early experience and the value of the social context of the total environment. This approach must be based upon the belief that although advanced moral reasoning depends on advanced logical reasoning the child must be provided with experiences in social living and social decision making much the same as the concrete operational child should be offered experiences that lend themselves to the development of the formal operational level with ideas cognitively. In addition, it must take into account the strong evidence as to the importance of modeling in the socialization process[18] and the influence of the interaction process of the child with the social structure of the environment.[19]

Basic Needs and Development

To wait for the child's cognitive level to reach formal operations is a serious mistake and is to wait too long. All development proceeds from one level to the next, and the child, because of his basic needs, is driven to learn from birth from those who represent the social order to him. Abraham Maslow's work on human social development gives us insight into this time period and how perfectly "Nature's plan" is mapped. According to Maslow there exists a hierarchy of needs which indicates the emphasis of an individual's efforts. He believes that "there is now sufficient anthropological evidence to indicate the fundamental or ultimate desires of all human beings do not differ nearly as much as do their conscious everyday desires."[20] Maslow theorizes that an individual's behavior is dominated by the need which is greatest for him at any given time. He believes that when a lower order "need is satisfied, a higher order motive (or class of motives) makes its appearance and demands satisfaction, and so on to the top of the hierarchy."[21] Through Maslow's hierarchy of human needs we are able to see, once again, Nature's principle of movement toward higher levels of existence.

The following is a brief summary of Maslow's hierarchy of needs.

1. *Physiological needs.* This level includes such basic needs as food, water, sleep, and other physical needs.
2. *Safety needs.* This second level reflects an individual's need for security and his dependence on others for meeting those needs.
3. *Love and belongingness needs.* This level reflects the need for friendships and belonging to a group.
4. *Esteem needs.* This level represents the need for self-worth, self-confidence, and capability for being useful and necessary in the world.
5. *Self-actualization needs.* This level represents the individual's need to do what he is best fitted to do. Maslow said, "What a man can be, he must be."[22]

It is our belief that there are two aspects of the hierarchy which have major import to understanding social-emotional-moral development. First, there is the aspect of the immediacy of the basic needs, and, second, there is the aspect of developmentalism in relation to the needs. The former expresses the idea that when an individual experiences a need, his powers are directed to satisfy that need. The latter expresses the idea that during particular periods of human development, certain needs are more prominent than others. For example, the newborn developmentally is driven to concentrate upon his physiological needs; the child from one year or so until about age twelve is driven toward safety; the early teen is driven toward belongingness and the late teen toward self-esteem. Each need builds on a partial satisfaction of the lower order ones.

When the two aspects are assimilated, a certain understanding of the emerging individual takes place. Accordingly, they provide society (in particular, parents and teachers) with the opportunity to focus upon those needs which are both immediately and developmentally prominent at any given time in the child's life. Furthermore, they provide an understanding into the process of discipline that children should experience for wholesome growth.

The following represents the developmental pattern of human needs in the emerging individual.

STAGE I (0–1)

Physiological needs are the most prominent during this stage. Both homeostasis and the individual's relatively helpless state cause his consummatory behavior for meeting his primary needs for air, food, water, sleep, and excretion.

STAGE II (1–12)

The most prominent need of the individual during this stage is security. He is concerned with both physical and ego safety. This is best provided for the child in an environment that has routine, consistency, and a properly constituted authority. The child thrives better in an environment that he perceives to be structured and safe. Indeed, he prefers, as well as needs, an environment which he can count on both in the present and far into the future. According to Maslow, "we may generalize and say that the average child in our society generally prefers a safe, orderly, predictable, organized world, which he can count on and in which unexpected, unmanageable, or other dangerous things do not happen, and in which, in any case, he has all-powerful parents who protect and shield him from harm."[23]

STAGE III (12–15)

During this stage, within the normal individual there emerges the need for belongingness, love, and affection, and the whole cycle already described repeats itself with a belongingness center. The child literally hungers for a place in his group. "He will want to attain such a place more than anything else in the world."[24] Thus the early teen is very concerned about his peers and their opinion of him.

STAGE IV (16+)

During this stage the individual develops the strong desire for a stable, firmly based evaluation of himself. He is driven by the need for self-worth, self-esteem, and the esteem of others. According to Maslow these needs can be classified into two subsidiary sets. First, the individual has the desire for competence, independence, and confidence in the face of the world. Second, the individual has the desire for prestige, status, recognition, or importance.[25]

When one examines the basic needs descriptions given by Maslow, the implications for development become clear. The environment must be planned in such clear directions that the child's needs are met and attended to in order for him to continue to develop as a whole human being.

The period of a child's life from one to twelve years is the time in which the foundations of conscience develop. Obviously the child's natural need for safety drives him to find limits and routines and to seek consistency from the properly constituted authorities in his environment. Furthermore, since the need for safety in the child is developmentally prominent and must be satisfied continually, the child is naturally driven to test the limits (the absolute boundaries) and the properly constituted authorities over and over again. Therefore, limits which are consistently enforced and the models that the properly constituted authorities exhibit are assimilated by the child and form the initial structure of conscience. Limits and boundaries which appear to be temporary and appropriate only to some situations or people are not assimilated into the structure of conscience.[26]

For example, if a school faculty has the rule (limit), "No running in the halls," and the limit is enforced, the child will indirectly learn a lesson in regard to not doing as he wants when he desires to run. He has to consider what his action will do to others. If, however, some teachers enforce the rule and others do not, or some teachers only correct a few children, the child learns that the rule is inconsistent and thus the indirect moral lesson is lost. In short, this time period provides teachers, parents, and other adults with an opportunity to educate the child and move him from his self-centered needs to a concern for others. Furthermore, it provides the fundamental experiences for the development of the conventional level of moral thinking, that is, ultimately toward the development of a respect for the law and order of society.

When the individual matures to the cognitive level of formal operational thinking and possesses the ability to reach the conventional level of moral thinking, he also begins seriously searching for his identity among others. Correspondingly, the basic need of belongingness intensifies and thus drives the individual to find personal meaning in relationship with others. Also, during this time period the person begins to satisfy more intensely his safety found through consistent limits that are guided by properly constituted authorities. Still, the individual needs limits but may not necessarily *consciously* want them or *act* as if he does. Indeed, it is the time in which the individual and his peers try out and expand upon what their individual and collective consciences have acquired. Consequently, if they have not had a firm foundation of conscience laid—that is, one which ties them to the culture through its moral foundation (work ethic, perseverance, constructive self-criticism, cooperation, and respect toward family)—a severe identity crisis occurs and the symptoms of juvenile delinquency, pessimistic individualism, pervasive materialism, or a combination of them may develop.

From approximately age sixteen, the individual is haunted by the prominence of the basic developmental need of self-esteem. After trying himself out with and among others he begins to find himself as a contributing member of society. In his search for self-worth through the moral aspects of the culture, the individual gains identity and an understanding of his culture.

In summary, as can be seen through the works of Teilhard, Hegel, Piaget, Kohlberg, Erikson, and Maslow, the basic principle of growth is that of movement toward higher levels of existence and knowing. From the physical to the cultural there is evidence of this growth process. Furthermore, this principle is seen in the existence of the individual, from the cognitive to the moral, from basic needs to social development.

By understanding this principle and the aspects of development within the emerging individual in relation to it, the mature members of society can provide experiences through which the potential of the young is brought to intellectual, moral, and social fruition. Each sign of disregard for the potentialities of Nature's plan drafts both the individual and future society away from movement toward higher levels of existence. Although an understanding of this basic principle will not assure us against failure, it does provide a means by which we can locate points of effective endeavors and focus available resources upon them. Furthermore, it will enable us to render failure a source of instruction for future practices.

Indeed, it is the intelligent acknowledgment of the continuity of Nature's plan for the individual and society which will secure a growing morality that will be "serious without being fanatical, aspiring without sentimentality, adapted to reality without conventionality, sensible without taking the form of calculation of profits, idealistic without being romantic."[27]

Notes

1. Barbel Inhelder and Jean Piaget, *The Early Growth of Logic in the Child* (New York: Norton, 1964), pp. 1–16.

2. Barry J. Wadsworth, *Piaget's Theory of Cognitive Development* (New York: Longman, 1971), pp. 39–91.

3. Erik Erikson, *Childhood and Society* (New York: Norton, 1950), p. 258.

4. Ibid., p. 260.

5. Ibid., p. 259.

6. Ibid., p. 261.

7. John Dewey, *Theory of the Moral Life* (New York: Holt, Rinehart, and Winston, 1908), p. xii.

8. Ibid., p. 142.

9. John Dewey, *Moral Principles in Education* (Boston: Houghton Mifflin, 1902), p. 43.

10. Dewey, *Theory of the Moral Life*, p. x.

11. Lawrence Kohlberg, "The Cognitive-Developmental Approach to Moral Education," in *Phi Delta Kappan* LVI (June, 1975), pp. 670–677.

12. Ibid., p. 671.

13. Reginald D. Archambault, editor, *John Dewey on Education: Selected Writings* (New York: Random House, 1964), p. 207.

14. John Dewey, *Democracy and Education* (New York: Free Press, 1916), p. 17.

15. Ibid., p. 18.

16. Ibid., p. 19.

17. Ibid.

18. Albert Bandura and Frederick J. McDonald, "The Influence of Social Reinforcement and Behavior of Models in Shaping Children's Moral Judgments," in *Journal of Abnormal and Social Psychology* LXVII (September, 1963), pp. 274–281.

19. Jean Piaget, *The Moral Judgment of the Child* (New York: Free Press, 1948), p. 14.

20. Abraham Maslow, *Motivation and Personality* (New York: Harper & Row, 1954), p. 67.

21. James Chaplin and T. S. Krawiec, *Systems and Theories of Psychology* (New York: Holt, Rinehart, and Winston, 1960), p. 429.

22. Maslow, *Motivation and Personality*, p. 91.

23. Ibid., p. 87.

24. Ibid., p. 89.

25. Ibid., p. 90.

26. Kevin Walsh and Milly Cowles, *Taming the Young Savage* (Huntsville, Al.: Strode, 1981), p. 13.

27. Ibid., pp. 88–89.

CHAPTER 4

The Trinity of Discipline

Reconstruction of the American culture demands a discipline process through which the fundamental aspects of morality can be learned by children. It is not enough to develop children who are merely good; they must be good for something. To prosper, the American society needs children who possess a work ethic, the qualities of perseverance and constructive self-criticism, and a spirit of cooperation and responsibility toward family and society. Discipline techniques must always be designed and implemented to further the development of a social conscience.

Theoretically and practically, the discipline process must be in harmony with all components of human development. Therefore, it must be developmental. It must, to a great extent, be in harmony with cognitive-developmental theory, cognitive-moral-developmental theory, and both the immediacy and developmental aspects in the hierarchy of human needs. Discipline must help the child to develop his powers toward social ends, and it must be a process which brings the individual and the social values of the American society to fruition. In essence, then, the discipline process must develop an environment of selected influences that will positively affect the child and assist in his social development.

The first step a teacher or parent must take toward the use of social and moral discipline does not require any special capacity but rather a desire to participate. One cannot assume that the child is innately capable of total independence or that he has the power of mature reason, as many romantics have claimed. Teachers and parents must understand that this achievement must be coached and viewed as a developmental goal. The child is born neither good nor evil. He is born with the capacity to interact with his environment and to learn through experience. The foundation laid during the child's early years must help him to realize the limits of his own powers, as well as limits imposed by the social setting. Hence, the first step in the process of discipline is instilling a sense of right and wrong.

If "right" consisted in being quiet, immobile, and submissive, and "wrong" consisted in being active in speech and movement and inquisitive in nature, as some believe, the matter would be quite simple. However, the objective is to free the child for purposeful activity. He must have freedom from both the internal impulses that destroy his perseverance and the external fetters that stifle his creativity and curiosity if he is to produce work and be capable of constructive self-criticism.

Obviously, the child is born helpless. He is likewise helpless when he enters the social process. Therefore, parents and teachers must help the child to overcome, through the development of the power of reason, the barriers which inhibit his activity. A child cannot be molded like a statue, but must mold himself. This is accomplished through the guidance of adults and through his interaction with other children. A social being emerges; entirely limiting his interaction because of his lack of moral reasoning inhibits his natural desire to learn. On the other hand, permitting his unacceptable social interaction to go unchecked disrupts the sense of security the child needs, and fosters overdependence. It is the child's own experience, and not the commands or observations of outsiders, which facilitates the development of his freedom to think. Thus, an environment must be envisioned that not only allows the child to utilize his natural impulses, but also guides him in their use.

For example, the child enters school with the natural impulse to communicate. He expresses himself freely in a way which since his birth has been encouraged by his home environment. School must not truncate this impulse and ignore the experience the child has had at home; neither can the child in the school's collective social setting continue to speak whenever he desires. It is the teacher's job to expand, through the environment, the child's experience to fit the new social situation. Thus, the teacher should never physically contain the child's speech by use of force or tell him to "shut up." The teacher should instead work with the child to help him understand when it is appropriate to talk and when it is not. This education process takes patience and perseverance on the part of the teacher because the child is learning. Many times the teacher may have to use a form of social discipline to accomplish this aim; such use of social discipline is what total social education is all about.

Because a child is born with a natural impulse to be active, we must not stop his activity, but we should instead modify the environment to accommodate to this impulse and to help the child understand and control it in a social setting. We must not only develop an environment to utilize his impulses, but also help him to develop perseverance through control. Thus the social educator learns by watching children. Above all, the teacher must realize that although children exhibit common impulses, they are individuals and require a personal education. Step by step, day by day, as the child lives within an environment, his natural impulses will become more obvious to himself, thus allowing for personal control, freedom, and independence. Hence, the trinity of discipline—structure, intervention, and consistency—is quite a necessary element for social development.

Social discipline, however, should not be oppressive. It should not suffocate what the child is naturally; it should only help to modify him. The foundation of structure, intervention, and consistency is what eventually leads the child to freedom and independence. Without it, a total education is impossible, for the child develops without the self-control that is essential for true learning to take place.[1] These three elements must be considered and enacted as a total process, with each element being interdependent upon the remaining two. Through the harmony of the trinity of discipline the child comes to understand both himself and his social responsibilities. In short, these three elements, when rhythmically enacted, are a part of the transformation the child makes from being self-centered and uncontrolled to becoming socially conscious and self-disciplined.

Structure

Structure is that element which provides the overall limits to the child's environment. Through it comes the reality of social living as it comes to bear on the child. A structured environment not only allows the child to utilize his natural impulse (which is simply to be a child) but also guides him in the use of it.

Structure has two particular dimensions: *process* and *content*. The former refers to growth toward self-discipline and the latter refers to the various aspects of growth. The content of structure encompasses elements of limits, love, consequences, manners, responsibilities, and prevention practices. The factors involved in the concept of structure are tightly interwoven; therefore, one element of structure often serves to complement or strengthen another.

The need for safety on the part of the growing child emphasizes the crucial necessity of *limits* and *routines* in his life. First, growing children need limits set for them. The child needs to have *rules* and *regulations* to follow in his environment. The rules that are set should be clearly presented to the child and discussed with him at the earliest possible age. Certainly he will not be able to reason as an adult, as some psychologists believe, but the process of discussion begins to shift the responsibility of

discipline—following the rules and looking at their consequences—from the adult to the child himself. In short, the *rules*
and the clear *understanding* that they will be enforced provide
the foundation for self-discipline; they also establish the *limits* the
child so desperately needs for safety. Without clearly understanding the rules and limits, the child is driven by nature to try to find
them and will often perform socially unacceptable acts in hopes
of gaining attention. Such action, in truth, is his drive to find the
limits that let him know somebody really cares about him. Thus,
a child who does not go to bed when he is told to and has no
consistent parent follow-through will many times end up causing
a major disturbance of one sort or another in order to find his
limits. In other words, the child will continue to seek security in
his environment by going one step over the line until he realizes
that the parent means what he/she has said.

This need for safety is readily apparent in the natural development of a child. For example, very early in life many children
adopt a "security blanket" or a "teddy." This is evidence of their
need for safety, expressed by means of a real object. The blanket
or teddy provides them with security as they enter new environments, meet new people, or get tired. Likewise, they are in great
need of the safety of *rules* and *regulations* in conjunction with
firm and *consistent* discipline.

It has often been said that play is the principal means by which
a child learns. This is most certainly true. Furthermore, research
on child's play has revealed that from age two, the child, with
each stage of chronological development, is increasingly driven
to seek games and activities which have clearly defined rules and
regulations. The six- to twelve-year-old child often argues and
fights about rules being unfair, or being misinterpreted, when
they go against him and/or his team. This natural development of
play merely reflects the child's need for limits, which we have
stressed as being essential for wholesome development. In addition, the provision of limits serves as a way of bringing the self-

centered child into being a productive member of family and school groups. Irrespective of whether the child "hates" the rules when they go against him and "loves" them when they help, the fact is that the child desperately needs *rules* and *regulations*. The child cannot achieve his potential development without them. It is through his attempts at challenging the limits and the consistency of the consequences he encounters as a result of these challenges that his moral foundation begins to form.

Reconsider the previous example of limits. If a school has a rule against running in the halls, the child's self-centered freedom is curtailed. Inevitably, the young child in uncontrolled exuberance runs in the hall, and, if correctly disciplined after each offense, he will eventually learn not to run in the halls of the school. In addition, if there is consistency within the school, he is also indirectly learning two very important moral lessons. First, he is indirectly learning that he cannot just do as he pleases, but must consider what effect his actions may have upon others, that is, if he runs in the halls he could run into and hurt someone else. Second, he learns that in order for a society to exist, there must be law and order and respect for authority among its citizens. However, if some teachers consistently enforce the rule, others never enforce it, and still others enforce the rule only with their children while letting other students run wild around them, the child not only learns to continue to do whatever he pleases but also loses the moral lessons that the rule and its consistent enforcement would have indirectly taught him.

Concerning this need for limits on the part of the child, the parent and teacher should realize that the child should be gaining more and more responsibility and earning more and more freedom in his life with each passing year. Socialization can be born only on the plane of increasing responsibility and effort on the part of the child, not by blind obedience to rules imposed upon him. Freedom, activity, and decision making are processes which are vitally necessary for wholesome development. An individual can be considered truly disciplined only when he regulates his own actions. Therefore, limits should not be seen, except in dangerous situations, as a means of immediate control, but rather as a way of providing needed guidance for the child as he is growing into responsibility for his own behavior. The responsibility of the adults in a child's life is to prepare him for living, not to protect him from the process. It is vital that limit setting be a developmental process in which children participate for two very important reasons: first, eventually the child will be setting his own limits and will be a citizen in a democratic society in which active participation in rule making is essential; second, the child tends to see the limits that are established as being his own, not merely rules someone else is applying to him. This does not mean he should set his own limits before a reasonable degree of maturity is achieved.

Young children often set unrealistic limits with extremely harsh physical or humiliating consequences, while the adolescent in his drive for adulthood often will abolish all controls. The child needs to experience a process in which he develops responsibility for his actions.

A second important aspect of structure is that of love between the child and the parent or teacher. Without being able to give and receive love an individual spends a lifetime of frustration trying to fill this void. Love is much more than kisses and hugs and giving the child everything he wants. In fact, when parents and teachers give affection as well as material objects in an effort to "buy" love, they are often guilty of not providing the consistent limits which are essential to the wholesome development of the child. Love cannot develop unless it is nurtured in rhythm with limits. Love, for the child, emerges through his feeling of safety which results from routine and limits. There is nothing more sad than to hear parents say, "How could you have gotten into trouble? We gave you everything" and have the child respond, "But you never gave me the love and concern I needed." Being a "warm fuzzy" to the child does nothing but reinforce his self-centered attitude. When correctly employed, love becomes a vital part of the element of structure. The withdrawing of the expression of love, that is, attention, when the child misbehaves, and the giving of attention when he is being good, helps the child to understand his behavior and to realize that the parent or teacher truly cares about him. This can readily be seen in the actions of a young child after he has been disciplined and has finished pouting. He quite often becomes affectionate and gives love in order to gain the disciplinarian's attention once more. In such instances the child is giving love and finding limits, as well as learning that the parent or teacher genuinely loves him. Remember, the more the child is loved when he is behaving, the fewer times it is necessary to withdraw attention because of misbehavior. Too often the child is ignored when he is not causing a problem instead of being given the positive attention he deserves for being good.

One last word should be added about the aspect of love as it is employed in the structure of discipline. The child needs a great deal of love; to meet this basic need he requires just one person whom he realizes truly loves him. Consequently, a single parent or a teacher can successfully fill this need for the child if she is consistent and "has her own act together" to allow the child to experience love–safety from her.

The third major aspect of the element of structure is that of consequences in the child's life. Even children who are eleven, twelve, or in teenage years are often not yet capable of total independence, for they do not possess the power of mature reason. Therefore, independence of thought and action by the child must be perceived as a developmental goal by both parents and teachers. (Sometimes even as adults we lack maturity.) The child is born neither good nor evil. He is born with the capacity to interact with his social and physical environment and to learn through experience. Thus, the consequences which accompany his actions determine his perception of what is good and what is bad.

That there is only one hundred percent of behavior in a child's day seems to be quite a simple truism. However, this emphasizes the fact that the more time a child spends on being good, the less time he spends on being bad. The child should not be ignored simply because he is staying out of trouble. Although it is impossible and quite unnecessary to provide attention to every good action the child performs, it is at times necessary to let him know that being good is not only expected of him, but it also makes everyone happy. In this way, the consequences the child begins to look for are not strictly self-centered. He comes to realize that his actions are closely associated with other people and are not just based on what he wants for himself. In other words, self-discipline emerges as the child's actions, both positive and negative, meet consistent consequences through interaction with others, especially the parent and teacher. It is this action-reaction process that enables the child to feel secure and to learn what he must know in order to live in society.

The following section focuses primarily on techniques that may be used in dealing with problem behavior (more formally known as consequential discipline).

Ignoring a negative act by a child has probably been the most stressed consequence in recent years. Ignoring a behavior such as pouting is a realistic means of having a child learn that his behavior does not always accomplish what he thought it would accomplish. However, children at times need to experience unpleasant consequences when they have been "bad." For example, if a child threatens to have a tantrum in the supermarket to get what he wants, the parent has three possible alternatives: one, give in to the threat and buy the demanded item; two, ignore the tantrum, since after a number of tantrums the child will learn that this approach does not work; three, take action so that the child realizes his threat was not such a good idea. These last two alternatives are unpleasant but necessary consequences of the child's "bad" action.

The ideas and techniques for consequential discipline are used successfully only when the reader understands his children and the entire trinity of discipline. Otherwise, punishment techniques become reactions to problems rather than instruments insightfully selected and intelligently employed.

The following lists are presented for both parents and teachers. The first contains some overall procedures that can be followed to achieve social discipline; the second is comprised of punishment ideas that can be used as discipline consequences.

Procedures to achieve social discipline:

1. Discipline procedures should never be performed out of personal anger.
2. The initial aspect of the disciplinary action should be a reasonable, rational conversation between the child and his parent or teacher.
3. Embarrassment and humiliation should never be used as forms of punishment or motivation.
4. Parents and teachers should always refrain from using threats that can never be properly enforced.
5. Discussion with the child about his misbehavior should be done in private rather than in front of his peers.
6. The parent or teacher should avoid forming negative perceptions about the child as a person.
7. The parent and the teacher should attempt to understand the total context of the environment in which "their" child lives.
8. Teachers should never use threats of academic consequences as a form of classroom discipline.
9. The discipline of the classroom as a social entity should develop from the social life of the classroom.
10. Teachers and parents must be realistic and understand that some problems require assistance.

Discipline procedures should never be performed out of personal anger. Discipline must be seen as educative rather than as strictly punitive. It is perfectly all right for the parent or teacher to let the child know that she is displeased and that his negative actions are not only wrong, but personally unacceptable to her as an individual in the home or classroom. This kind of experience is necessary for the child to begin to understand his relationship to the social setting.

Whenever possible and appropriate, *the initial aspect of the disciplinary action should be a reasonable, rational conversation between the child and his parent or teacher* concerning the unacceptable aspects of the behavior. Many times this action will result in a possible solution to the problem that is developed by the child himself. At the very least, it will give the parent or teacher time to cool down and present the child with a good model. Furthermore, when this process is employed it virtually eliminates the possibility that the child may not understand what he has done wrong and why he is being punished. Although at early ages the child is incapable of total understanding, still verbal reasoning needs to be used. As the child grows older (eight years and beyond) he can also understand better what he has done wrong and why he is being punished. Thus, the conversation takes on more meaning. Of course, if the misbehavior is one that the child knows is wrong and the parent or teacher is absolutely sure the child knows that it is, the discussion process is not needed for his understanding of the decision. Discussion is still needed, though, for the model the process provides the child. As often as possible, unpleasant situations need to be handled with a rational discussion between child and adult.

Since their overall effect on the child is detrimental to the growth of a healthy concept of self, *embarrassment and humiliation should never be used as forms of punishment or motivation.* For example, although the child may stop talking if he is ridiculed in front of other people, the effect on his personal development is devastating. Embarrassment and ridicule drive the child back to his safety need, and protection becomes of major importance. The child's self-concept is being eroded and both social and personal development are severely hindered when embarrassment and humiliation are experienced.

Parents and teachers should always refrain from using threats that can never be properly enforced. For instance, it is meaningless to tell the child that he will write 1,000 sentences or that he will not have supper for a week if he is bad. One cardinal rule of consequential discipline is that the parent or teacher should always follow through with promised consequences. Speaking without thinking can result in statements that leave the disciplinarian with a "no-win" situation. The child learns that the adult does not mean what she says and that threats have little meaning, and he learns to "tune out" language at important times.

Whenever possible, discussion with the child about his misbehavior should be done in private rather than in front of his peers. This is especially true as the child reaches pre-adolescence and adolescence, for his image with his peers becomes of greater and greater importance to him as he proceeds into his teen years. Teachers must be especially aware of this idea. If possible, have the child wait in the hall or in an office or until class is over before confronting him fully. This practice greatly reduces his need to present a "tough guy" image and eliminates the teacher's need to react strongly if the child loses his temper in that her position as the properly constituted authority is not threatened in front of the class. (A word of caution: Do not use the hall as a means of eliminating the child's disruptive behavior for a long period of time; he may get into more trouble there or possibly even subconsciously realize that being "kicked out" gets him out of class and its requirements.)

The parent or teacher should avoid forming negative perceptions about the child as a person. When this happens a vicious cycle begins. That is, the parent or teacher sees the child as being hopeless and the child begins to live up to this expectation, deciding that a negative identity is better than none at all. This is why some children will say they are bad and fight to prove it. The best possible solution to misbehavior is for the parent or teacher to believe the child is striving to be good. When this belief is conveyed to the child, he perceives himself as striving to be good and wants to live up to this perception.

The child's world involves the home and the school. Therefore, *it is vitally important that the parent and the teacher attempt to understand the total context of the environment in which "their" child lives.* Through such activities as parent conferences, parent visitation days, school-sponsored parenting programs, and, in very special cases or relationships, home visitations, parents and teachers can begin to understand the child and also begin to achieve consistency in their relationship with the child.

Teachers should never use threats of academic consequences as a form of classroom discipline, such as telling the child he is going to fail just for misbehaving. Since there is not a justifiable relationship between earned grades and conduct, such practices are detrimental to the development of a social conscience.

The discipline of the classroom as a social entity should develop from the social life of the classroom. Misbehavior must come to be seen by the child as being unacceptable in the setting as a whole, not as simply something the teacher does not like. This can be accomplished by following the overall discipline process and most specifically by establishing classroom limits and activities through a class meeting strategy, as described later in this chapter. After all, both the teacher and the children comprise the social life of the classroom and both ought to have a vested interest in its maintenance.

Teachers and parents must be realistic and understand that some problems require assistance. When such problems occur they should seek help from appropriate sources, such as a guidance counselor, child psychologist, or the principal.

This second list presents some consequential discipline techniques that are social but not punitive in nature. The list is brief; many items can be added by the disciplinarian who understands the trinity of discipline.

Suggestions for discipline consequences:

1. Taking away the child's privileges
2. Isolation
3. Having the child write
4. Having the child make amends for his misbehavior
5. Physical punishment

Loss of privileges is an excellent means for having the child realize that his negative actions bring personal consequences. This technique is effective because it takes away from the child something he has or an activity he likes to do. The privilege taken away from the child must be some object or activity that he truly enjoys and will miss. Also, as with other consequential discipline techniques, the child must earn the right to have the privilege once again. What generally takes place, then, is a developmental process that requires an ever-increasing payment for return. For example, the child makes verbal gestures of repentance as an initial strategy to regain the lost privilege. He says, "I'm sorry" or "I won't do it again." Since his thinking is immature and not adultlike it is easy to understand that these gestures are really quite superficial and usually contain very little lasting sincerity.

The taking away of privileges in all probability will not correct the behavior problem for long, but it does provide the means for leading the child toward greater social awareness. The next time the child misbehaves in the same way, the parent or teacher should not accept the child's word so easily, and should explain to the child that he does not do what he says he will do. The child then, over time, comes to realize that his words are neither accepted nor respected by the disciplinarian and that he must therefore think about what he will do to regain his lost privilege and his parent's or teacher's trust. Hence, the process leads the child from words of what he will not do, to thoughts of what he will do, to actions. Indirectly, through these discussions he also begins the social process of realizing that words of promise must be followed by actions of living. Once again, patience and consistency are needed by the parent or teacher in order to change the child's thinking as well as his behavior. In the long run this is what is important to overall, wholesome social development.

Isolation is many times a discipline technique that brings positive results. Isolation can be perceived and enacted in three possible ways:

a. Isolation can be used for an *immediate calming effect.* Many times discipline problems are caused by temporary exuberance, and putting the child in the "think chair" (an early childhood name) gives him a needed break from an activity in which he is engaged. Isolation for an immediate "calming" effect can also be used to separate two combatants after the physical struggle has been halted. Putting them in isolation provides the time needed for hot tempers to cool. Exit from an immediate calming isolation should always be done through a discussion. In the early years this can be done by moving the child to another chair titled the "talk chair." Calming isolation serves a purpose that is often needed in rearing a child and should be used frequently.

b. Isolation can be employed with an *exiting time duration.* With this technique the child is told he will sit for five minutes or until an activity is over.

c. Isolation can also be employed with *no definite time for release.* This technique is usually accompanied by a commitment from the child to do what is expected before he returns to an activity.

The isolation strategy follows the developmental process we have discussed in the section on loss of privileges. With each isolation the child has to work harder and harder to return to his former position in his parent's or teacher's eyes as well as to gain his own "release."

There are two basic ideas concerning the structure of the isolation area. The first one sets forth that the isolation area should be an attractive and appealing area to the child. This idea contends that many children who perceive themselves as bad need to realize and believe that they can be nondisruptive. This strategy provides them an opportunity to do so if they are nondisruptive when put in this isolation area. The idea is also that the child will come to realize that even though the isolation area has great appeal, it is actually "dull" compared to being in the social mainstream.

The second and more commonly accepted idea concerning the structure of the isolation area is that it is simply an area to which the child goes when he has lost the privilege of interacting with other members of the family or class. Parents and teachers must be sure that the area they choose is in harmony with what they intend as discipline for the child. Very simply, if the parent or teacher wants the child to be isolated in an unappealing way, then he should place the child in a chair or at a desk and not in an "entertainment center" such as his room.

In junior and senior high schools, the concept of isolation takes on a certain significance in the process of discipline. Isolation can be seen first as a detention hall procedure whereby students are removed for a time as a consequence for misconduct. Effective detention halls must be designed in such a way that the environment is highly structured and totally teacher-controlled. They have been shown to be most effective when conducted after school or even on Saturdays.

The second practice of isolation at this level is in-school suspension. This practice should, in effect, take all aspects of school life away from the student except responsibility for studies. As with detention halls, this process should be highly structured and teacher-controlled. In some situations a special teacher may need to be hired to conduct the in-school supervision program. In addition to the suspension, parents should be notified as to the seriousness of the behavior and informed of the next practice in the process of discipline through isolation. That practice, the third in the isolation series, is out-of-school suspension. Although this practice is unsuccessful most of the time, it does make the statement that the school as a social setting with limited resources cannot deal with all antisocial individuals and that at this point the parent must take full responsibility for the child in school. The fourth and final practice is expulsion from school.

Although teachers, administrators, and boards of education should determine what acts would warrant each practice, there are two points which must always be considered. First, the quality of the act (such as selling of drugs, violence, weapons) should have a bearing upon whether or not the series should be followed. Second, quantity has a bearing upon the use of the isolation series presented. That is to say, tardiness in itself is a relatively minor act; however, when repetitive, the collective nature of the act makes it quite serious.

Having the child write is another acceptable consequence to use in discipline. Statements that this process will hinder the child in his creative writing are simply not true. There is nothing wrong with having the child write sentences or compositions as a form of punishment. However, it is desirable to use positive sentence writing rather than the writing of negative ones. The child should write positive sentences such as "I will try to work with my brother" instead of "I will not fight with my brother." Using "positive plans" rather than composition writing as a discipline consequence is also advised. Positive plans are written plans containing what the child is going to do in order to be successful in staying out of trouble. This strategy makes the child think as well as write and contributes to the child's thought process concerning the way he should be acting. In addition, written plans serve as concrete reminders for the child when he is back in action again and is beginning to behave inappropriately. Furthermore, this strategy provides the disciplinarian with both a qualitative control over the results, by accepting or rejecting the stated ideas, and a quantitative control over its length or the number of copies. A copy of the plan should always be kept by the parent or teacher, and, when duplicates are necessary, the child should keep one as well. The positive plan strategy takes advantage of writing as a means of punishment and, in addition, forces the child into thinking about what is expected of him. It is a strategy that deals with the child as an individual who has a responsibility to others in his society.

One of the most essential practices of consequential discipline is that of *having the child make amends for his misbehavior.* For example, if the child throws something in a rage, he must be made to pick it up, even if the teacher or parent must take the child's hand in her own and put the object back. Only through this process will the child come to realize that fits of temper and thoughtless actions result in consequences that are unacceptable to those around him.

The aspect of *physical punishment* in the discipline process will be discussed in the section on intervention.

Disciplinarians can and often should use different techniques in harmonious union, such as isolating the child in conjunction with a loss of privilege.

In summary, the most important points for parents and teachers to remember about consequential discipline are: first, always be firm; second, follow through with promised consequences. Furthermore, they should always express to the child their personal displeasure with his negative behavior in order that the child will realize that it is the action that is unacceptable, not the child as a person. Finally, the parent or teacher should describe or have the child describe the exact behavior that is expected from him as a substitute for the undesirable behavior that has gotten him into trouble.

Dealing with negative actions is, to many people, what discipline is all about. This conception is grossly shallow. If discipline is thought of as merely modifying behavior, throwing all thoughts of consequence and moral development to the wind, we will tend to perceive discipline as control rather than as a process of social development. Many consequences may bring about changes in behavior, but only certain logical and social consequences will bring about changes in attitude and wholesome development. After all, changes in attitude leading to permanent behavior changes can be made *only* by the child. The end result of successful discipline is a person who controls his behavior through the thinking process. When techniques are used that develop a person's ability to think through his actions, the individual is prepared to live a constructive, healthy life. Teachers and parents must take the time and make the effort to constantly provide a set of activities designed for social development. The only way one learns to become ethical and moral is to practice daily toward reaching those ends. Discipline is an important element of this practice for the child. In essence, a person will never develop a social conscience without discipline, and discipline has no meaning if it does not result in a socially conscious person.

The fourth element necessary for the development of structure in the child's life is that of manners. Although in recent years many writers and psychologists have portrayed the idea of developing manners in the child as being meaningless indoctrination, or some other such notion, this is simply not true. Manners are, in a sense, minor morals for the young child. That is, they form a sound foundation for morals as the child matures. Having the child learn to say "thank you" and "please" and other manifestations of manners during the years when he is most anxious to learn and to please is extremely beneficial to the development of character. In short, manners help the child to develop a positive attitude of respect for others, care about his environment, and pride in his work, which later provides the core of his moral reasoning.

Under the major category of manners there are four general

areas which should be developed in the young child. Like the child himself, each of these four areas is developmental and is only healthy when it is practiced in harmony with the child's own development. In each area there is an ever-increasing rate of responsibility as the child grows. It is through these four areas of manners that the child begins to establish the attitudes necessary for the later development of good character and self-discipline.

Consideration for others. Since he is self-centered, the child will naturally act without concerning himself about others. From the very beginning, one should always emphasize "the others" to the child in all decisions he makes and in the discipline he encounters. Such practices as teaching young children to say "yes" instead of "yep" and teaching older children to wait until it is their turn are mannerly acts that have very meaningful effects on children's overall social development. Furthermore, if parents and teachers emphasize "the others" in the discipline conse-quences children encounter when they misbehave, they will eventually learn that they must consider the feelings and rights of others before they act.

Respect for property. Most children have little respect for prop-erty; objects to them are primarily a source of pleasure. Thus, it is the responsibility of the parent and the teacher to teach the child respect for materials. Of course, this is not to become something which completely hinders the child from being a child. For example, putting things back where they belong is a good lesson for the young child; getting upset every time he breaks some-thing, however, is detrimental to his growth.

Two major lessons a child must learn concerning respect for property are: first, that objects are not always readily available; second, that objects are not always easily replaceable. Too often parents and teachers give children anything they want and re-place objects that children have destroyed through total neglect. When this is the case children do not learn to respect property, for ownership ought to exist only with responsibility. Parents and teachers must make a determined effort to have children learn to turn pages properly, return materials to their proper place, and take care of their possessions. In this way children learn to respect property and become aware of their responsibility of ownership.

Neatness. It is important for wholesome development that a child learns to take pride in what he does and how he does it. This is essential not only for the eventual development of self-discipline, but also for the establishment of a good self-concept in the child. Because of the child's makeup, he often becomes impatient with performing responsibilities which he does not "have time for" or does not like to do. Hence, he often does them without any consideration of the quality and/or appearance of the final product. In such cases he will give just what is acceptable. Furthermore, as a consequence of this, he never really takes pride in such work for he knows that almost anything will be accepted. It is the responsibility of the parent or teacher to have the child learn that his best effort should be given on everything he undertakes. However, driving the child to be perfect is just as detrimental to his self-concept development as is accepting inferior work. Therefore, the parent or teacher must know the child's capacities and continually be aware of his development in order to avoid extremes in her expectations of the child regarding perfection, neatness, or totally sloppy work.

Punctuality. Although the child does not truly understand the concept of time until about ten or eleven years of age, we should begin to have him experience the limits of time as early as possible. There is no doubt that children should not be rushed and hurried into doing things. However, the child needs to realize that he lives in a world of time as well as space. Thus, through the process of time schedules, activities in time, and the telling of time, the child begins to encounter the necessity of punctuality. This aspect is not only "politely" necessary, but it is crucial to the development of a work ethic, respect for others, and self-discipline. From such experiences as having a family dinner at a set time, going to bed at a designated time, and being home when the street lights come on, the child learns to relate time to social demands for punctuality and getting things done on time. In short, he begins to recognize that time places demands upon freedom; this helps him to establish self-discipline.

Although we began by describing manners as minor morals for the young child, it should be noted that consideration for others, respect for property, neatness, and punctuality are still important in the development of self-discipline in the preadolescent and the adolescent.

Responsibility is the fifth aspect of the element of structure within discipline. There is nothing more cruel in life than freedom without responsibility. If the child is expected to be responsible for his actions, he must be given many experiences in which he can be responsible. From a very early age the child should be given tasks he is capable of performing on a regular basis and should be held responsible for completing them successfully. As the child matures there should be an ever-growing number of duties added to his life. Parents and teachers should draw out natural impulses, respect the child's curiosity, and innovatively play upon the child's creative abilities. However, this should never mean the withdrawal of social responsibilities. Without having responsibilities, the child will never develop the values of hard work, perseverance, and self-criticism that also constitute self-discipline.

Seemingly small responsibilities such as having the two-year-old put his toys away when he has finished playing with them, having the three-year-old help set the table for dinner, and having the child dress himself are examples of actions which are reasonable for the young child. An older child should take care of younger siblings, be responsible for maintaining a respectable room, help with home maintenance, and generally contribute to the family's well-being.

There are three major points concerning the responsibilities that children are given. First, responsibilities which have natural consequences, such as setting the table or bringing in firewood, are much more effective toward the building of character than are responsibilities which have inspection or imposed consequences like cleaning a room. This does not mean the latter responsibilities should be excluded, but rather that the former ones are clear-cut in that dinner cannot be served if the table is not set and the house gets cold if there is no wood for the fire in this time of energy conservation.

Second, children should *not* be paid for performing their responsibilities to the family. Since responsibilities are essential to the development of self-discipline and the importance of family life, monetary incentives merely feed the child's self-centeredness and become a deterrent to attaining the goal of self-discipline. Paying children to do their work in school or for getting "A's" on their report cards, and so forth, may gain immediate results and seem to be a simple solution. But in the long run, "buying the child off" not only becomes too expensive as he gets older, but, more importantly, it seriously interferes with the child's overall development of character. This is not to say that reinforcement is not necessary to keep the child going. The child will respond to smiles, words of praise, and adult attention as readily as anything else, for what he is searching out is approval from those he feels are properly constituted authorities. Giving the child a cookie for doing his work or a star for a job well done is not wrong, but when material or monetary rewards are all he ever experiences, they are all he will ever respond to as he gets older. For this reason, the idea of an allowance for the child should never be associated with responsibilities to the family. The child needs to feel he is responsible to the family, not to the dollar. As a child feels responsibility to a group or organization, he feels more loyalty to and involvement with the group. Thus, parents who help their children feel a sense of family will find it fairly easy to counter the classic line, "Everybody else is doing it." They will be able to answer with another favorite: "In this family, we do this. We don't always do what others are doing." However, it will only work if the child feels he is contributing and is a valued member of the family. Then when he hears the words, "In this family . . ." something registers with him.

An allowance is a good means for teaching the child the value of money, but should only be used for this purpose. Since this is the only good reason for an allowance, the amount given to the child should be realistic in terms of the child's age and not governed by family income. Giving the child an exorbitant amount of money in most cases leads to a loss of the value of money rather than appreciation of its value.

Third, the model the individual gives to the child is extremely important. In order for responsibilities to have a meaningful effect upon the child, he must see those in charge as being very responsible. For example, if a teacher wants the child to be on time she must be on time herself; if parents want the child to make his bed they must model the same behavior consistently.

The sixth and final elements of structure is prevention of problems. Practices that parents and teachers can employ to minimize the problems which occur in their environment are in the general category of preventive discipline. This section is structured into two distinct parts for the convenience of the reader. The first is written for the parent and the second is written for the teacher. Many of the practices are similar. However, we suggest that teachers and parents read both sections, since consistency between the home and the school is vitally important for the wholesome development of the child.

For the Parent

1. All children must have their safety needs met in order to begin true social development. As indicated already, parents must consistently provide limits and routines and represent a

properly constituted authority for their child. If this need is met through the enactment of the trinity of discipline, a parent is establishing an environment that is conducive to the prevention of many discipline problems.

2. Good examples set for children are extremely important in the preventive discipline process. The modeling process for the child is crucial in his social development. The child tends to imitate what he sees and experiences; therefore, parents must "practice what they preach." Of course, there is nothing wrong with having some practices which only adults can do. Certainly, parents need not give up their adult life to live as children, but being honest with the child and showing him the right way by example is necessary for his wholesome social growth.

For example, if a child learns a few off-color words from a parent who did not realize he used them that often, the problem can best be solved by the guilty parent's controlling his own language first. Very simply, the parent should tell the child that the words are ones that neither of them should be using and that they will not say them again. In this way the child learns the unacceptable nature of the words from the person from whom he learned them and also has a new model to successfully imitate.

3. Most parents realize that childen need love and attention. In addition to these two vitally important needs children must be treated with dignity. Dignity is found when a person knows that his thoughts are respected. This does not mean parents must accept the child's thoughts and allow him to act exactly as he pleases. What it does mean is that parents must demonstrate a sincere concern for their child's development and allow him to express himself. Children want to belong to a family. They need a home that is both loving and receptive. Thus, parents must *allow* the child to be part of the family, rather than *make* him part of it. This is done through listening to the child and by guiding and respecting his contributions.

4. All families should have scheduled family meetings once a

week. Discussion of rules, responsibilities, and family happenings should provide the focus. For the five- to twelve-year-old child these meetings provide an element of routine, enhance decision-making abilities, and enable him to contribute his ideas. Furthermore, the models of communication and concern for family togetherness that are being practiced serve to help the child reach out from his self-centeredness and take into account the feelings of others.

An agenda for the meeting should be drawn up throughout the week by way of a "meeting sheet" which is put on the refrigerator or in some other area of the kitchen. Family members should then put down topics they would like to discuss and sign their name. (If the child is too young to write, an older child or a parent may put his idea down for him.)

One major point to be remembered by parents is that the meeting should not be forced or rushed. That is, if there is only one thing to discuss and it only takes ten minutes, then so be it. On the other hand, if someone wants to talk, let him. Throughout the family meetings, the child must learn to listen to and respect other family members. Do not be surprised if it takes quite a long period of persistent "direction" to have the children learn to respect each other and to participate in the meeting in the desired way.

5. Periodically parents should monitor the quality of the parent-to-child and child-to-child communication within the family. This can be achieved by making either mental or written notes of the communication that takes place in the home. For example, a parent can monitor the communication between two of his children or a child and himself between 4 p.m. and 8 p.m. or from after dinner until bedtime. The monitoring or observation should include positive as well as negative comments on behaviors, such as: helping each other, playing together peacefully, deciding on television shows together, fighting, yelling, arguing, and being totally uncommunicative. In short, parents who em-

ploy this strategy are exploring the social atmosphere of the family. The observations are used in order that adjustments can be made to improve the quality of the family interaction. Although some days are "better" than others, this random monitoring practice allows parents to gain an accurate family atmospheric pressure reading over a period of time and focus on specific problems that seem to be more prevalent and are the cause of family unrest.

6. Children need many opportunities to develop pride, significance, and a positive self-image. These feelings can be nurtured through practices that we have termed "pride-builders."

Responsibility is the most direct way for a child to feel that he is an important part of the family. Whether the child is two years old or twelve years old there is no substitute for his having responsibilities and doing them correctly. They are the primary medium for his developing pride, significance, and self-worth. Parents should therefore be sure to provide the child with an adequate number of responsibilities (not too many—not too few) for his age. We also suggest that responsibilities be listed on a check-off sheet that is taped on the refrigerator. Although this appears to be a simple managerial practice, it is in fact an instrument for having the child be responsible for doing his "chores." In most homes the parent has to "inspect" to find out whether or not the child has completed his responsibilities. This inspection is not only time-consuming and therefore not consistently done, but it also tends to prompt the child to take a chance on getting away with not doing his chores. By keeping the checklist in the kitchen the parent can easily keep up with the child's responsibilities, and in addition, the child sees the list and is reminded of his responsibilities throughout the day. This does not mean parents should be naive enough to believe that the child will refrain from checking off items when he has only "kind of" met his responsibilities. However, periodically checking to see whether or not the child performed his chores and how well he did them will increase the honesty of checked responses. Furthermore, when parents discover a disparity between what the child has checked and the actual completion of his responsibilities, it provides them with a concrete means of having the child face his deception.

Another pride-builder parents should provide for their child is support for chosen hobbies and interests. All children have activities, hobbies, and interests. Furthermore, they want to share these interests with their family. Parents should therefore listen to their child's discussions of his interests and achievements, no matter how small they may seem. They should praise, support, and encourage his endeavors. Too often parents try to determine what interests their child should have. This practice is totally wrong. Parents can "open new worlds" to the child, but should never force the course of his journey. The child should have a part in the decision-making process.

Parents should also avoid making judgments as to which interests are the most valuable for the child. (Of course we are taking for granted that interests are positive activities, not negative ones such as smoking.) Some children will like sports, others will like music. Certain children will choose group interests, while others will prefer individual activities. The major consideration of parents should not be what particular interest a child has chosen but rather how they can involve themselves in the child's interest, at least from the standpoint of giving support. Parental involvement should never take the form of forcing a child into joining every league, group, and club in the area. Many children today have very little time to be children because they become overburdened with activities. Children need to play in trees, under bushes, and in "special" places; through these activities nature teaches them many things leagues and clubs never can.

If a child "wants" to become involved in an expensive hobby such as piano lessons, parents should not rush out to buy a piano and hire a piano teacher. As most parents are fully aware, children are quite spontaneous and often *want* something but do not really *desire* it. *Wanting* something is merely an impulse, a whim. *Desiring* something is an impulse followed by thought. Therefore, waiting a few weeks—even though this time will probably be filled with promises, pleas, and even fatalistic prognostications, such as, "I'll just die if I don't get it"—gives the parent an opportunity to add some thought to his child's impulse. By telling the child how expensive the impulse is and how many hours are involved in practice, the parent is performing the necessary act of helping the child process the *want* into a *desire*. If after two or three weeks the child is still interested in the activity, parents should help to get the child started. But start small. For example, do not buy a piano; rent one. No matter how much thought a parent believes he has added to the situation, it is hardly a substitute for reality.

Finally, once a child begins an interest be sure that he does not quit on an impulse. He may *want* to quit, but not *desire* to quit. Again, parents should have the child wait before quitting and try to add some thought to the quitting impulse. Many times the child is struck by a "new" impulse or he becomes frustrated. The child often wants to be good at something immediately. When this happens some directed perseverance is quite necessary. However, if the child continues to resist over a considerable period of time (at least a month) there is not much that can be done. Undoubtedly there are cases in which a parent has been persistent and great things have resulted; however, these instances are few and far between, for interest and effort are directly proportional.

There are many ways for parents to help their children gain pride and significance in the home. The nucleus of these ways is the time that the parents spend with them and the concern that they show.

7. Parents should be aware or at least appear to be aware of what is going on in their home and in their child's life. Many discipline problems occur because parents have not paid enough

attention to the child and what he is doing. In this day and age when mothers as well as fathers work outside the home, this lack of awareness has become a continuing factor in discipline problems. With the present economy and the predicted future economic situation, mothers are forced to work outside the home if there is to be a vestige of the "good life." What this means for the family is that today's parents have to provide safe, consistent environments for their child during the time when they cannot be with him. They must find a situation that gives the child many if not all of the processes he is given at home. Such concern might seem to be asking a great deal, but in truth, the consistency it will provide is vitally needed by the child. The parents must constantly be aware of the other environmental settings in which their child lives.

Another point which parents need to consider concerning the awareness factor is the "everybody else declaration." This is a practice which children use to fool their parents. It goes something like this: "You tell your folks I can do it and I'll tell mine you can," or, "Everybody else can stay out until eleven o'clock on Fridays, why can't I?" In most instances, the "everybody" includes children who have used the same line on their parents and children whose parents let them decide, without guidance, what they will and will not do. Parents should move firmly and show courage by drawing the line with their preadolescent. They should check out stories of "everybody else is" and not hesitate to call other parents who have been referred to in the discussion. Finally, parents should not be swayed, even if other parents are allowing their children to do something, if they do not believe the occasion or the time is right for their own child. After honestly considering the importance the event holds for the child, the parents should establish their own reasonable requirements and expectations. In most instances, a mutually agreeable compromise can be developed from open discussion between child and parents. The process requires patience and attention to the child's thoughts.

Consider again the example given in chapter three of the twelve-year-old and her attitude toward the curfew set by her mother. Even though she resented having to be home by ten, she recognized that she needed this limit, and the curfew helped her realize that what "everybody else" was doing was not necessarily right for her. The point of the example is that parents must understand their child's need for both freedom *and* limits, but they must also recognize that the child may not seem to appreciate those limits.

8. All families should have a "quiet time" without television, loud music, or loud games. This is a good time for family members to do homework, talk with each other, get responsibilities done, help each other, play quiet games, and have family meetings.

The best period for quiet time is usually right after dinner, which should be a meal in which every family member participates. The length of quiet time is dependent upon the age of the oldest child. That is, if the oldest child is six or seven, twenty minutes would be advisable. On the other hand, if the oldest child is ten or eleven, quiet time should be one hour. Of course, as children get older, they often have things to do outside the home immediately after dinner. Therefore, one should not make quiet time a prison-like atmosphere. Allow the children to do what they must do and find another time to "really talk" to them. Likewise, if younger children have special things such as Cub Scouts to attend, allow them to go, for quiet time is meant to be a time to be oneself within the family, not a mandatory silence.

Parents should use quiet time to talk sincerely with their child and show a genuine interest in whatever he chooses to discuss. If the child goes to his room, the parents should occasionally drop in and talk with him or help him with his homework. Quiet time enables parents to follow up family communication conducted at the dinner table with personal communication. Also, it is a time that gives both the child and his parents an opportunity to step back from things and activities and to know and understand each other.

9. Parents should always provide realistic and reasonable alternatives to the child's present unacceptable action. For example, if a child has gotten a "D" on his report card in reading, parents should not demand an "A" for the next marking period, unless his "D" came after a previous "A." Directing the child to do such a complete turnaround in most cases is so overwhelming and unrealistic to the child that it leads to frustration and can become the nucleus of a discipline problem. Telling the child that the "D" is unacceptable and that he must do better the next time, in conjunction with monitoring his study habits, leads the child in the right direction, and is a first step toward improvement in school.

The concept of reasonable demands also includes moving the child into situations with realistic expectations; for example, leaving a nine-year-old in charge of a six-year-old and telling him to make sure that everything goes smoothly and without any problems is obviously unrealistic. The six-year-old (who is probably jealous) will, in all probability, not let him achieve this goal anyway. Children need to know what is wrong and then what they "should be" doing. If the alternative presented to the child is realistic, this process will bring positive results. If the alternatives are not clearly presented and realistic, change cannot and will not take place.

10. Mountains should not be made out of molehills. There are many times that parents can avoid problems by not becoming too involved in certain situations. For example, children will have many arguments and fights with each other. They will also forget their differences, in most instances, in a short period of time. However, if parents become involved and order their chil-

dren not to play with a certain child or children, the conflict intensifies. Usually other children become involved as sides are drawn. In addition, the families themselves become enemies and the models that are portrayed to the children are of the worst kind. In short, a volcanic mountain has been made from a molehill.

Another mountain-making practice parents often participate in is that of becoming too emotional over very common and normal childlike acts. For example, it is quite common for children, especially boys, to experiment with foul language as early as seven or eight years of age. This experimenting occurs as a natural result of development, for children during this time period begin to realize that words are a way of having an effect on others, and they begin to discover that there are certain words which are taboo or somehow adult in nature. Sexual interest is expressed in words, and even "hidden pictures" are somewhat common for children as young as seven or eight years old, although nine or ten years of age is a more likely time for these problems to emerge. In any case, neither the experimenting with foul words nor the expressions of sexual interest should send adults into total shock or lead them to believe their child is somehow abnormal or perverted. Simply using a rational, conversational intervention technique about such words or an honest discussion, appropriate to the child's age, about sex is quite sufficient after the first incident. Chances are that he will use the language again and then punishment is in order; that is, unless he often hears this language in the home. In this case, he is only modeling what he believes to be a correct behavior. Parents who drink may be able to say that drinking "is for adults" and get away with it, but language they use in conversation is vastly different. Children seem to have an innate need to experiment with language and their doing so is vital for wholesome language development.

There are many times when parents read too much into their child's actions and thus expand problems beyond their true dimensions. When a problem occurs that seems to be beyond the norm, parents should consult someone such as a guidance counselor before becoming too upset.

11. We have stressed the importance of responsibility in the wholesome development of children. A child should have a pet. In addition to gaining responsibility for its care, the child learns to relate to animals in a positive way. That is, he learns not to fear animals and also to have a humane concern for them, both of which are very important for a child's wholesome development. Furthermore, pets provide a child with a way to experience and express many emotions, such as love, sympathy, sorrow, and joy.

We include the idea of a pet under preventive discipline because it allows a child to release frustrations and cope with many new experiences. Thus, if it is at all possible, parents should provide their child with a pet. Whether it is a dog or a cat, a hamster or a bird, a pet will help the child grow emotionally and gain responsibility, and will therefore prevent many discipline problems.

12. Parents should realize that social education and discipline are part and parcel of the same developmental process. Because this is true, patience is not an option but a necessity for parents to possess. Patience requires self-discipline. All parents seem to take great pride when their child learns a new letter of the alphabet or a new number. They even take great pride when their child learns some simple little verse or how to catch a ball. However, because the child's antisocial acts embarrass parents they often forget how extremely complex seemingly simple social behaviors such as table manners really are. Patience seems to be a little easier to find and positive results seem to occur more often when parents realize that social learning (discipline) is a complex process that takes time and deserves at least as much attention as reading, writing, and arithmetic.

13. We have stressed already the importance of communicat-

ing with other parents to avoid becoming victim of the "everybody else declaration." However, communication among parents should go beyond the awareness factor. We believe that parents should have "parent get-togethers" at least twice a year to learn about their children and to share frustrations and ideas. There are many resource people in schools, universities, and churches who are available to conduct seminars for parents, and there are organizations such as PTAs that need interesting programs. The time parents spend participating in such discussions and seminars is well worthwhile and returns big dividends in presenting discipline ideas and strategies.

14. The most successful preventive discipline practice parents can employ is spending time with their children. In today's society, time is at a premium for most adults. However, it is the responsibility of parenthood to give time to children. Year after year discipline is the number one concern of both parents and teachers, as evidenced in the Gallup polls. Year after year we hear repeatedly about the disintegration of the family and we note an ever-increasing divorce rate in America. No doubt there is a direct relationship between discipline problems and family life.

The necessity for routine in a child's life has already been stressed. Family routines are of utmost importance. Families should, if at all possible, have their evening meal together. Families should work together, have picnics, and go places together as often as possible. Family failure is the cause of problems throughout life. Too often a parent's occupational success is achieved at the expense of a family and the lives of its children. Parents should never waste the most important years of their child's life by not being there to meet his needs. Successful parenting demands a great deal of time—there is no alternative.

"An ounce of prevention is worth a pound of cure" is certainly true in parenting. Preventive discipline not only helps to avoid problems but meets the child's needs and assists in his social development as well. Parents must use preventive discipline techniques to develop a successful total discipline program for their child.

For the Teacher

In many schools there is one person who is perceived by the administration, and often by his or her colleagues, as being the best disciplinarian. In most instances, however, what such a dubious honor really means is that this person maintains the most apparent and strict control or domination over students.

The major question that educators should consider in relation to discipline is how the essential processes used can contribute to a high level of intelligent socialization in students. All too often the problem seems to be viewed only as how students can be controlled. For example, being physically stronger than the students and using this physical power over them can be a successful means of maintaining sheer control in the classroom. But such practices do not contribute any positive aspects to the social development of the students. Although some control is often necessary, if educators hope to contribute to the development of self-disciplined, socially conscious graduates, settling for an approach to discipline which results merely in control of students is not good enough in today's society.

Discipline ought to be viewed as a necessary part of the entire *schooling* and *socialization* process. After all, discipline is operating in all classrooms every minute of every day, at least as far as the students are concerned. If the teacher is the only person responsible for discipline and socialization in the classroom, the inevitable result is an "us" (the students) against "you" (the teacher) situation. In such cases, the development of both social consciousness and self-discipline is impossible. The solution, then, is that through the classroom environment—its rules, privileges, and activities, plus the student's active participation in this environment—discipline (the social life and the structure) becomes the responsibility of every member of the class, not just the teacher's. In other words, discipline and socialization come from the life of the classroom, with the teacher being a member (albeit the major member and properly constituted authority) of that environment.

When this point of view is held, discipline becomes an evolutionary process whereby students throughout their education experience gain more and more responsibility for their actions and the operation of the classroom. When the only interest is to control the students, persons who set the tone in the school environment show more and stricter control over children as they get older, whereas the truth in social development is that the older and more mature people become, the more they can be expected to assume responsibility for moral, ethical, productive behavior. This does not mean the children run the classroom but rather that they participate in classroom meetings conducted appropriately to their social stage. Through structured developmental processes, children participate in discussions about classroom life and slowly through the school years earn more and more responsibility for the development and practice of sound, self-directed behavior. Students must learn to respect others and assume their responsibility for the life of the classroom. This kind of classroom environment provides the activities students need in social decision making and the opportunity to experience the consequences of the decisions that are made.

Corporal punishment serves the teacher and the school far better than it serves the education of the student. The use of force is not usually initiated in the name of education, but rather in the name of control. Punitive action, on the surface, appears to be quite successful, especially for those who have a need to possess a physical dominance over the student involved. However, since the action is individual and is based upon a hierarchical power structure rather than a social relationship, the result is fear, which is often confused with respect. Corporal punishment is situational; for this reason it is often (erroneously) interpreted as a contributing factor toward the development of self-discipline. Neither fear nor physical control by others helps a child develop responsibility for his own actions.

The process for the development of a social education for students calls for the establishment of a social consciousness within the student through social interaction and social discipline. This interactive, socially consequential process is a necessary part of an educational process that is concerned with developing a total being who is capable of existing within and contributing to a democratic society.

The student must be free to move rather than having to feign paralysis. He must live in the real world, not in an artificial school structure, for his efforts are intrinsically social. The discipline through which he develops must contribute to this end. The individual can only be considered truly disciplined when he can regulate his own actions. Therefore, it does little good (although it is sometimes required) to forcibly stifle some activity of an individual when the consequence is, simply, immediate control. Can we ever consider ourselves to be educators when we *force* our students to do their work?

For an individual to benefit educationally from any discipline procedures taken, he must perceive his actions in continuity with their realistic social relationships and consequences, as opposed to contrived physical consequences. For example, if a teacher spanks a child with hand or board, the child is usually controlled, for the moment, but a more important dimension is the consequence of such an action. In most instances, the student realized his action was wrong, but only when an enforcer was present. There also is the tendency for the student to believe that his specific act, rather than his lack of social responsibility, is the cause of the teacher's displeasure.

If, however, the teacher interacts with the student and discusses the action itself, as well as its relationship to the other students, the individual tends to begin perceiving his actions in relation to the social setting. If the student's action, in the teacher's opinion, warrants a consequence, it should be social in nature. In this way the student comes to develop an understanding of the continuity of the act itself and its social ramifications.

Since the school is by its very nature a social institution, education must be a social process. In effect, it must assist the student in developing his powers for social ends. Values can truly mature only as the individual enters into a proper relationship with others in a unity of sharing work, play, and thought. Then, and only then, does the individual begin to think in terms of self within society. Therefore, it is the teacher's duty to create an environment of selected influences which affects the individual and assists in his social development. The responsibility for the rules, ideas, and values must be shared by all members of the classroom environment.

For the teacher, preventive discipline is both a list of strategies to be employed and the establishment of a consistent social environment. Preventive discipline is used every minute of every day in the classroom; therefore, preventive discipline and consequential discipline are joined together as a whole package. Discipline should be viewed as part of the overall social development of the child. The following eighteen practices are specific techniques whereby the teacher can develop classroom discipline that is both preventive and consequential in nature.

1. Teachers who construct a dynamic social environment obviously understand the developmental aspects of the students they are teaching. They also know and practice the trinity of discipline. This knowledge enables the teacher to establish an environment in the classroom which is advantageous in preventing many discipline problems. We strongly believe that teachers, as a faculty led by a competent principal, must establish a *process* of discipline (not just a set of school rules) that will be practiced by

everyone throughout the school. Until this is accomplished, discipline problems will continue to occur and will be handled for immediate control, rather than for the long-term social growth of the students.

2. A weekly classroom meeting is an essential part of preventive discipline. The need for limits in the student's life and the developmental aspects of these limits have been stressed. The classroom meeting is an excellent strategy for setting limits.

The meetings should be conducted as early as the kindergarten year and continue through high school. They should start simply and change as the child develops toward maturity.

For example, in kindergarten the meetings are held daily as part of "show and tell" time. The teacher should envision show and tell as a developmental learning process. Initially she helps children to be quiet while others are showing and telling. Next, she coaches children to listen while others are showing and telling by simply asking general questions about what the child has presented. Finally, she teaches the children to listen and think by asking specific questions about the presentation. This process generally takes around three months to accomplish. Through this growth of listening and thinking in the kindergarten year and in the child's development, the seeds for the classroom meeting are planted. When the children have reached this point the teacher tells them, "Starting today we are going to talk about our room and how we can make it a nice place to be." She then talks to the class about one of the rules (limits) that they have been following since the beginning of the year. There should be sufficient time to ask the children why they have the rule and how they can follow it as individuals. Over a period of time the teacher should cover all of the rules and have each of the children talk about himself and his relationship to the other children through the rules.

As can readily be seen, the kindergarten teacher is simultaneously teaching the children the process of the classroom meeting and giving them a continuous experience with their social relationship to others. Of course, as in the other grades, the classroom meetings can and should include all social interests of the children and the atmosphere of the classroom, for example parties, field trips they would like to take, and things they would like to learn.

First grade through third grade children (provided they have experienced the kindergarten process just described) should have a weekly classroom meeting. We suggest late Friday afternoon for the meetings, since it may be an appropriate time in classrooms and also because decisions reached during the meeting can be implemented in the following week. The teacher should be the leader of the meetings and should have the final say as to whether the rules which are passed will be accepted. Although this may sound autocratic, it provides a structure from which the children can operate. Certainly, if a teacher allows the children to determine what will be done, the results are often disastrous. As we have already explained, children, in a savage way of thinking, believe the harder the rules and the more cruel the punishment, the more the teacher will like the decisions and like them. When the teacher allows children to make classroom rules and consequences without guidance, the results usually are brutal and are impossible to implement successfully. We have found that when the teacher provides an overall structure for the children through an approved policy and guides them during the meeting, social growth is enhanced tremendously.

After rules and plans have been passed by the students and accepted by the teacher, they should be printed on a "class news board" and given individually to students for "class journals."

Fourth grade through sixth grade students should have multi-age group meetings. Once again we suggest that the meetings be conducted on Friday afternoons and follow the "town meeting" model that the children have experienced in the earlier grades. There are three important factors which differentiate these "town meetings" from earlier classroom meetings. First, the children experience social interaction and decision making in a larger body and with children of different ages. Second, an elected child-leader assumes the leadership role for the meetings. Third, the teacher joins as a participant in the meetings and the principal becomes the overall executive through whom all policies must pass.

The multi-age meeting is an important social development activity for the children. In many schools, this is the first and only time children have an opportunity to experience democratic social interaction with children of different ages. Furthermore, it broadens the children's perception of the school itself and their relationship to it. The multi-age meeting experience, just as the classroom meeting, helps the children to understand that the rules as well as the happenings of the school are theirs to live, not just something for the teacher to enforce.

If the total number of children in the multi-age group exceeds one hundred seventy-five, as it will in many of today's "school-factories," we suggest having several smaller meetings and a combined representative body to draw everything together.

From seventh through twelfth grades the classroom meetings should be enacted weekly, with students in each homeroom electing representatives to form what is traditionally called a student council. In this way, the student council reflects the ongoing active involvement of the entire student body.

3. Being a good model for students is an extremely important role for the teacher in the preventive discipline process. Since the student imitates what he sees and experiences, modeling is crucial to his social development. When the teacher exhibits good models and praises children for being good examples, she is taking a significant step toward helping children develop attitudes that are conducive to proper behavior and wholesome social development. In addition to the obviously appropriate and inappropriate models, the teacher must become aware of the "hid-

den" models she projects to children. For example, if a teacher uses embarrassment as a means of motivation, students will view this as an acceptable way to treat others. Therefore, the teacher must not only think in terms of actions she performs or avoids, but also of the social environment she is developing in the classroom.

4. In addition to love and attention, students need to feel equality of dignity in their learning environment. All too often classrooms become places in which curiosity and thinking are expelled in favor of giving right answers and fitting in. Being wrong is seen as a personal humiliation rather than as part of the learning process. For both preventive discipline and sound education it is necessary that the teacher respect students' beliefs and ideas. This does not mean the teacher has to become a "warm fuzzy" and accept anything and everything in the name of helping the child build a good self-concept. What it does mean is that the teacher must allow children to express themselves and also demonstrate a sincere concern for their unique development. Students want to feel as if they belong and therefore need a learning environment that is both caring and receptive to them. The teacher must allow students to participate in the classroom by providing a structure that establishes social order as she listens to them, guides them, corrects them, and respects their contributions.

5. Teachers should periodically monitor the quality of the teacher-to-student and student-to-student communication within the classroom. This is accomplished by using formal sociometric instruments, such as a sociogram, and by using an informal process of keeping notes or a diary of the communication that takes place in the classroom. For example, communication between and among students should be noted at different times during the day and with different activities. This monitoring process should include positive as well as negative comments about such behaviors as helping each other, playing together in

harmony, fighting, arguing, making fun of others, and being uncommunicative. This strategy will explore the classroom's social atmosphere. After data are obtained, adjustments should be made to improve the quality of the classroom interaction. Although some days are "better than others," this random monitoring practice allows teachers to gain a classroom atmospheric pressure reading over a period of time and to focus on specific problems that seem to be more prevalent and cause many of the disturbances in the classroom.

6. Students need many opportunities to develop pride, significance, and a positive self-image. These feelings can be nurtured through "pride-building" practices.

As we have already stressed, responsibility is the most direct way for children to feel as if they are important, contributing members of the classroom. Whether students are in preschool or twelfth grade, there is no substitute for having responsibilities and meeting them well. For the development of pride, significance, and self-worth, students must participate. Therefore, each child must be provided with an adequate number of classroom responsibilities.

We believe that housekeeping activities should be used as a primary source of classroom responsibilities. Elementary students should be responsible for putting things back where they belong and for sweeping and cleaning their classroom at the end of the school day. Also, elementary children should work as partners and teams at being responsible for keeping orderly desks and the school property clean and attractive. They should be responsible for attendance taking, lunch count, and many other classroom managerial tasks. We suggest that all responsibilities be listed on an individual check-off sheet located near the teacher's desk. This simple managerial practice provides organization and shifts the responsibility for task completion to the children. Often children will fail to meet their responsibilities correctly before checking them off; however, with periodic and judicial inspection by the teacher, the shift in responsibility for completion of the task does successfully take place in almost all instances.

Pride and significance for the elementary child are certainly nurtured through teacher recognition. In addition to the common focus of praise that we have already mentioned, we strongly suggest that teachers employ the "special message" technique of sending a child a written note telling him how well he is doing. Done spontaneously and at random, this technique is a highly successful means for motivating children as well as for giving them pride and significance.

A pride-building activity for all students is that of multi-age tutoring. For many students the opportunity to help others provides a tremendous boost to their self-concept. Even students who are having learning problems can and should be used as tutors with younger children. Indeed, in many instances the "below-average" student is a more successful tutor than the "average" or "above-average" student because he better understands how hard the work is to do and therefore has greater patience with the tutee. Success as a tutor builds the student's self-pride and, quite often, helps him to increase his own academic achievement. In addition to the tutors' personal development, multi-age tutoring provides a tremendous social experience for both the tutors and the tutees. It should be remembered that, like everything else involving students, the tutoring program must be highly structured and well-organized in order to be successful.

Another pride-building activity for elementary students is the Expert Helpers Resource Directory. Very simply, this activity is the development of a directory that includes every child in the class with two areas of expertise after his or her name. The area may be, for example, basketball dribbling or creative writing, just as long as every child has two and only two areas listed after his or her name.

In junior and senior high schools, students should be utilized as office workers, assistants to teachers and administrators, and monitors. However, most important for the adolescent is the feeling of group pride that can be developed and nurtured by clubs, music, art, and organizations and teams of all kinds.

In order to build pride in students there is one basic rule that must be followed. Students take pride in work into which they feel they have put an effort. Therefore, personal quality (how the student has grown) in his work is a major criterion of praise. Students are looking for support and praise from their teacher, but can only gain pride when they have earned it. The "giving" of grades and lowering of expectations have probably done more to destroy pride within students and schools than any other single factor.

Pride-builders are an important dimension for providing significance to students. When a student feels significant in a classroom he not only stays out of trouble but also becomes a positive force in the social atmosphere of that classroom. Thus, the more students who gain significance in the classroom, the greater the incentive for other members to join in a positive perception of classroom life.

7. The teacher, as the properly constituted authority, must be aware, or at least appear to be aware, of what is going on in the classroom. When the teacher is seen by the students as being "with it," their little subversive acts are curtailed significantly. Hence, teachers should try to keep "an eagle eye" on all classroom happenings and become familiar with phrases, sayings, and interests of the students they are teaching. Nothing will lead to "nuisance activities" by the students more quickly than a teacher's being perceived as someone who does not know what is really going on. Although this is true with all levels, it is especially true for teachers of junior high school students.

8. All teachers must have a classroom arrangement that is in harmony with the social development of the students, the number of students in the class, and the activity planned. Many times

teachers expect too much from their students by requiring them somehow to possess a sense of responsibility that they have not yet developed. As we have stressed, responsibility is gained gradually through experience. Students who have never worked independently or on group investigations will not be able to immediately begin to work productively in such situations. Therefore, teachers should begin any new experience in a structured way, both in time and in teacher control.

Numbers also play an important part in what the teacher can do. Many of today's classrooms are overcrowded, and that condition limits some activities that demand space. However, an amazingly wide array of activities can take place, even in overcrowded, poorly equipped classrooms, when the teacher realizes that socialization requires both time and controlled experiences. With this realization comes an awareness that planning should always include considerations of who will be where, what "movement system" will be employed if the students are to move, and how the teacher can maintain contact with all of the students involved.

The simplest rule for classroom arrangement is not to try too much, for too long, too soon. The variables we have emphasized—classroom and multi-age meetings, pride-building practices, monitoring of communication, and so on—should be implemented one at a time and must be used only to the point appropriate to the student's social development, with increased student responsibility as a goal rather than as an expectation.

9. Teachers should try to place the instructional process at the top of the list and subsume discipline underneath; otherwise, the structure of the classroom is eroded. Sometimes this is not possible, but by using a nonverbal technique to handle a problem the teacher can prevent the kind of major disruption that sometimes breaks the rhythm of classroom organization. In short, it keeps the teacher's attention focused on those who deserve it.

10. Teachers should establish an environment filled with sus-

pense and excitement. Although the need for routine has been stressed, if every day is "the same in every way" students become very bored and very sure of what they can "get away with" and when they can get away with it. Dull classrooms are the result of unimaginative planning. The energy of students should be an asset to learning and should be used to the fullest rather than viewed as an element to be controlled. Teachers should realize when their students need to release "bursting" energy, and they should respond by allowing spontaneous activities. Surely, creative energy should be used to tap the student's interests and keep the classroom spontaneously alive.

11. Since students are dynamos of energy, they need action times during the day. One of the worst beliefs that has developed is that students' time is wasted during recess, especially after the third grade. This is totally untrue. Children throughout elementary school need recess and also need other planned times when they can be active. Energy not spent in the playground will often be spent in trouble.

In junior and senior high schools, students also need time when their energy can be spent on informal social activities. Hence, these institutions need to provide times when opportunities are available. One way is to make study halls optional. However, the students should not be allowed to go wherever they please. Designated areas should be established and supervised by student monitors with teachers and administrators providing support when needed.

12. If at all possible, every elementary classroom should have a place in which the children can go to be alone at times. In early childhood classrooms it can be a cardboard castle or cave; in the upper grades an area in back of the room that is sectioned off by formal or informal partitions will suffice. The teacher and the children should set up rules concerning the use of the "alone area." Finally, the teacher should try to make note of the children who use the area most often and the time when it is most

used. This can provide valuable insight into the children and their needs during the day.

13. Teachers should try to provide a special time for conversation with each student. Of course this is in addition to being available at all times, but this time is provided to allow the student to feel as if he has the teacher's full attention. This special time will probably never be long enough in the early grades, and in the upper grades it might hardly ever be used; however, it does provide an opportunity for the student to reach out and be heard. Quite obviously this time can be assimilated with the "alone time," if the teacher can continue to function well without having her own time to be alone.

14. Sometimes teachers involve themselves in situations when it would be better to stay out of them. For example, once we were in an elementary school in an urban area and two older boys were at the end of a hall having a private conversation. A teacher who was quite a long distance away yelled, "I heard that," and proceeded to tell the boys they were in trouble for using "filthy language." The boys denied this vehemently. When they realized it was not doing any good, they became defensive and fought back with a "who cares what you think" attitude. Since the boys were being quiet and private in their conversation, the teacher should have ignored the situation. This does not mean that teachers should ignore foul language or insults when they are directed at someone else or even at themselves. They should not; however, such was not the case in this situation. The teacher really did not know what the children were saying and assumed the worst.

Sometimes teachers become too serious. Laughing with the students rather than becoming upset and blowing things out of proportion can often solve an immediate situation and prevent future complications as well.

15. All teachers should realize that social education and discipline are part and parcel of the same developmental process.

Then, discipline does not seem as if it is such an isolated waste of time. In truth, *discipline may be the most important basic a student will learn, for it is the beginning of moral and conscience development.* Quite often discipline is the most exciting part of education, for it is usually the time that the student is most creative and also the time the teacher becomes most meaningful in the education process. Since this is true, teachers should take great pride in a situation in which a very young student yells at rather than hits another child, when hitting has thus far been his social behavior pattern. Self-discipline is a *process* rather than a *product.* Therefore, when the student's success is measured by his growth, reinforcement of a present level of socialization can lead to the positive continuation of the growing process itself.

16. Teachers must give students realistic alternatives to their present unacceptable behavior. Teachers often point out to the student his bad behavior, but they ignore clarifying what alternative exists for him. For example, if a student is frustrated and asks another student to help him, he is told to stop talking and keep to himself. This kind of statement leaves the student without any alternative but to try again or to release his frustration in some other (more than likely unacceptable) way. When the teacher intervenes, she must consider the student's action and the alternative she can suggest to solve the problem. Providing one realistic idea is usually sufficient; presenting too many alternatives is confusing and overwhelming. Thus, even while using a corrective action the teacher can be either preventing or nurturing future problems.

17. Teachers should always make reasonable demands in all situations with their students. For example, during the times a teacher has to leave the room, it is more realistic and socially better to allow the students to talk quietly than to forbid them to talk. Although some teachers can intimidate the students into silence and others leave a "special guard" to report the talkers, it is far better socially to allow the students to take responsibility for

"quiet" talk. This does not mean that their idea of "quiet" talk will be the same as the teacher's. However, through the experiencing of the teacher's pleasure and displeasure and the giving and taking away of privileges, success does come. This success promotes social growth and allows the teacher to leave the classroom when it is necessary without fearing what will happen during her absence.

18. Teachers in the elementary school often deal with complaints by having students write them down. This strategy has three major advantages. First, providing the students with a complaint box gives them a release for problems they are experiencing. Second, it provides teachers of children who are in the tattling stage (usually late first and second grades) with the best means of dealing with this problem. It is the best way because, on the one hand, if the teacher discourages tattling by telling the egocentric child not to tell on others and only be concerned about himself, he may do just that. On the other hand, if the teacher reinforces the tattling process the child will continue to try and make himself look good by "putting down" others. By having to write the complaint, with no names mentioned, the child realizes that the teacher is interested in the social climate of the classroom but that he gains no personal praise. Most teachers find it amazing how quickly the tattling comes to an end. Third, the written complaints are an excellent source for discussion at classroom meetings.

In summary, preventive discipline techniques are vitally important aspects of the overall discipline process. They help avoid discipline problems and establish a positive home and classroom environment. The techniques given here are examples of what can be done by both parents and teachers to develop a positive atmosphere in their home or classroom. Through social interaction with their children, they can and should continue to try new preventive ideas and do away with others that have grown old and seem to work less well.

Finally, the more positive actions parents and teachers take with children, the less negative actions they will need to take. The more time parents and teachers spend getting to know their children and building a positive social climate, the less time they will have to spend punishing them. Failure to give children the time they need can never be corrected by punishing their bad behavior.

Structure is essential in a student's life. Even the teenage child is not capable of total freedom in his social decisions or problem solving. However, structure does not mean total restriction. The individual must be allowed to assume more and more responsibility for his actions and hence more freedom as he grows to maturity.

Intervention

Intervention, as the second component of the trinity of discipline, pertains to the various ways of interacting with the structure that has been established for the individual by the parent or teacher. Too often parents and teachers only interact with the structure when problems emerge; they react to the problems without thinking and, consequently, end up punishing the child without any rhyme or reason. Therefore, successful maintenance of the structure, through a repertoire of intervention techniques and the knowledge of how and when to use them, is of utmost importance to all disciplinarians.

The following list provides the seven intervention techniques that we consider to be necessary for parents and teachers to possess if they are to maintain a wholesome structure of discipline.

1. *Observation intervention.* One of the hardest discipline intervention techniques for adults to learn is patient observation. Most of the time, it takes skillful observation on the part of the parent or teacher to determine what has actually caused the be-

havior problem. No doubt many problem situations do not provide for the luxury of watching what is taking place. If, however, the opportunity to observe does exist, one should not rush to actively intervene. On some occasions, for example, when children are arguing, growth comes from the process of the disagreement. That is, in some circumstances children will come to a solution which is acceptable to all parties involved. In such instances, the social development which takes place for the children is far greater than could be accomplished by any adult intervention. Furthermore, if your children argue but do not turn to physical aggression (fighting) out of hopeless frustration, a great deal is being achieved as far as social growth is concerned. It is even advisable to intervene positively in situations in which the children would ordinarily end up hitting each other but do not. This is accomplished by stating that arguing is not polite, but that it is right that the children did not try to solve their problem by hitting each other. In this way, there is a condemning of the negative behavior of arguing, but also a recognition of the positive behavior of physical restraint. As an added bonus, children are usually so totally shocked by this intervention strategy that they very rarely continue their argument, even when told to do so.

In any given day some of the child's behavior will be good and some will be bad. It is the parent's and teacher's responsibility to react to the bad behavior with discipline and, just as importantly, to take time to let the child know when he is doing the right thing.

As an observer, the parent or teacher should take note of two broad areas of concern: first, *when* the problem generally occurs, and second, *where* the problem generally occurs. *When* the problem occurs refers to time of day and to such other aspects as *when* he is hungry or tired; *when* he is doing a certain task; *when* he is with certain children; *when* he is in a large group; *when* he is jealous; *when* he is bored; or even *when* he just seems to need some attention. *Where* the behavior problem occurs simply refers to the location of the trouble time. For example, the problem might occur only on the playground, or in church.

The combined information of these two elements assists the disciplinarian in formulating an overall picture of the problem and helps him to focus upon the specific causes of the problem. The parent or teacher should rely on recorded observations. Therefore, keeping a record of the *when* and *where* data of the observation is a vital aspect of observation intervention, especially when there is a continuous or recurring problem. It provides the disciplinarian with the means of stepping back from the immediate, disturbing situation and looking at the problem in its total perspective.

In addition to the recording of the *when* and *where* data of the problems, the disciplinarian also should record the discipline procedure used in each circumstance and the duration of the success, if any, that has resulted from the specific procedure employed.

Since the whole point of observation intervention is to allow children to develop socially through peer interaction and to provide the disciplinarian with a vehicle for discovering the cause of the behavior problem, it cannot be stressed strongly enough that the recording of observations is essential. The brief time spent on recording exactly what happens usually pays big dividends in return to the disciplinarian.

2. *Physical intervention.* Physical intervention is a commonly practiced form of discipline used by parents and is probably the most longed for by teachers of all ages when they get frustrated by problem behavior. Whether it is the belief that "every kid needs a good strapping now and then," as one parent said, or "controlling children is easy. I just make them kneel on rice when they're bad," as a teacher stated, physical intervention is perceived by most people who deal with children as either the way to successful "control" or as a last-resort measure. However, the major

issue that parents and teachers should consider in relation to discipline is how the essential processes used can contribute to a high level of intelligent socialization in children. All too often the problem of discipline seems to be viewed only as how children can be controlled. For example, being physically stronger than the children and using this physical power over them can be a successful means of maintaining sheer control in both the classroom and the home. Such practices, when exclusively used, do not contribute any positive aspects to the social development of children. They only control for the moment.

On the other hand, many parents and teachers today have been so intimidated by psychological publications and by legal action resulting from child abuse that they are, in fact, afraid to assert themselves with their children. In short, in this country there is a large number of parents and teachers who are not sure of what is right and what is wrong when physical punishment is used as a means of discipline.

Let us review two major points we have already made which pertain to this issue. First, physical punishment in many instances gets results or at least appears to get results. Since the child is self-centered, he wants to avoid all discomfort and gain as much pleasure as possible. Physical punishment hurts and the child will do what he can to avoid it. This accounts for the simple fact that physical punishment works *on* children. But, in addition to learning that certain behavior will bring on physical punishment and pain, the child learns that the way to deal with something he does not like and/or something which he thinks is "bad" is by hitting or hurting it. Quite obviously this is not what children should learn. Grown people who murder, abuse their children, or physically fight with others, are prime examples of people who never learned to handle their feelings through reason and rational action. Rather, they learned as children that problem behaviors are solved through lashing out and hurting others physically.

The second related point concerning physical intervention is that, especially between five and ten years of age, boys are in a "power phase." That is to say, they usually begin a phase in which displeasure is demonstrated in physical ways. Rebellion to direction is often exhibited by means of a physical challenge, for example, refusing to sit when told to do so or refusing to move when asked to do so.

Since the basic frustration many parents and teachers are feeling concerning physical punishment as a means of discipline stems from confusion over its appropriate use, we must emphasize that there is a big difference between physical intervention and child abuse. In some situations, disciplinarians are left with no other alternative than to use physical intervention. After all is said and done, the child who is in a power phase needs to realize that the disciplinarian too can use power (although he does not want to) to accomplish his directions. Furthermore, physical intervention may sometimes be necessary to protect the young child from hurting himself (for example, by running into the street).

Thus, physical intervention is a legitimate means of dealing with behavior problems in young children. However, when considering physical intervention the disciplinarian should keep three important things in mind. First, physical punishment is indeed a two-edged sword. Since discipline must be envisioned as a necessary part of the socialization process for children, one must thoughtfully weigh whether a particular situation merits physical punishment at the cost of giving the child an extremely poor model of the way adults handle their displeasure. Second, there is a limit to physical punishment. Very simply, such obviously abusive acts as washing a child's mouth out with soap, hitting a child with a belt, or slapping the child across the mouth can never be justified. Physical punishment means "placing" the child down when he refuses to sit or giving a spanking on the bottom when he continues to run into the street. Third, physical intervention should be the last resort rather than a common practice. Quite frankly, when an adult has to use physical intervention to gain a desired response from the child, he has failed in every respect of discipline-socialization, other than getting a desired result through fear and hurt. Physical intervention is indeed the lowest level of intervention between a parent or teacher and the child. Therefore, if physical intervention is the only technique used that seems to work, the relationship is in serious trouble.

Physical intervention is never recommended as a technique to be used by parents and teachers of teenagers. First, since the individual at this age is so peer-conscious, he is often "forced" by his fragile image to take "action." Second, the adolescent considers himself to be an adult and to be treated in such a way is viewed by him as being totally degrading. More appropriate procedures for enforcing limits must always be used with the adolescent.

In summary, physical intervention is a sometimes necessary evil, but it is necessary only when there are situations with no other answers. It is an evil because of the many inherent consequences which are detrimental to the socialization of the child involved. Physical intervention is the lowest level of relationship between the parent or teacher and the child. Physical punishment should never be performed out of anger, and when physical punishment is chosen it is always wise to remember that there is no relationship between the severity of the pain and gains in positive results. It is the physical action itself that brings results. Therefore, the parent or teacher should always consider the physical results of his actions. For example, the disciplinarian should hit the palm rather than the back of the hand because of its bone structure. If physical punishment is, after thoughtful consideration, deemed necessary, then the action should be planned for its safe effect rather than for severity of pain. Finally, the goal of any intervention technique is to gain the tremendously necessary feeling of love and respect from the child and to assist in his social development, until eventually he can and will control his own behavior through thought, reason, rational actions, and "talking out" problems.

3. *Verbal intervention.* Verbal intervention is the most commonly used form of discipline. The verbal actions included in this technique range from very patient discussions with children to screaming and yelling. In the section on physical intervention, children between five and ten were said to be in a power phase. Likewise, during this time period they enter a "verbal assault phase" by which they learn that words can hurt. This phase, however, seems to be more prevalent in girls than in boys. Girls usually employ language rather than power to assault others. They form groups (cliques) and can be quite vicious to each other. Adolescents as well are very prone to use verbal abuse against people with whom they disagree. In such cases, verbal intervention is a most appropriate means of dealing with the problem.

There are three specific techniques which can be incorporated in forming verbal intervention strategies that work. They are rational discussions, direct statements, and controlled emotional outbursts.

The *rational discussion* technique is an approach which is of utmost importance in the discipline process. Although children are not capable of reasoning as adults can in problem situations, the model a parent or teacher sets for the individual by using rational discussion is extremely advantageous to social development in children. Just as the model of physical control indirectly teaches children to be aggressive and hurtful when they are displeased, reasoning and rational discussion indirectly assist them in learning socially acceptable patterns for problem solving.

When one chooses to use the rational discussion technique there are two important dimensions to consider. First, rational discussion cannot be undertaken with an individual who is emotionally out of control. Getting the individual's attention is the first step in discipline. This is especially true in employing verbal intervention with rationality. If the person is emotionally out of control he is not only unable to participate in a discussion but is even unable to gain the major benefit from the model the disciplinarian is setting. If the child is in such an emotionally charged state, the disciplinarian must delay this approach until he is reasonably under control. This is usually accomplished by stopping the negative behavior and by directly telling him that it will be possible to talk with him about the problem when he is "ready" to talk about it. If he continues to "carry on" then other steps should be taken and rational discussion delayed until another incident occurs at a later time. Also, the adolescent may sometimes employ the passive resistance technique of not truly participating in the discussion. As with the emotionally charged situation, rational discussion cannot be successful in this situation and thus must be postponed.

Second, rational discussions demand two-way communication. The student and the adult must be ready to listen to each other's point of view. In addition to telling the individual what is wrong during the discussion, it is absolutely essential to ask him to present alternative solutions to the problem at hand. Through this strategy, not only does the child come to realize that adults are willing to listen to him, but there is also occurring a vital shifting of responsibility toward him to help solve the problem. Many times the child is merely presented with a parent's or teacher's solution, which he passively rejects, since he had no part in the process. This severely hinders the child's developing social responsibility. Therefore, disciplinarians should be hesitant in trying to provide an answer for children's problems. Children should participate in the rational discussion technique by deciding what they can do to avoid the problem in the future and even the kinds of punishment that should be given if the problem happens again. As a word of caution, children, even teenagers, will many times say "I don't know why I did it" or "I don't know what I can do to stop the problem." This is an easy "cop out" for them. Such statements should not be accepted at face value; rather, it is necessary to pursue more thoughtful solutions to the questions. It is probably true that he does not know why he "did it," but thoughts as to what he may do in the future are vitally important for the child's thinking and actions. One should also be aware that when the young child initially gives a punishment consequence for a negative behavior, he is probably going to suggest a very harsh punishment. That is, he will attempt to provide a severe punishment consequence, thinking that this is what is wanted. He thinks in terms of pain and its severity as a means of stopping him from doing something which is wrong. Disciplinarians should try to ignore these overdramatized solutions. After the child has given a solution which is too severe in nature, the conversation should be extended. In this manner, a great opportunity for a social development lesson is given to the child.

Adolescents, on the other hand, are not prone to giving severe solutions. In fact, they are more likely to try to avoid any consequence whatsoever. However, adolescents need very much to express their feelings and ideas. Therefore, verbal communication is an essential component of discipline for this age group.

In summary, the rational discussion technique is employed to provide a good model and to help the individual think in terms of logical consequences and personal responsibility for actions.

Using *direct statements* as a verbal intervention technique is almost self-explanatory. This technique is to be short and to the point. It is employed as a vehicle for getting actions accomplished and letting the individual know, beyond any doubt, who the properly constituted authority is.

There are many times when the individual knows exactly what he has done wrong. He knew before he acted in a certain way that, if he got caught, his actions would get him in trouble. Also, there are times when he is just being bold and is seeing how far he can push or how much he can get away with before something happens to stop him. (Psychologists call this process "testing his limits.") In such cases, direct statements are very appropriate and highly successful intervention techniques.

There are three rules that must be followed in order to use the direct statement technique successfully. First, the disciplinarian must use a stern voice. Second, the disciplinarian must state the point in as few words as possible. Third, the disciplinarian must have an outcome which he expects from the individual.

Direct statements are also the means whereby disciplinarians should explain and clarify consequences. Many times an individual child or adolescent will intentionally or unintentionally "forget" a rule which is part of the limits he needs and requires. In such instances, directly stating what the rule is and what will happen to the child if he persists in breaking it is usually sufficient for dealing with the problem.

The *controlled emotional outburst* is our third verbal intervention technique. It should be used very sparingly, since its effectiveness and value are totally dependent upon the shock factor. If the outburst is employed too often, the child gets accustomed to the adult's being in this state and is not usually very impressed or guided to positive behavior through its use.

The most important aspect of this technique, as with all other discipline techniques, is that the disciplinarian must be under control when utilizing it. Although the child should think that the disciplinarian is "ready to explode at any minute," the truth of the matter should be that the adult knows exactly what he is doing and what effect his behavior will have on the child. Emotional outbursts, when professionally performed, should involve piercing eyes, a loud voice, and arm gestures to add some flair to the whole technique. Also, just as with the direct statement technique, the disciplinarian should not waste words but rather succinctly dictate what has driven him to this point and what he now wants to have happen, immediately. Used wisely, the emotional outburst technique has a valid place in the classroom and in the home. If used more than occasionally, however, it produces little other than a headache for the one trying to use it and does not provide a healthy model for the child. (The controlled emotional outburst technique is rarely successful with adolescents, since developmentally they are in a stage of emotional turbulence.)

In conclusion, verbal intervention is an extremely important discipline skill for parents and teachers to possess. Through three techniques, it provides a means of listening to the individual, presenting a positive model, shifting responsibility to the child for his own behavior, gaining respect from the individual, and achieving needed results. It is highly important that disciplinarians use verbal intervention, but only as a result of thinking. It cannot be stressed enough that uncontrolled and unplanned verbal strategies do not work; when the parent or teacher is not in control of her words and actions the child learns quickly that she seldom means what she says and that she does not have control of her behavior. Neither of the two conditions promotes wholesome social development.

4. *Nonverbal intervention.* Nonverbal intervention is another strategy which is, and should be, commonly employed by both teachers and parents during the discipline process. When successfully used, it demonstrates the disciplinarian's relationship to the individual as the properly constituted authority in his life. It also shows the individual that he can operate on a high level of understanding about his own behavior and the consequences it brings. If the disciplinarian can bring about a change in an individual's negative behavior, gaining his attention without speaking, the relationship is operating on a high level of respect.

Whenever one thinks of nonverbal communication as a method of discipline, nasty looks, snarls, piercing stares, and the "evil eye" come to mind. Indeed, all of these are effective nonverbal techniques, but should only be employed by people who have the ability to perform these techniques successfully. For example, a person with a "baby face" who is trying to look mean is using a technique that simply does not work. In most instances, the facial expression results in a joke and little is accomplished in the name of discipline.

Children and adolescents will often use joking or kidding as a defense mechanism against adult discipline intervention techniques. If successful, they realize that they have manipulated the disciplinarian and have merely proven to themselves that what they were doing to warrant the intervention was not really all that bad. There are, however, certainly times when laughing at ourselves with the child is not only acceptable, but needed. Being a good model is, again, very important. Hence, being human by showing the individual a sense of humor is most definitely a model which should be demonstrated frequently. However, it should not happen too often at the "wrong" times. Most adults have to cultivate effective facial expressions.

Finally, one must remember that nonverbal intervention is on a scale that includes many strategies in addition to facial expressions. Stopping speaking until attention is gained, flashing lights on and off, having a hand signal that means attention is called for, and clapping out rhythms are also highly acceptable strategies which should be included in nonverbal intervention. One must remember that the less aggressive the action taken, the higher the level of operation between the disciplinarian and the individual. Thus, in nonverbal intervention, looking up is certainly on a higher level than having to give an awful stare or a sad face to gain the child's attention and respect.

5. *Removal of object intervention.* Removal of object intervention is the most appropriate for parents and teachers of young children. One must be careful to understand what it means, since the technique appears on the surface to be very obvious and easy to use. Parents and teachers, for some unexplainable reason, seem determined to play Solomon in every squabble that devel-

ops between and among children. A child's greatest social growth takes place during a problem-resolution process with his peers. In most instances, the adult is not able to solve the problem. Often children present differing stories of the same situation, since they are naturally self-centered. Thus, when the adult renders a verdict, it is usually unsatisfactory to all parties involved, including the person who makes the decision. Parents and teachers should therefore stay out of as many squabbles as possible.

When involvement of the adult seems absolutely necessary in children's disputes, removal of the object or activity is the most realistic intervention technique. The removal should be accompanied by a statement which informs the children that when they are able to decide how to share or take turns, the object will be returned or they will be able to resume the activity. If an injustice is seen, however, such as one child pushing another off a bike that he has been riding for a while, take action against the aggressor, rather than removing the object. Finally, one should remember that children forgive and forget most conflicts rather quickly. In too many cases, adults blow things out of proportion by telling the children not to play with each other again. It is very common for little squabbles between children to turn into family feuds, and this is quite needless.

Extrapolation of the removal of object intervention technique leads to the idea that with both young children and adolescents teachers and parents can and should stop an activity which is resulting in problems. For example, if a teacher realizes that an activity-centered lesson is resulting in more confusion than learning, she should stop the lesson and tell the students that since they do not seem able to behave responsibly during activities, a more structured lesson is more appropriate for them. This is not to say that activity-centered lessons should not be used; indeed, sometimes a person has to experience what can exist in order to appreciate it fully. By using less structured lessons, even if they have to be discontinued, the teacher provides incentive for students to assume the responsibilities of activity.

6. *Positioning intervention.* Another intervention technique which is appropriate for teachers, and to some extent for parents, is positioning. This technique lets the individual know that the adult is aware of exactly what is happening, and it is used to prevent problems as well as to deal with them as they occur. There are two major strategies related to positioning intervention: (a) positioning before interaction, and (b) positioning as a result of the interaction.

a. *Positioning before interaction* refers to the thoughtful planning of exactly where the teacher or parent should be located to insure the successful completion of the planned activity. It includes the thoughtful planning of room arrangement and, in some cases, a movement-management system which provides a way for students to work, move, and be active in their tasks without running into each other or turning the activity into utter chaos. Several aspects must be carefully considered in planning a "special" activity with a group of students: (1) the social developmental level of the students, (2) the number of students involved, and (3) the area needed for the activity. (The word "special" merely refers to any activity which is outside the students' routine.)

1. The social development of the students refers more to the ability of the students to work together than to their chronological age. Even young children (five- and six-year-olds) can successfully perform activities that require movement and cooperation if they have been taught and held responsible for doing so. On the other hand, sixteen-year-olds who have never been taught and held responsible for working in groups find it very difficult to have freedom and accept any responsibility.

   Freedom is born on an increasing plane of responsibility. That is, a person is only truly free when he can be responsible for that freedom. It was the lack of an understanding of this principle that led so many so-called "open educators" into socially unhealthy "nonlearning environments." Whether working with one child of five or a group of thirty teenagers, teachers must be aware of the group's social development which is measured by their ability to be responsible for freedom. Therefore, parents and teachers should initiate any activity out of the regular routine for short time periods and use a highly structured mode of operation. If students are to learn to work in "learning centers," the procedure must be introduced gradually. They should begin by spending only fifteen minutes in a learning center with the teacher showing the students how the system works. This may continue for many days before the length of time is increased and the controls are loosened. Ability to work independently rests on social development and the assumption of responsibility by the student. Sometimes stressful endeavors may be necessary for the student to grow into the culture, but all activities and expectations must be geared to the social developmental level of the student.

2. The number of students to be involved in a group activity is important and is closely related to their social development. With students who have a low level of social development, it is extremely difficult to do any activity with even as few as four group members. However, these students are the ones who need socially developmental activities the most. Instead of giving up—which can, and too often does, happen—the teacher should begin with a few of the stronger students and, for very short periods of time, begin some structured-independent activities. The plan of attack is "divide and conquer" by bringing a few at a time into the social order.

3. The area used for an activity is also important. Quite obviously, it must be large enough to accommodate the activity planned. Too often parents and teachers try activities which require much more space than exists. Therefore,

one must be sure to plan activities which fit into the available area at the same time that they fit the students' social development. The teacher should design a room arrangement on paper before undertaking any new endeavor so that problems can be anticipated and avoided. Making the design ahead of time also gives an indication of where the adult should be positioned to keep the activity going smoothly.

b. The second major aspect of positioning intervention is essentially *movement to achieve intervention*. Quite often during an activity (lesson), minor disturbances develop in different sections of the activity area. In such instances the teacher or parent should continue what she is doing and try to move herself to a position directly in the heart of the disturbance. By doing this the disciplinarian can usually stop the disturbance without giving too much recognition to the "troublemakers." Furthermore, it allows the disciplinarian to use other intervention techniques, such as direct statement or that special "glare," if they are required.

7. *Positive intervention*. The final intervention technique all disciplinarians should use regularly is positive intervention. In addition to ways of intervening when problems occur, intervention should also include techniques which tell the individual he is doing a good job and that the adults are proud of him. Too often parents and teachers only intervene (communicate) with their children when something has gone wrong. Since children need a great deal of attention as a natural part of their development, this practice can result in a very serious problem. Children who learn that they can only get needed attention when they are "bad" will create problems just to be recognized. In the thinking of children, any type of attention is better than none at all. Therefore, positive intervention is the first and most important discipline intervention technique. Parents and teachers must communicate with their children at all ages and stages.

Young children enjoy material rewards for their concrete value, but these rewards also provide needed attention and say indirectly to children that the adults both love and approve of them. Withdrawal of positive intervention can be successful in dealing with some disturbances; that is, of course, if the child is experiencing positive intervention in his life. Withdrawing positive attention and affection in relation to a child's negative behavior can serve as a stimulus to his realization that what he has done is not very good, *but* this can only happen when the child has a lot of love in his life. Finally, punishment is much more effective when the child realizes the consequences of his actions—that is, when he comes to know that good behavior results in positive consequences and that bad behavior results in negative consequences.

Positive intervention comes in many forms and is both qualitative and quantitative. Kind words, congratulations, words of encouragement, hugs, kisses, pats, smiles, nods of approval, and tangible rewards all constitute positive intervention.

Parents and teachers should become aware of the forms of positive intervention to which their particular children respond. All too often children are hugged and kissed by people whom they would rather not have hug and kiss them. Children will let disciplinarians know exactly what they need in their own way. They will look for smiles, they will come up very close for a hug, or they will look for special praise of their work. The adults must be totally sensitive to those signs and vary the positive intervention techniques that are used in line with their success with the children.

Finally, parents and teachers should never be overly critical of their child's endeavors. Neither should they always be telling him how great he does everything. Positive intervention means working and communicating with the child and it praises, it helps, it gives suggestions. Positive intervention is, in essence, a process for developing constructive self-criticism.

In summary, intervention comprises the various ways of correcting the child and communicating with him. When employed intelligently, it provides parents and teachers with the means for both intervening in the child's positive and negative actions and helping him to grow into his culture successfully by focusing experientially on the aspects of morality of that culture.

Consistency

Consistency is the third element of the trinity of discipline. Emerson once said, "A foolish consistency is the hobgoblin of little minds." Wise and insightful consistency, however, should be thought of as a vital ingredient for the wholesome development of the individual and the key to successful discipline. Ideally, consistency should exist in every aspect of the individual's life. In particular, there are seven areas of consistency that parents and teachers should be constantly aware of.

Area One

First, there must be consistency between the expectations parents and teachers hold for the child and his ability to achieve those expectations. Too often expectations are held for children which are totally unrelated to their capabilities. In some cases, children are forced to engage in activities which they simply cannot perform because they are not developmentally ready. Not only is this true of the child who is failing in school; often it is also true of the child who is being forced into "gifted" programs to run the race of champions. In other situations, too little is expected of the child. Accepting the individual's most minimal efforts is unfortunately a very frequent occurrence in today's families and schools. Such classic lines as, "He's going to have everything I never had" reflect a dangerous parental attitude which leads the parents to spoil and misdirect their child.

Many people believe that children are more mature now than they were in the past, and that they are capable of total freedom and self-determination. This belief is not only incorrect and grossly unfair but is detrimental to the child's wholesome development as well. Children will develop the capacity for total self-determination through proper discipline and experiences, but the process is gradual, lasting through the teenage years.

In classrooms in which this understanding is not put into practice, discipline problems emerge. Children are either bored with the simplicity of the required goals or frustrated because they are totally incapable of achieving them. Both boredom and frustration are feelings that demand release.

Teachers must develop individualized instructional programs to meet the needs and abilities of their students. This does not mean that the teacher has to plan thirty different lessons for thirty different students. There is social and intellectual need for students to work together. Thus, individualized instruction means grouping children in various patterns that will allow them to grow. This can mean having them skill-grouped for some activities and at other times working in peer tutoring or partner learning situations. It is only the nature of the traditional classroom environment that allows one student to get ahead by "beating" the others. If the environment is to be one in which the students learn that sharing and working together are measures of achievement, grouping and partner learning are most beneficial and feasible strategies for teachers to employ.

Area Two

Second, there must be consistency between and among teachers. All teachers must be concerned with the entire school environment. They must communicate with their colleagues and support the process that the personnel of the school, as a whole, have decided to use. This means that they talk to students from other classrooms whenever they see them and that everyone assumes responsibility for students who are misbehaving.

Consistency is a vital factor in letting students know how they are to behave. When students realize that everyone believes in and follows the same rules to build a social order in the environment, discipline problems on the whole are substantially reduced throughout the entire school. By working as part of a faculty the teacher does not lose her personal identity and beliefs. Rather, she contributes to the development of the social atmosphere of her school. Too often in today's schools faculty members have been encouraged to be concerned only about their own students. This "closed door" practice is more than a little responsible for the increasing disorder within schools and the increasing number of discipline problems in education.

Area Three

Third, there must be consistency between the principal and the teachers in a school. The students view the teachers and the principal in power circles and are therefore driven to test the consistency between them. If the principal approaches discipline from a different conceptual point than the teacher—even if he supports her actions—consistency is not firmly established. Therefore, a school must have a totally consistent discipline *process*, not just a discipline *policy*.

Area Four

Fourth, there must be consistency between the mother and father. Both parents are responsible for disciplining the children in a family. It is not a duty that can be borne solely by one parent or shifted from parent to parent. Actions such as saying, "Just wait until your father gets home" not only are unfair to the father, but they also delay the consequences for the act and tend to make the child see his father as the only properly constituted authority in the home. Also, in many homes one parent will say one thing and the other will say something else. In addition, children will often be unchecked when they try the subversive act of asking a "second opinion" on an already answered question or request, hoping to pit one parent against the other. When successful, such practices serve to confuse the child and to erode his sense of safety, his structure of discipline, and his overall social development. Communication and shared responsibility for discipline, between parents in the home as among teachers in the school, are of utmost importance for the development of consistency.

Area Five

Fifth, in consistency as in all the other elements of discipline, modeling is highly important. The child has a great gift for imitation and tends to learn from what he sees as much as from what he hears. If the child comes from a family that consistently condones fighting and hitting, stealing, or lying, a family in which the consistent models are themselves fighting or untruthful, then that is what the child will accept as a normal way of life. People are sometimes amazed by the fact that most abused children become abusing parents. Logically, most people tend to think, "If I had been abused, I'd want to be good to children." They are forgetting two factors: The models the children grew up with were those of abusing parents; and the conscience and beliefs that they developed tell them that abuse is a way of life. Abusing their own children is something they do almost unconsciously.

Conscience is formed through consistency—the models and morals that parents and teachers consistently present to their children. The models should show the child right from wrong, good from bad; they should illustrate love and affection, and their values and morals should exemplify what they truly want their children to be when they mature.

Area Six

Sixth, consistency must go beyond the home. Society will never be able to solve discipline problems until there is much more communication between the home and the school. Such communication would lead to consistency between what the school expects and what parents expect. Teachers and parents must agree upon what should be expected of the children at school.

Parents and teachers must be consistent for good discipline to develop. They must be patient with each other and patient in their plan of attack, for once they falter in their consistency the child begins to drift away from the direction that will lead him to conscience development and self-discipline.

Area Seven

Seventh, consistency means honesty in what is expected from children. Parents and teachers sometimes use deception to gain results. The inherent danger with this practice is that the values and ways of behaving that a child learns during the foundational years of conscience development prepare him to deal with the "identity crisis" associated with the teen years. If the child discovers when he is older that some of his values started with lies and deceptions, he tends to doubt his beliefs altogether and also begins to doubt himself. Thus, the emerging adolescent is unarmed, so to speak, as he enters the phase of life when discovering his identity is so important. In short, the use of deception can lead to a severe identity crisis. Children with this problem take a much longer time in growing to a healthy adult life.[2] Honesty is absolutely essential to teenagers as they question and attempt to make real their social world.

The trinity of discipline is a highly complex triad. Each element plays a key role, but success is totally dependent upon the whole system. Structure is worthless without proper intervention;

intervention is ineffective without consistency; and consistency can become the "hobgoblin of little minds" if it lacks structure.

The trinity of discipline describes the elements of discipline and how they work. Yet it is another trinity that makes the discipline process successful: Thought, love, and patience are as necessary as structure, intervention, and consistency in making the trinity of discipline work. All of these factors are needed to bring the social consciousness of the child and the adolescent to a sufficient level that will enable them to be productive members of society.

Notes

1. Kevin Walsh and Milly Cowles, "Social Consciousness and Discipline in the Urban Elementary School," in *Urban Review* II (Spring, 1979), pp. 29–30.

2. Kevin Walsh and Milly Cowles, *Taming the Young Savage* (Huntsville, Al.: Strode, 1981), pp. 16–40.

CHAPTER 5

Civic Education and Discipline

The two correlative aspects of the process of education are the child who is born immobile, helpless, and ignorant, and the culture embodied in the surrounding life of society into which the child must be initiated and guided. Education can only be considered successful when the child ultimately becomes an effective member of the social order. "This he does, while he matures physically, by gradually acquiring the group culture as he lives in and with the group and takes over progressively its ways of acting and thinking."[1]

The process of acquiring the various aspects of the culture to which he belongs begins within the family and expands outward to society. By means of his basic needs the helpless child experiences the world through his mother, father, siblings, school, and community and gradually comes to accept the ways of the social order to which he is exposed and then assimilates. Through consistency the child comes to know what is right and what is wrong. He learns the tastes, attitudes, values, and morals of his people. He may learn "that foreigners or out-groups are persons undesirable or even dangerous; that the republican form of government is the only really good one; that cheating (dishonesty) is wrong, always wrong, or that it is wrong only if practiced within the group, or that it is acceptable and even clever if practiced against customers and within business dealings."[2] He may learn

125

to contribute to the overall good of his family and the society or to look out only for his own interests. These examples of behavior show that it is through individuals and the manner in which they act that the society is maintained. Therefore, the culture molds the child to its model.[3]

Traditionally, citizenship or civic education has been perceived as the process by which the young will become productive citizens for the American society. For example, the following statement was issued by the Council on Civic Education:

Civic education is a process comprising all the positive influences which are intended to shape a citizen's view of his role in society. Civic education is, therefore, far more than a course of study. It comes partly from formal schooling, partly from parental influence, and partly from learning outside the classroom and the home. Through civic education our youth are helped to gain an understanding of our national ideals, the common good, and the processes of self-government. . . . They are helped to understand the various civil liberties guaranteed in our Constitution and Bill of Rights and the accompanying civic responsibilities by which alone they can be achieved.[4]

Civic education in America means the development of character, efficient habits of work, proper conduct, consideration for others, and orderly democratic living. However, as Kilpatrick so eloquently put it: "Democracy is at once a faith, a hope, and a program."[5] As stated by Chase and John, "If students come to value democratic ideals, they need to have direct experience with these ideals."[6] Again, according to Hanna, Potter, and Reynolds,

Children learn democracy only as they live it; they develop moral and spiritual values only as they experience them and have opportunity to generalize from their experiences. This means that schools must provide many opportunities for children to work together, to assume responsibility, to respect each other and to be respected for themselves and what they can contribute to the welfare of the group, to experience success and failure, to meet situations requiring poise, to be leaders and followers, to share ideas and search for truth, to solve problems scientifically, to be self-reliant and self-disciplined, and to make ethical judgments.[7]

Schools must provide abundant opportunities for pupil responsibility, initiative, and action for true citizenship to be nurtured.[8]

Civic education is the process of developing a good citizen for American society. Sound discipline is the process for bringing an individual into the culture. Consequently, both discipline and civic education are concerned with the social development of those who will inherit the American culture. As such, both the discipline process of the school and the process for citizenship development must be seen as aspects of the same whole. To speak of democracy, the work ethic, respect for others, cooperation, and responsibility means that in the form of subject matter and instruction, as well as the means of dealing with children, the climate and environment of the school must be in constant cooperative movement. Unless the content, methods, and overall school climate are in total harmony with the conditions the student experiences within his life in the school, civic education is quite meaningless. It cannot be taught in isolation from what the child experiences totally; this includes the models provided both by students and all school personnel.

The Goals of Civic Education

Any time a process as complex as civic education is expressed in a limited number of goals it is subject to criticism of being too broad or too narrow, too liberal or too conservative. Nevertheless, in the words of Paul R. Hanna, "We believe that no society can survive and advance unless its citizens understand its underlying purposes and values; unless they know where we are going and why."[9]

The following list contains eleven goals of civic education which were developed by the Council on Civic Education. They reflect the best thinking in the area. Each item may be found in good citizens in varying degrees; collectively they represent the ideal of citizenship in the American society.[10]

Each of the goals is equally important, but as changes occur in our schools, our nation, and our society, reexamination and revision of goals and the relative emphasis placed on each should be subject to constant analysis.

The Goals

1. Knowledge and skills to assist in solving the problems of our times
2. Awareness of the effects of science on civilization and its use to improve the quality of life
3. Readiness for effective economic life
4. Ability to make value judgments for effective life in a changing world
5. Recognition that we live in an open-ended world which requires receptivity to new facts, new ideas, and new ways of life
6. Participation in the process of decision making through expression of views to representatives, experts, and specialists
7. Belief in both liberty for the individual and equality for all, as guaranteed by the Constitution of the United States
8. Pride in the achievement of the United States, appreciation of the contributions of other peoples, and support for international peace and cooperation
9. Use of the creative arts to sensitize oneself to universal human experience and to the uniqueness of the individual
10. Compassion and sensitivity for the needs, feelings, and aspirations of other human beings
11. Development of democratic principles and application to daily life[11]

Developmental discipline is in total harmony with the goals of civic education. The end result of discipline must be the development of a social conscience, and a social conscience can only be developed through sound discipline procedures. Furthermore, developmental discipline provides insight into the developmental aspects of the person and provides a means by which the goals of civic education can be experienced by the individual. The work ethic, perseverance, constructive self-criticism, cooperation, and responsibility toward family (which leads to patriotism) are lived by the students as they actively participate in the life of the school. If we truly want students to learn about and grow in their responsibilities as citizens we must allow them experiences in real situations and the process of collectively finding solutions to the problems they face in their society. Therefore, critical thinking and group processes are essential both instructionally and in the process of discipline. Otherwise, there exists the possibility that both will be reduced to a process of indoctrination. Democracy and indoctrination are totally incompatible concepts. Democracy "must reject such enslavement as partisan exploitation of the individual's right to be educated to do his own thinking and make his own decisions."[12]

However, to believe that discipline and resulting social education must be delayed until the time the individual reaches a level of cognition by which he is able to understand fully his actions is an absurd notion. Furthermore, such a belief is in total discord with the manner in which children develop socially and cognitively. To wave the banner of the sanctity of personality and to proclaim the "self" as the ultimate aim of education is to cheat the child out of his proper social inheritance and to contribute to social destruction.

Some indoctrination is inevitable with younger children, but its ultimate intent should be to the contrary. For example, quite obviously the self-centered young child cannot fully understand the concept of honesty, but he can understand to some degree how he would feel if someone took an item he treasured. Habits of social living must sometimes be developed prior to full intellectual understanding of them. "In all cases where habits are desirable, we teach the habit even though the 'why' has to come later."[13] Even when there exists controversy as to the absolute right of a habit, the parent and teacher must impart their best insights as to the properness of the habit. However, as soon as the child develops a habit he should be helped to gain intellectually what is socially and morally involved with the habit he has already acquired. Later, when he reaches adolescence and possesses the logical stage of formal operations, he should be provided experiences through which he can review critically his habits and their meaning. In this way he possesses the habit; the habit does not possess him. "Previously, he had learned them as a child, when he thought as a child. Now he must rethink them, to make them his own or to reject them or revise them on his mature level."[14] If discipline and education are not enacted developmentally, the individual will be enslaved to ideas he acquired as a child and will behave in an immature, childish way.

Correspondingly, the formal subject matters of civic education (examples: history and government) are not to be considered in an either-or dichotomy with instructional practices. The child's factual knowledge about his social inheritance and the necessity of his developing the ability for critical thinking are not in polarity one to the other but rather are part and parcel of the same whole. Learning such facts as George Washington's being the first president and the branches of the American government are not wasted on young children but can provide a foundation upon which they later will understand and apply the doctrines of democracy intelligently, if such facts are used to support meaningful critical thinking experiences for the students both as they study and live in the school.

Many of the discipline practices we have stressed as being essential are means by which the students utilize what they have learned in harmony with real issues of concern. Such experiences as the classroom meetings and the assumption of responsibility, combined with proper guidance provided by the teacher or parent in the form of intervention, assist the student in developing proper habits and the means to apply them intelligently in the future.

In conclusion, civic education and the process by which the individual is disciplined must be in total harmony with one another. "To teach democracy in an undemocratic fashion, in a way to foster uncritical acceptance, would seem an odd way of fostering democracy."[15] Furthermore, to ignore the essential values, attitudes, and aspects of morality of the culture within both the civic education content and the discipline of the person is to believe erroneously that somehow the culture will be transmitted a priori. For as Piaget has stated, "Man's social behavior is less the result of hereditary transmission than an individual's interactions with others. Just as is the case in language acquisition, social experience plays a powerful role."[16] Since democracy is a program as well as a hope and a faith, it is incumbent upon parents and teachers to intentionally provide experiences through which the ideals, attitudes, and morals of democracy are transmitted to the young people who will inherit the American society.

Notes

1. William Heard Kilpatrick, *Philosophy of Education* (New York: Macmillan, 1951), p. 71.

2. Ibid.

3. Ibid., p. 72.

4. Donald Robinson, *Promising Practices in Civic Education* (Washington, D.C.: National Council for the Social Studies, 1967), p. 10.

5. William Heard Kilpatrick, *Group Education for a Democracy* (New York: Association, 1940), p. 1.

6. W. Linwood Chase and Martha Tyler John, A *Guide for the Elementary Social Studies Teacher* (Boston: Allyn and Bacon, 1972), p. 136.

7. Lavone Hanna, Gladys Potter, and Robert Reynolds, *Dynamic Elementary Social Studies* (New York: Holt, Rinehart, and Winston, 1963), p. 417.

8. W. Linwood Chase and Martha Tyler John, A *Guide for the Elementary Social Studies Teacher*, p. 136.

9. Robinson, *Promising Practices in Civic Education*, p. 13.

10. Ibid., pp. 15–16.

11. Ibid., pp. 16–17.

12. Kilpatrick, *Philosophy of Education*, p. 123.

13. Ibid., p. 124.

14. Ibid.

15. Ibid., p. 125.

16. Jean Piaget, *Intelligence and Affectivity: Their Relationship During Child Development*, translated by T. A. Brown and C. E. Kuezi (Palo Alto, Ca.: Annual Reviews, 1981), p. 19.

CHAPTER 6

Discipline and School Administration

JAlan Aufderheide

The implications of implementing effective developmental discipline within the public school structure are mind-boggling for school administrators. To begin with, *any* sort of meaningful change is not for the faint of heart. Further, implementation of social discipline requires a well-conceived, broadly accepted, and heavily theoretical basic philosophy of discipline upon which sound application of a multitude of practical day-to-day activities must be based over a long period of time. The possibilities for success are innumerable, and despite a careful analysis of the pitfalls, one must never lose sight of the fundamental optimism which underlies first the call to public education, and beyond that the challenge of public school administration. We will come back to such optimism later, but in the meantime let us explore some of the major stumbling blocks which must somehow be overcome.

Elements of the Problem

1. The "Quick-Fix" Syndrome

On the one hand, there seems to be widespread agreement among administrators, board members, teachers, parents, and the general public as consistently reflected in Gallup polls, for

133

example, that discipline in the schools is a significant problem which ought to be given high priority in the distribution of scarce resources of time and money.

Unfortunately, in many respects we in education reflect a characteristic desire exhibited all too often by our society in general in that we keep looking, sometimes frantically, for that "quick-fix" which will set right a problem which has been years in the making. Beyond that, the "quick-fix" syndrome can lead us to the false belief that application of a little pressure in the right direction will offset massive pressure from many sources in the wrong direction.

The facts of the matter, which must be recognized up front by those of us who would be social discipline advocates, are that the shambles of discipline in the public schools did not happen overnight and the problem cannot be "fixed" overnight. Furthermore, the status quo—whatever you assess that to be—has been "achieved" by the application of many pressures coming from many different directions.

Perhaps the analogy of an economic model is appropriate here. The economy of this nation in the eighties is the result of decades of economic decisions (many contend they have been poor decisions) made by a half dozen Presidents and Congresses over decades. However because perhaps we are a people who have been "sold" the idea that miraculous things come out of spray cans, we have a tendency to believe that a little oven cleaner in the right place will dissolve all that baked-on crud by tomorrow morning.

Much to our own dismay, or to those with whom we are working in the public schools, the truth must be known—there just is no quick fix.

2. The "Discipline Without Discipline" Myth

Paralleling the Quick-Fix Syndrome is the myth all too often exhibited by the educational community that somehow we can have "Discipline Without Discipline." That is, there must be a way to create this thing we call discipline and stamp young people with it, but at the same time never have to exhibit such a characteristic ourselves.

Again using the economic analogy, this is like saying there must be a way to cure inflation and lower interest rates with little unemployment and no slowing of the economy, while federal budget deficits continue or escalate and no programs get cut, or if they do at least not mine. The *fact* of the matter is that such "double-speak" has been perpetrated by the American people for years and sooner or later reality is going to have to creep in.

If we really want the public schools to *do* something about discipline, then we in the educational community must at some point begin to exhibit characteristics of discipline ourselves. Among others, we will have to give up the luxury of each going our separate ways. *Somewhere*, there must be a building principal and his/her staff (better yet a board/superintendent and their buildings/staffs) who will give up some of their individuality to pursue the common goal of a thorough and consistent program of instituting developmental discipline.

This will require that we exhibit enough discipline to close ranks behind an identified common good which enough of us subscribe to, that "critical mass" is reached and an explosion of positivism occurs. This can never take place without leadership, for the bottom line of a successful school is whether or not the administrator leads or not.

In fairness, we must admit that this process *is* occurring in a few places. It just hasn't occurred in enough places yet to make, over time, a significant difference.

3. The "Who Needs Theory?" Trap

If we in education were nearly as bright as we think, we would have realized long ago that theoretical models need practical application and that practical models need sound theoretical bases.

How often do we hear of the latest grand plan of some theoretician which, when tested, lacks workability in the real world of schools? As practitioners we are quick (especially with 20/20 hindsight) to point, even with some measure of glee, at the folly of some great theory which obviously will not work in our schools.

The irony is that many of us as practitioners are guilty of the same, albeit reversed, illogic. We fly a kite with no tails, only to be surprised that the thing pitches and dives madly, not at all responding to the controls we so sincerely attempt to apply.

"Theory . . ." we snort, "Who needs it?" and continue to march in many directions at once. The reality is that *every* practitioner who purports to move our schools toward social discipline in practical ways needs to know how the various steps fall in concert with Maslow's hierarchy. We need to know (that is, have a *working knowledge of*, in practical terms) Kohlberg's comments on moral development and the stages thereof. Or what of Freud and Erikson regarding personality? Piaget and mental reasoning?

All of this asks a great deal of us as practitioners, with the threshold issue being whether we will open our minds enough to admit that our kite in fact *does* need a tail. That question would appear to be truly an open one, even with some whose kites are momentarily about to cross some power lines.

4. The "What Is Discipline, Anyway?" Argument

There is just enough apparent credibility on the several sides of the "What Is Discipline?" argument to convince us that the argument is worth having and, once having taken the fatal first step, to then become convinced that it will be impossible to agree on anything, as in fact it truly will be.

The irony is that the major blocks of which discipline is comprised are discernible, if not self-evident, and are of such a prima facie nature that quick consensus can be achieved *if* we are willing for the time being to put off, perhaps forever, the arguments about how I achieve that in *my* room versus how you do it in your room.

This is similar to the panic-become-paralysis which grips education in the area of teaching values. The illogic goes something like this: Because there are a *few* really sensitive and explosive issues on which we are sure to get burned, we will just ignore the whole mess and not teach values at all.

Yet, if we were to sit down and list all the values we could possibly teach, and then strike from the list those which *anyone* objected to, a substantial number would remain. Moreover, the list would curiously enough have much to do with discipline—honesty, respect for self, respect for others, manners, the value of hard work, perseverance, and on and on.

So the "What Is Discipline, Anyway" argument *can* be beaten. It simply requires a simplistic agreement not to beat it to death.

5. The "Don't Teach It But They'll Get It Anyway" Fallacy

The public schools of this nation rightly believe that reading is a very important thing for young people to learn, and, understandably, significant amounts of time are therefore set aside to that end. Reading blocks occur almost daily in elementary schools at least, and tremendous resources via teacher time, basal series, consumable workbooks, machines, aides, and the like are expended in this cause. Should it appear that, despite all these normal efforts, some youngster is not "getting it," special efforts (Title I or otherwise) are made to rush some "CPR" to the scene to see if the failing patient can be revived and helped to struggle on. This is all very good.

Now, math is really important, too, so we should also set aside time for that, and, yes, we should even go so far as to have computer-assisted instruction to that end. Now come language arts, general science, social studies, music, art, and P.E., each in due course according to whatever pecking order has been worked out locally. All of this would indeed work out just fine if it were not for this chapter, and this book, and this whole flap about discipline.

No, by and large we do not set time aside for it. We just take some time out when a problem occurs. You know, if a kid needs it we keep him in at recess and talk to him. And we do send kids to the principal if it is that bad.

No, we do not spend money on it, but we did send several of our teachers to a conference once. What do you mean, anyway—a *program* to teach discipline? A K-12 concerted, articulated program? We do that in math, but not in discipline. They'll get it anyway.

That is the fallacy. The public schools must decide that discipline is important enough to set time aside for it, spend money on it, and *teach* it. Then, and only then, will it be fair to expect results. Otherwise, we should continue to spend little, if any, time, money, and effort in a K-12 articulated program. Then, when the results are dismaying, we can at least be assured we got our money's worth.

6. The "Cognitive Domain" Hoax

One should not engage in a conscious effort to raise anyone's hackles or step on toes, but the emphasis which the educational community often places on the worship of the cognitive domain borders on a cruel hoax. To be sure, the hue and cry throughout the land often rings around the crisis of falling standardized test scores. No one advocates abandoning or watering down academic standards. But let us, for one sane moment, examine just what kind of fix we have ourselves in.

The American people can send men and machines in orbit or to the moon where they will be safer than walking a city street after dark. We can, if the need arises, transplant virtually every organ in the body except the brain and make a person well enough to be run down by a drunk driver. We can crank out as many fine doctors as we need, one or more of whom will surely soon achieve a cancer breakthrough. Yet those same fine physicians will be as likely, or more so, to suffer the drug addiction which stalks our society generally.

The point is that, in our pursuit of the cognitive domain, we may have created a problem—a gap between our knowledge and our ability to use such knowledge in human caring ways. If we were to list *all* the ills of society, or at least the top ten, how many of these ills would be solved by greater strides in the cognitive domain?

Or would we find that major advancements in the development and use of social skills (discipline?) by our young people constituted the greatest need?

7. The "What's The Problem?" Problem

Too often as school administrators, or as any other of the actors in the educational community, we fail to adequately describe the problem of discipline in the schools beyond simplistic terms. It is easy to recognize the youngster who has problems because he/she is the one giving *you* problems. But *what's the link* . . . what is the point of breakdown . . . what is the failure of execution that gives rise to the passive or active, individual or collective symptom of "he/she/they didn't get it"—the "it" being acquisition of social competencies of discipline.

A good set of descriptors, among many others available, comes out of the Family Development Institute (Washington, D.C.) as a hierarchy of characteristics which could serve as the basis for a problem attack model. Generally speaking, it would appear that individual, or for that matter school-wide, discipline programs could be designed around preventing/ameliorating these six characteristics of persons or categories of persons with discipline problems.[1]

A. Weak Identification with Viable Role Models
Such identification may be external (e.g. hero worship) or internal (what I want to be) or a composite (best of others plus best of myself). Lacking such identification with viable role models, a young person is far more likely to exhibit behavior which deviates from that asked for/expected in the program of discipline.

B. Weak Identification with, and Responsibility in "Family" Processes
The concept of "family" can be used in the literal, narrow sense or in the more generic sense of group identification with the classroom or school as "family" or even at highest levels with mankind, universe, and so on. The need is to identify with family processes which are greater than self.

C. Poor/Misdirected Problem-Solving Skills
Skills needed in this area have to do with positive attitudes toward individual or group problem solving—I/we *can* make it (the situation) better. The negative alternative is escapism (e.g., alcoholism) where things just "happen to me beyond my control."

D. Limited Use of Intrapersonal Skills
Skills used to communicate with self lead to self-discipline (self-control), self-assessment, goal setting. Inabilities in these areas lead to stresses, tensions, and dishonesty, thus low self-esteem, inability to defer gratification, and the like.

E. Weak Systemic (Situational) Skills
Networking of skills builds into decision-making systems. These systemic skills involve abilities and skills responding to the limits inherent in a decision-making situation, including the ability to modify behavior according to a situation in order to get one's needs met.

F. Weak Judgmental Skills
Weakness in this area is characterized by repetitious, self-

destructive behavior which feeds upon itself (e.g. "See, I told you I couldn't do it"). The ability to recognize, understand, and apply judgmental relationships is impaired.

If these six characteristics could be generally accepted as deficiencies most common in students who lack "discipline" then major components of the attack model could be planned to simulate and practice positive experiences rather than to reinforce negative ones by *happenstance*.[2]

Elements of the Solution

Douglas McGregor's Theory X, Theory Y approach to management studies provides an interesting overlay on which to examine some of what we are doing or not doing in our approaches to discipline in the public schools. It would be unfair to say that there are substantial portions of the American educational scene which subscribe to the Theory X format, but it is interesting nevertheless to compare approaches X and Y to see where we might fall as individual educators or where our schools as collectives might fall.

Approaches to Discipline

THEORY X	THEORY Y
I go to a school where . . .	I go to a school where . . .
1. Most students are "bad actors" who have to be watched constantly.	Most students are "good actors" who can learn to be responsible.
2. Discipline consists mainly of external control(s) which are imposed on me.	Discipline consists mainly of learning to develop internal control(s).
3. Discipline is a "product."	Discipline is a "process."

4. The quality of the "product" falls most heavily on the Authority Figure(s).

The quality of the "process" falls most heavily on me.

5. Therefore, I must be a passive participant.

Therefore I must be an active participant.

6. As long as I keep my mouth shut and my nose clean, I'll be OK.

I have to dialogue with others and learn from mistakes.

7. Learning is absorbing facts and recalling them on command. The cognitive domain is eminent.

Learning is questioning, discussing, and socializing. The affective domain is just as important as the cognitive.

8. I am one of a number in this institution where we do things "by the numbers."

I am a vital part of a social community which is a warm, exciting, pleasurable place to be.

9. Somebody else makes the rules; all I have to do is follow them.

I have to help make the rules, and I have a stake in seeing that they are good rules.

10. The Authority Figure(s) is/are watching and waiting for me to make a mistake.

The teachers are my friends who really care about me and want to help me overcome my problems.

11. If I break a rule, I hurt the Authority Figure(s).

If I break a rule, I hurt myself and the school society which includes my friends.

12. If I break a rule, I will experience the fate of all

If I break a rule, I will learn some consequences of

rule-breakers: punishment, often corporal in nature.	having made a bad decision: social consequences which adversely affect my privileges and responsibilities.
13. If I make a mistake, I'll be punished, and the Authority Figure(s) won't like me.	If I make a mistake, I'll have to admit it, and my teacher will still like me but won't like what I've done.
14. After all, this is the Authority Figure's school and I'd better not mess with it as long as I have to be here.	After all, this is *my* school and I *can* make it better because I *want* to be here and *want* to make it better.
15. When I get out, I'll be ready to take my place as a socially competent, productive member of a free, open, and democratic society. After all, I *have* learned how to be a good citizen!	When I graduate, I'll be ready to take my place as a socially competent, productive member of a free, open, and democratic society. After all, I *have* learned how to be a good citizen!

In this skeleton we see a number of key issues emerging as elements of the solution:

1. Good Actors Or Bad Actors?

     Children must be viewed as good actors to the extent that they have not yet learned the skills to proficiently operate within the system and still have their needs met. The program of discipline must be based upon the assumption that they *can* learn to be responsible.

2. Discipline—Internal Or External?

     While there may be need for external controls (to a high degree at a young age, less so at later stages) the goal of the program or system of discipline must be the removal of external controls as internal controls are phased in. To the extent that external controls are left in place after they are no longer necessary, the growth of internal controls will be stunted (a la training wheels on a bicycle).

3. Discipline—Product Or Process?

If discipline is a *product* (quiet in the library) then it is achieved when it is achieved, regardless of how or why, and regardless of whether any learning has taken place. Rather, discipline should be a *process* which is ongoing and transferrable (being quiet in the library is like not throwing food in the lunchroom).

4. Discipline—Whose Responsibility?

The need for a Properly Constituted Authority is indispensable. *Someone* must be in charge ultimately, and young people must know that, if the need arises, the PCA can and will be there to step in. Under that umbrella, however, the system must train for the assumption of responsibility by the individual. If a PCA *always* steps in, why should such responsibility be assumed by anyone else?

5. Active Or Passive Participants?

The normally healthy active condition of young people must be capitalized upon to incorporate them in a dynamic system. Their activity within that system must have viable and visible results (see previous systemic skills comments).

6. Monologue Or Dialogue?

Education generally, and learning the disciplinary system specifically, must be viewed as a series of dialogues rather than monologues. In one sense, in a monologue the listener does not have to worry about making mistakes—because he/she won't have the chance. It is an important element of the solution that young people learning "the system" have an opportunity to dialogue . . . to learn that it is not the end of the world to err, but the beginning of the end if we do not learn from our mistakes.

7. Cognitive Or Affective?

The cognitive domain is important, and, in the right context, so is memorization. But this element of the solution calls for a *socialization* process which demands questioning, discussing, debating pros and cons. Such socialization in the affective domain is just as important as the cognitive.

8. By The Numbers or Unpredictable?

Shall our schools be institutions where we do things by the numbers? Or shall we create a social community which is growing in responsibility for their environment?

9. Whose Rules?

If somebody else makes the rules, the only decision I have to make is whether to break or follow. Rather, a system of social discipline provokes questions like: Why should we have rules? What would happen if we didn't have *any*?

Okay, if we're going to have rules, what would be some good ones? Thus, the "trainee" begins to see that he/she has a stake in the rules.

10. Authority Figure—Friend or Ogre?

The Properly Constituted Authority is a necessity and at times may have to be something of an ogre if negative consequences for a bad decision are in order. But the pervasive spirit should be that of the PCA being the friend who can be counted on to give assistance in working out problems.

11. Who Hurts When A Rule Is Broken?

An act of vandalism in a Theory X school is a perfectly natural and predictable consequence. An effective system of social discipline should try to find ways to show young people that a torn-up bathroom hurts all of us in this "family."

12. What Consequences For Rule Breakers?

Shall the consequence of rule breaking be externally imposed punishment? Or shall we try to find ways to show young people in training that adverse social consequences to them are natural outgrowths of decisions which *they* made, whether such decisions were conscious and logical (at the time) or unconscious and illogical?

13. Separate Me From My Mistakes

It is crucial that an effective social discipline system separate disapproval of an action (bad decision) from acceptance of the person who made the mistake.

14. Whose School Is It Anyway?

If your school belongs to the principal or the superintendent, or to the teachers, a serious mistake has been made which needs immediate remediation. The most effective social discipline system promotes the ideal that the school belongs to the young people. This is *not* to be viewed as synonymous with the permissiveness of the sixties which allowed for self-destruction in the name of freedom.

15. Which System Shall It Be?

Who can argue that we want our young people to eventually take their places, as socially competent, productive members of a free, open, and democratic society? The question is "What kind of training model—X or Y—will best get them there?" All of the participants in the educational community must share the optimism we spoke of at the outset that it *can* be done—and done well—by sharing of commitment, pride, and problem solving, with kids ending up the winners.

16. What Does Reality Tell Us?

Speaking realistically, there are a number of issues that must be faced by educators in today's schools.

  a. Without proper resources, reality tells us that there are certain students that the school cannot help. That is, these students need an environment that can deal with their particular problems. Without such an environment the school is not helping the problem individual, and, furthermore, is often hurting the education of the other thirty or so students who are in class with him.

b. In many districts, a teacher unit will need to be established to conduct an in-school suspension program to work with disruptive students.

c. Schools need a process which will show boards of education and communities each step the system will take to deal with problem students, in order that when expulsion is necessary there is evidence that the school has made every effort to help the student.

Where Do We Go From Here?

A potential weakness of all of the previous discussion may be that it does not go far enough from theory and generalizations into the practical world of specific workable models. Practitioners frequently seem to say "Tell me exactly how to do it, and I'll do it" without realizing that such a posture is more befitting an aide than a professionally trained educator.

What is needed is an intensive series of discussions by a building administrator and his/her staff (or alternatively by the administrative team of a district and district staff) to put together a model which is workable for that specific school or school district. In this light, the previous sections have merit as guidelines for discussion or even as the beginnings of "decision rules" to choose this model-option over that. Eventually, the series of discussions must lead to acceptance of an overall model to which the staff must be committed.

There are, fortunately, many readily available "canned" models or model components which can be drawn in to help overcome potential frustrations over reinvention of the wheel. Professional organizations including, but not limited to, NEA, NAESP, NASSP, AASA, ASCD, and the like, have veritable gold mines of excellent material. Private efforts like Glasser's *Reality Therapy* and *Schools Without Failure* are excellent sources. Other resources, such as the Charles F. Kettering Foundation, have a long menu of books, reprints, monologues, and working papers which will be of assistance. Still other program-specific packages such as *Tribes*, *Ombudsman*, and *Quest* have much to offer. And, of course, excellent guides in the form of people or print are also available in many states with more aggressive state departments of education.

In short, there is no want for readily available ideas and suggestions. Whether a "canned" program is adopted largely intact or several are blended together, a uniquely local flavor must emerge as the intensive discussions of a local staff proceed.

The crucial question—in the final analysis—is not *whether* an effective program of social discipline can be designed and implemented. Neither is the question *whether* it can succeed. Practitioners are in the process of devoting their careers in the conviction that education does make a difference. Nor is the question *how* it shall be done, because there are many different paths to success with no one being exactly right and the others wrong.

Embarrassingly enough, the *real* question simply distills down to . . .

Will we do it?

Notes

1. E. Stephen Glenn and Joel W. Warner, "The Development Approach to Preventing Problem Dependencies" (Washington, D.C.: Family Development Institute, n.d.), monograph.

2. Douglas McGregor, *The Human Side of Enterprise* (New York: McGraw-Hill, 1960).

CHAPTER 7

Discipline in a Moral and Religious Key

James Michael Lee

The Nature of Discipline

Some teachers and parents regard discipline as a precondition for learning. "There must be discipline before learning can occur," they say. But this view is erroneous. Discipline is not a precondition to learning. Rather, discipline is a way in which learning itself takes place, the way in which a person learns.[1]

Unless and until teachers and parents truly understand what was written in the preceding paragraph, it is highly unlikely that the discipline which they attempt to implement will even be genuinely educational.

Because the point made in the opening paragraph is so central in effective developmental discipline, I will reiterate it in a slightly different form. Discipline is not something prior to the learning process or outside the learning process. Discipline is the learning process itself, or more precisely, a manner in which the learning process occurs. In a word, discipline is purposeful, goal-directed, channeled learning. Discipline is learning at its highest, most effective form.

Since discipline is purposeful learning, it is both a major goal of education and an indispensable way in which education takes place, rather than a tool to bring education to pass.

Discipline is the way in which a person harmoniously mobilizes his resources as he learns. *Basically considered, then, discipline is a way of life.*

Awareness of the etymology of a word often provides a valuable key to unlocking the intrinsic meaning and basic import of that word. The ultimate root of the English word discipline comes from the Latin verb *discere* which means to learn. Of all the Latin verbs directly pertaining to learning, *discere* is the most general.[2] *Discere*, then, refers to all kinds of learning, in contrast to other Latin words denoting one or another specific form of learning, such as cognitive learning, perceptual learning, affective learning, motor learning, and the like.[3]

Discipline and Discipleship

Virtually every major moral system and universal religion places great stress on two central human activities, namely discipline and discipleship. This fact is hardly surprising, since every major moral system and universal religion urges persons to learn the teachings and the conduct of that moral system or universal religion. As we have already seen, to learn is *discere* in Latin, and the two principal etymological Latin derivatives of *discere* are *disciplina* (discipline) and *discipulus* (disciple).

The Latin word *disciplina* (discipline) means every kind of purposeful learning, including humanities, natural sciences, affects, conduct, and so forth. Indeed, famous Roman writers ranging from Plautus[4] to Cicero[5] often use the word discipline in the sense of character, conduct, or way of life. The monumental and authoritative Oxford English Dictionary states that etymologically speaking, discipline is the contrary of doctrine, because discipline is that which the *discipulus* (learner) does, while doctrine is that which the *doctor* (teacher) does. (In Latin, the word for teacher is *doctor*, a noun derived from the verb *docere* which means to teach.) "Hence in the history of words, doctrine is more concerned with abstract theory and discipline with practice or exercise."[6] For many centuries the English word discipline meant learning in the general and comprehensive sense. It was only much, much later that the English word discipline lost its exclusive identification with learning and came to assume its present connotation of order and control, usually maintained and enforced by others.

The Latin word *discipulus* (disciple) means a learner. More specifically, this Latin word connotes a person who devotes a considerable portion of his time to learning a particular area of life, especially a practical area such as that of an apprentice in a trade, a student in a school, or a seeker after a particular way of life. A *discipulus* might become a follower of a person or of a way of life *if* such followership significantly enhances the disciple's own learning. Learning, then, rather than followership—and certainly not blind followership—is the hallmark of a true disciple.

The Romans sometimes called a gladiator a *disciplinosus*, a noun which means the very disciplined person. By using this term, the ancient Romans indicated that the gladiator represents the ultimate in the effective, harmonious, purposeful mobilization of all one's human capacities. The gladiator, in the sense of *disciplinosus*, is the quintessential learner (*discipulus*) because he has learned through prolonged personal activity to felicitously maximize and coordinate his body, his mind, his heart, and his will in order to successfully combat whatever hardship he might be called upon to face.

Virtually every major moral system and universal religion takes pains to emphasize that discipleship in a moral system or religion inevitably involves large and small sacrifices at every turn. The word sacrifice is derived ultimately from the Latin words *sacrum* and *facere* which mean to make holy. Moral systems and universal religions typically assert that the learning process involved in disciplining oneself in a moral system or religion necessarily brings with it as both process and product the increased holiness of the disciple. In this way, authentic learning or discipline is its own reward because learning or discipline itself sanctifies the person and the activity.

Discipline has always constituted a cornerstone in moral systems and universal religions because of its developmental, self-fulfillment nature. Discipline is learning to activate and coordinate all of one's human powers to achieve a desired objective. Discipline is learning to harmoniously mesh oneself with the realities and imperatives of society in such a way as to simultaneously bring about personal self-fulfillment and societal enrichment. Discipline makes the person better and holier because it involves a constant sacrificing of his impulses to the ordered upward flow of the best personal and communal perfection.

Discipline in Moral Thought and Moral Education

While moral thinkers and moral educators often do not use the specific term discipline, nonetheless the concept and flow of discipline is very important in their theorizing and research. To be sure, discipline is essentially integral to moral education. After all, moral education necessarily involved purposefully learning (*discere*) moral principles and values, purposefully learning (*discere*) the bases of these principles and values, and purposefully learning (*discere*) to live up to these moral principles and values in one's everyday life.[7] In its totality, moral education is itself fundamentally discipline—the discipline of learning and living a good moral life.

Act Theory and Rule Theory

Moral educators generally adhere to one of two conflicting views on the source and norm of morality. These two divergent views are called rule theory and act theory.[8] The rule theory of morality holds that an action is judged moral or immoral on the basis of whether or not it conforms to a set of universal constitutive moral rules. An example of a rule theorist is Lawrence Kohlberg. The act theory of morality maintains that an act is judged moral or immoral on the basis of the moral dimensions of the here-and-now act itself and not on the basis of a set of previously devised universal constitutive rules. In this view, moral rules are quite useful as starting points and signposts in properly ascertaining the morality or immorality of a given act; still, moral rules are essentially only indicators and hence are not in themselves normative or even necessary benchmarks of morality. John Dewey exemplifies an act theorist.

Regardless of whether they espouse the rule theory or the act theory of morality, virtually all moral theorists and moral educators place discipline at the center of their views on moral development and their proposals for moral education.

Responsibility

Moral educators of all persuasions are united in claiming that responsibility forms an essential and pivotal dimension in the work of moral education. Such responsibility is total, in that it embraces responsibility to self, responsibility to others, responsibility to society, responsibility to one's job, and so forth. Responsibility necessarily entails obligations and duties, both general and specific.[9] It is eminently true that responsibility is one of the primary forms which discipline takes. Where there is responsibility there is discipline, and where there is little responsibility there is little discipline.

Moral Writers

To further illumine the centrality of discipline in moral thought and moral education, it is helpful to look at the pertinent views of three of the twentieth century's most important writers on moral development, namely John Dewey, Jean Piaget, and Lawrence Kohlberg.

John Dewey is a philosopher for whom morality and education occupy a preeminent place. For Dewey, philosophy is life, and life is education, and education is the progressive never-ending growth in a morality which is at once personal and social. For Dewey, then, education in its every aspect is fundamentally a moral activity. Discipline is that which enables education to be fruitful and moral. Dewey regards true discipline as that kind of present learning process in which the individual achieves such a fluid mastery over what he has previously learned that he can now effectively control these past learnings for the sake of worthwhile personal-social goals. Far from denigrating or disposing of discipline as some of his uninformed critics erroneously contend, Dewey strongly insists that discipline is the form which growth-producing learning takes when such learning is purposeful and goal-directed.[10] The process, end, and criterion of human morality for Dewey is that which is educationally growth-producing for persons and society simultaneously. He is therefore firm in insisting that any attempt to separate teaching from discipline inevitably results in separating teaching from morality.[11]

In his classic empirical study entitled *The Moral Judgment of the Child*, Jean Piaget identifies discipline with morality in the sense that the foundation of both is to be found in a system of rules.[12] Piaget contends that all morality consists in a system of rules, and that the essence of morality lies in the respect which the individual acquires for these rules. In other words, discipline constitutes the essence of morality since discipline is the positive cognitive-learning and action-learning of the rules of life. Among the many important points Piaget makes about discipline in *The Moral Judgment of the Child*, two are particularly germane, namely, the way in which a person acquires discipline and the sources of discipline. Because discipline is part and parcel of the learning process itself, it is not surprising that Piaget's research concludes that just as all learning occurs gradually, so too a child acquires discipline developmentally in a series of successive stages.[13] The source of learning the rules of life (morality, discipline) may be either external to the child such as parent or teacher or clergyman, or internal to the child. Piaget states that his own research unambiguously indicates that the child acquires genuine morality only when the parent or the school see to it that this morality is learned gradually in a manner which will inevitably lead to internal autonomy. In other words, the parent and the school should not attempt to supply the child with a total set of rules all at once, but rather act in such a way that the child learns these rules inchmeal in the very manner in which his own organism is slowly evolving and developing. Also, the parent and the school should avoid persistent external coercion or punitive learning procedures as far as possible when endeavoring to systematically teach children the rules of life because persistent external and punitive procedures inevitably lead children to adopt a morality which is external and punitive. Discipline, after all, is goal-directed learning, and the way in which a person learns will be the way in which he conceptualizes and practices his own discipline, his own way of life. Piaget specifically endorses Deweyan activity schools as one of the best ways in which society can effectively organize its educational endeavors so as to teach morality in a gradual, internally-based fashion.[14]

Lawrence Kohlberg denies that morality consists of an external order imposed from outside on a person's basically selfish and often unruly impulses. Rather, morality is the way in which an individual developmentally learns to harmoniously order his own relations with others in such a disciplined way as to become progressively altruistic. Kohlberg's "research suggests that moral judgment, like overall moral development, is the process of personal self-constructed and self-regulated advance as one interacts with the environment."[15] Thus, discipline is at the heart of

Kohlberg's system of moral development because the inherently purposive processes of personal self-construction and self-regulation are themselves the discipline process. The moral development process, which is to say the discipline process, takes place in six successive hierarchical invariant stages.[16] The fundamental moral principle or most basic moral value for Kohlberg is justice. It is from justice that all moral rules eventually flow, and it is in justice that a person is enabled to formulate his own moral rules.[17] Because justice and discipline form the twin base of Kohlberg's theory of moral development, it is only natural that justice and discipline form the twin base for his moral-education curricular and instructional proposals. Kohlberg's curriculum is called the "Just Community Curriculum," and his instructional procedures include role-taking,[18] dilemma discussions,[19] and +1 matching.[20] Thus schools which implement Kohlberg's moral education views thereby become shot through and through with discipline: the self/group discipline involved in carefully reasoning about real-life moral issues, the self/group discipline involved in taking the roles of others, the self/group discipline involved in exposure to the next higher stage of moral reasoning, and the self/group discipline involved in actively participating in group decision making for devising and enforcing its own rules.[21]

In summary, then, moral education and discipline go hand-in-hand. Each is ontically inseparable from the other. There can be no morality without discipline, and no discipline without morality. Morality is fundamentally a discipline process, and discipline is fundamentally a moral process.

Discipline in Religious Thought and Religious Education

The reality and also the term discipline loom large and recurrent in the history of religion. Because religion above all means purposefully learning (*discere*) a particular way of life, it is only fitting that religion accords a heavy emphasis to discipline. Indeed, discipline is probably the most ecumenical dimension of religion, since each and every universal religion, regardless of its beliefs, places discipline at or near the center of its activities.

So intrinsically intertwined are discipline and religion that the rise and fall of any particular religion is in large measure due to the degree of discipline which it enjoys. This historical fact is not surprising, since discipline is essentially learning (*discere*) and discipling—the essence of religion. A great deal of the strength and vitality of American evangelical/fundamentalist Protestant denominations in the post-World War II era is directly attributable to the relatively high degree of internal doctrinal and lifestyle discipline which these denominations require. Conversely, much of the loss in active membership and religious ardor of many American mainstream Protestant denominations in the post-World War II era can be directly traced to the significant erosion of doctrinal and lifestyle discipline which these denominations have experienced during this period.

To further appreciate the depth and variety of discipline, it is helpful to examine how some of the world's great universal religions treasure discipline and how they place discipline at the center of their educational efforts.

Hinduism

Hinduism, the oldest of extant world religions, places immense store in discipline.[22] This is evident both from the ancient sacred writings of the Hindus as well as from current Hindu practices.

The mystical and lofty *Upanishads* deal with the nature of ultimate reality and the way to achieve this reality in one's own personal life. Only in a personal, intimate, lived experience of the Brahman can the person existentially know and then answer the most basic of all cosmic/personal questions: "What is it that which, being known, everything is known?"[23] Through experiencing the Brahman, a person dissolves into all reality so that every dualism is swallowed up in the sea of fundamental Oneness.[24] A person can know and be absorbed into the Brahman only through meditation and asceticism, both of which are discipline in that both encapsulate the only real kind of learning, namely learning which is aimed at attaining the authentic good by means of intentionally eliminating any detours and distractions.[25]

In the sacred Hindu writings known as the *dharmashāstras*, a person's life is catalogued into four chronological and hierarchical stages. The last and highest stage is *sannyāsi* (literally, the person who has renounced everything). In this stage, the person is so disciplined that he breaks all attachments to the world and lives as a wanderer and beggar. Thus, discipline liberates the person from any worldly attachments which might hinder him from finding and being his true self.

In what is perhaps the most famous Hindu sacred writing, the *Bhagavad Gitā*, the great goal of life is regarded as attainable by every person, no matter what that individual's state of life might be. Every human activity can become a means to ultimate personal perfection if the activity is undertaken not for personal gain but for the sake of selfless love. This kind of love is a highly disciplined love because it learns (*discere*) life and learns the union with the Brahman in a pure way.

Though Hindusim is an extraordinarily elastic religion and admits of an immense variety of ways of reaching union with the Brahman, still personal discipline is central to each and every way.[26] One of the most well-known Hindu practices to enhance discipline is that of yoga, an activity which continues to flourish down to our own time. Every form of yoga basically is the discipline (learning) of systemmatically subordinating lower desire to higher desire. Thus yoga is essentially "a disciplined, soul-searching path that one must travel alone."[27] The purpose of yoga is to set the soul free from material concerns and indeed from matter itself.[28] Yoga is quintessential discipline because yoga is not merely a combination of exercises and ascetic techniques; rather yoga, as is true with every authentic form of discipline, is fundamentally a way of living.[29]

Yoga focuses on the study of human nature and its intrinsic unfolding from primary consciousness. Yoga seeks self-perfection. "In order to achieve this integral goal, a person must consciously activate those inherent laws of his or her multileveled nature. To embark on the practice of yoga, one enters not an intellectual adventure, but a transformative process that systematically awakens, coordinates, and realizes the latent resources in human nature for peaceful living in self-awareness."[30]

Classical yoga, sometimes called Pātañjali Yoga or Rāja Yoga (the latter meaning the royal path) is an overarching discipline strategy in which the person controls body and mind, conscious and unconscious, until the mind attains that liberated state in which it is no longer controlled by the body.[31] At the height of the last of the eight stages of classical yoga discipline practice, the person is able to be so liberated from his material accoutrements that he can transcend the normal condition of mortal life and become swallowed up in Being itself. All this occurs within the context and along the axis of discipline.

In Hinduism, discipline is more than simply conquering self. To be sure, this great religion looks on discipline as the only true form of learning, namely learning to be who one is and who one can be through conquering oneself.[32]

Zen Buddhism

Zen is the Japanese translation of a Sanskrit word meaning meditation.[33] Specifically, Zen is a school of Buddhism whose axis is a well-developed set of discipline (learning) techniques for meditation.

The ever-present and overriding purpose of Zen is to attain the experience of enlightenment (*satori* in Japanese, *wu* in Chinese). *Satori* consists in a luminously clear personal experience or intuitive vision of the original oneness of all reality. *Satori* is attained only through discipline (controlled and goal-directed learning). The intent of this discipline is to enable the person to radically break through the inherently tangled web of his rationality so as to arrive at the personal intuitive experience of the seamless fabric of all reality. By use of discipline techniques, Zen endeavors to jog loose and free the seeds of enlightenment which lie hidden in the unconscious, seeds buried under the rubble of conscious reason. An overriding purpose of all Zen is to provide the disciple with a deep experiential awareness of his own consciousness and also with a being-with his own consciousness. [34] Zen seeks *satori* by seeking things as they truly are. To accomplish this goal, discipline (learning) is required. All learning exercises (discipline procedures) are designed to crush every false duality, such as mind and body. Indeed, one of Zen's essential features is its methodology or discipline procedures for learning. These procedures, besides being made up of a series of paradoxes, contradictions, and irrationalities, operate in intimate connection with the learner's (disciple's) own experience. [35]

Above all and through all, Zen is discipline, a purposeful and controlled way of life. Zen is not a revelation of enlightenment (*satori*) but rather a way to enlightenment. [36] The way of enlightenment is essentially a path of discipline, and specifically a path of definite discipline practices. The two primary discipline techniques used in Zen Buddhism are *zazen* and the *kōan*.

Zazen means the sitting position in which the disciple (learner) meditates. *Zazen* is done in an upright sitting position with the legs crossed. This is the famous lotus position, and is regarded as more conducive to depth meditation than any of the other yoga sitting positions. At the outset, the practice of *zazen* is difficult. Sitting quietly for hours meditating deeply in the lotus position is hard work, and involves a great deal of personal discipline.[37] But as the individual sits quietly and does *zazen* for hours, the unrelenting discipline (learning) involved in this activity tends to bring with it a physical and psychological relaxation which significantly aids the individual to empty his psyche of conscious rational forms and to break through to *satori*.

A *kōan* is a verbal paradox or riddle which either contains a blatant logical contradiction or which inevitably leads to a logical dead end. In a *kōan* "there is no direct connection between question and answer. And if a [logical] connection should arise, then a *kōan* would no longer be a *kōan*. The *kōan* should put the disciple in a blind alley, with no way out."[38] The *kōan* can only be solved when the learner so disciplines himself as to put to rest his analytical mind with its processes of discursive reasoning, and instead relies on his own experience, on his own being-in-reality, on his own nonrationality.[39] The more the learner intensifies his rational discursive powers to solve the *kōan*, the more he discovers that reason is of no use. The recurrent experience of the utter futility of reason to solve the *kōan* prepares the ground for the letting go of reason, a letting go which is indispensable for solving the *kōan*. The solution can be experienced only in a sudden breakaway flash of intuition which tends to bring enlightenment (*satori*) with it. One of the most famous of all *kōans* is: "What is the sound of one hand clapping?" There is no universally "correct" response to a given *kōan*. Rather, each person authentically responds to a *kōan* when he addresses it from out of the existential wellsprings of his own disciplined silence.[40] The ultimate purpose of the *kōan* is to bring the person to enlightenment. The discipline of the *kōan* is grounded in the Zenist belief that personal, lived inner experience is the only true path to *satori*. The *kōan* is discipline especially when a person silently reflects on it and, indeed, lives it throughout the day and days. In this connection, Daisetz Teitaro Suzuki quotes Tai-hui: "Just steadily go on with your *kōan* every moment of your life. If a thought rises, do not attempt to suppress it by conscious effort; only renew the attempt to keep the *kōan* before your mind. Whether walking or sitting, let your attention be fixed upon it without interruption. When all of a sudden something flashes out in your mind, its light will illumine the entire universe, and you will see the spiritual land of the Enlightened Ones revealed at the point of a single hair, and the great wheel of the Dharma revolving in a single grain of dust."[41]

Zen stresses that enlightenment is attainable by any disciplined person in any state of life. Nonetheless, for the individuals who wish to orient their whole lives around the discipline (purposeful learning) of Zen, monasteries have been established. Every aspect of the Zen monastery reflects the discipline which is quintessentially Zen: the carefully manicured garden, the well-ordered ceremonies, the superbly crafted decorations and works of art, the pedagogical activities among monks and disciples, the five meditations before each meal, and so forth.[42] Zen monks engage in hard manual labor daily to further grow in discipline (learning).

The discipline of Zen promises what all discipline promises, namely learning in the most efficient and most fulfilling way possible.

Islam

The very term Islam pinpoints the intense and all-pervading discipline nature of this universal religion which arose from the preaching and teaching of Mohammed. In Arabic, Islam means surrender.[43] A believer in Islam is called a Muslim, an Arabic word which means a person who has surrendered to God. The surrender of a person to God in Islam is total and complete in that it takes place in every phase of the individual's personal and social life. The total surrender which constitutes Islam is not only accomplished by discipline, but in fact is itself discipline.

A Muslim practices continuous self-surrender to God in a

variety of complex religious practices which run the gamut from purely voluntary acts of discipline, to necessary but not obligatory acts of discipline, all the way up to the completely obligatory five classes of discipline (learning) acts—the famous "five pillars of Islam." These five obligatory pillars are profession of faith in Islam, prayer, almsgiving, fasting, and pilgrimage. Each of these five pillars represents a different but complementary form of learning (*discere*) how to surrender oneself more fully to God.

The first pillar of Islam is profession of faith. This profession consists in reciting the simple, well-known formula, preferably before witnesses: "There is no god but God (*Allāh*), and Mohammed is his prophet." With this simple statement, a person becomes a Muslim. But throughout his life, the believer must make a continuous intellectual surrender to six basic articles of faith dealing respectively with God, the angels, scripture, prophets, judgment and resurrection, and predestination.

Prayer comprises the second pillar of Islam. Prayer in Islam is not only a discipline, but it is done in a highly disciplined way. A Muslim prays five times a day at a prescribed time. Prayers are preferably said in community at a mosque, preceded by ablutions (ritual cleansing). When this is not practicable, then prayers are to be said wherever the believer might be at prayer time, be it at home, in a marketplace, playing sports, or the like. There is a set ritual, including deep bows (*rak'ah*), for the five prescribed forms of prayer. The discipline of prayer (learning to be near God) is obligatory for everyone. Even sick persons in bed must pray in the prescribed manner, and may pray while lying down only if it is absolutely necessary for them to do so.[44]

The third pillar of Islam is almsgiving (*zakāt*). As often as possible, believers must make free-will offerings to the poor, to beggars, to travelers, and so forth. Almsgiving is no easy discipline practice because it involves sacrificing a portion of one's money for the welfare of others.

Fasting constitutes the fourth pillar of Islam.[45] For the average

Muslim, fasting takes place chiefly during the entire month of *Ramadān*, which is the ninth month of the Muslim calendar. The *Ramadān* fast begins at daybreak and ends at sunset. During the daytime hours of the *Ramadān* fast, all eating, drinking, and smoking are strictly forbidden. Fasting is obviously a discipline practice. Its purpose is to purify oneself by denial of ordinary required material needs, to repent, and to learn (*discere*) more of *Allāh* and his ways.

The fifth pillar of Islam is the pilgrimage (*hajj*) to Mecca which every adult Muslim is expected to make once in his life if he possesses the means.[46] The formal pilgrimage takes place during a set number of days during the final month of the Muslim calendar. There is an entire discipline ritual involved in the formal pilgrimage.[47] The pilgrimage to Mecca and its rituals involve a high degree of discipline.

Because Islam is fundamentally a religion of law, it is fundamentally a religion of discipline.[48] The ultimate source of Islamic law is the *Qur'ān* (Koran), which is regarded as the word or speech of God delivered to Mohammed by the angel Gabriel through the power of the Holy Spirit. The *Qur'ān* is amplified and supplemented by three other sources: *sunnāh* (traditions), *ijmā* (community consensus), and *ijtihād* (individual reflection). Islamic law, or *shari'āh* as it is known, is not so much the letter of the law as the total interlocking system of specific values which the law endeavors to promote. The spirit and authentic discipline (learning) character of *shari'āh* shines through the very word itself. *Shari'āh* is an Arabic term meaning "the way leading to the watering place," that is, the source of life.[49] The law is total and complete, covering not only a person's relations with others but also with his conscience and with God.[50] The law is an expression of God's will; hence to learn to follow God one must discipline oneself to follow the law as carefully as possible. Law is necessary because, as the *Qur'ān* states, man is prideful and sinful; consequently the discipline of the law is necessary in helping the person surrender to God.

Sufism (from the Arabic word *sūf* meaning wool) is the name given to a major mystical and ascetical movement within Islam. The origins of Sufism go back to the eighth century. Sufism typically centers around intense discipline.[51] This discipline is geared at enabling the devotee to learn of God more deeply and more experientially.[52] Beginners who enter Sufi orders undergo rigorous discipline in order to learn the mystical way of experiencing and living. Through ascetical practices, meditation, and other forms of purposeful learning (*discere*), the disciples eventually become full-fledged mystics and spiritual leaders.[53] Sufi imagery, poetry, and the like are produced out of a context of mystical growth-producing discipline, and have become highly regarded by many Western intellectuals and seekers.

Judaism

The indisputable fact that Judaism is essentially a religion or discipline can readily be appreciated when one recalls that Judaism is essentially a religion of the *Torah*.

The Hebrew word *Torah* is sometimes used to refer specifically to the Pentateuch, the first five books of the Bible. At other times, the word *Torah* is used to refer to the entire written and oral body of Jewish teaching.

Etymologically, the root meaning of *Torah* is not law, but rather teaching. If a Jew wishes to be authentically taught by and in God, then he must learn (*discere*) the *Torah* and submit his whole self to its prescriptive teachings. To learn (*discere*) God is to carefully follow his laws, to be disciplined. Thus the *Torah* as law is not an oppressive yoke but a liberating discipline, the way par excellence to know and love and serve God. Only by holistically living the *Torah* can a person be rendered acceptable in the eyes of God.

The *Torah* is law precisely because the *Torah* is God's teaching and God's wisdom. The essential rule for personal living in Judaism is to discipline oneself productively according to the teachings of the sacred *Torah*.[54]

The *Torah* is the embodiment of Judaism because it contains the terms of man's covenant with God. All life is basically a covenant relationship with God, and the *Torah* sets forth the spirit, goal, and specifications of this covenant relationship.[55]

The *Torah* is sacred teaching—teaching which everyone should learn (*discere*). This teaching and this learning are preeminently holistic in that they involve every aspect of a Jew's personality acting in disciplined concert. Thus, the *Torah* is the teaching not of an intellectual perspective but of an entire way of life.[56] Because Judaism is basically a way of life governed and interpenetrated by the *Torah*, "no confession of faith by itself can make one a Jew. Belief in the dogmas of Judaism must be expressed in the acceptance of its discipline rather than in the repetition of a verbal formula."[57] The essential meaning of the *Torah* as teaching/learning is nicely expressed in the words of the prophet Isaiah which the editorial board of the *Encyclopedia Judaica* chose to emblazon on both the outside and inside covers of all sixteen volumes of this monumental work: "Come ye and let us go up to the mountain of the Lord to the House of the God of Jacob and He will teach us of His ways and we will walk in His paths for out of Zion shall go forth the Law and the word of the Lord from Jerusalem."

The *Talmūd* is a cornerstone of Judaism.[58] The *Talmūd* is a compendium of interpretation of oral tradition and law by generations of Jewish scholars and legal experts in many centers of learning over a period of several centuries.[59] (The law which is set forth in the *Talmūd* was first codified in the *Mishnah*.) The word *Talmūd* means learning or study—in short, discipline (*dis-*

cere). The *Talmūd* has exerted enormous influence down through the centuries in shaping the spiritual, moral, and social life of Jews.[60]

The *Talmūd* clearly indicates that the means and end of all education and all life is learning/doing the *Torah*. Because education is something which takes place over an entire lifetime, learning/doing the *Torah* is an activity which perdures throughout a person's life. To authentically learn/do the *Torah* is both to learn/do the *Torah* on its own terms and also to discipline oneself to faithfully observe the commandments (*mitzvot*).

Also central to Judaism is the *halakhah*. The word *halakhah* (plural *halakot*) is specifically used to designate an official, rabbinically defined law.[61] The discipline texture of *halakhah* is amply revealed in the etymological root of this word, namely to go or to follow. In the Bible, the authentic religious life is often referred to as the way in which a person is supposed "to go" or "to follow." Thus, for example, Exodus 18:20 states: "Teach them the statutes and the decisions; show them the way they must follow and the work they must do."

Halakhah is an amalgam of five principal elements of unequal value: the written law found in the Bible; interpretations of biblical written law; oral law; statements handed down by tradition; custom.

In short, *halakhah* is the legal side of Judaism as distinct from *aggadah* which is the nonlegal side. The essential discipline character of Judaism again manifests itself in that *halakhah* is considered to be far more important and valuable than *aggadah*. To be sure, *halakhah* is so important because obedience to the word and way of God (discipline) is a supreme hallmark of Judaism. *Halakhah* reveals how and in what way a Jew can purposefully learn (*discere*) to pattern himself after God's word. The discipline specified in *halakhah* is as comprehensive, rigorous, detailed, and meticulous as that in some austere religious orders of Catholic monks. Jewish rules of discipline apply to all areas of life. "So far as its adherents are concerned, Judaism seeks to extend the concept of right and wrong to every aspect of their behavior. Jewish rules of conduct apply not merely to worship, ceremonial, and justice between man and man, but also to such matters as philanthropy, personal friendships and kindnesses, intellectual pursuits, artistic creation, courtesy, the preservation of health, and the care of diet."[62]

The centrality of discipline in Judaism also reveals itself in the observance of the *mitzvah* (plural *mitzvot*). A *mitzvah* is a commandment, prescription, or injunction. With respect to its source, a *mitzvah* may be biblical or rabbinical. A *mitzvah* may be grave or light. *Mitzvah* may also refer to a good or charitable deed, a fact which clearly reveals how discipline is regarded in Judaism as a positive rather than as a negative force. A *mitzvah* is implemented, focused, and fulfilled in and through *halakhah*. The heavy emphasis on *mitzvot* in Judaism shows anew that Judaism is essentially a religion of discipline.

It would be a major mistake to regard Judaism as a religion of empty, barren, dry legalism. The purpose of law in Judaism is to produce a disciplined life, one which enables a person to learn deeply about God and thus live a deep personalistic existence. *Halakhah* "serves to make concrete that which is otherwise in the realm of the abstract, while serving to sanctify that which is otherwise in the realm of the mundane."[63] In the words of a particularly spiritual and learned modern Jew, the surest way for a Jew to forfeit personal faith and an inner spiritual life is to do away with *halakhah*. "Without *halakhah*, [inward faith] loses its substance, its character, its source of inspiration, its security against becoming secularized. By inwardness alone we do not come close to God. The purest intentions, the finest of devotion, the noblest spiritual aspirations are fatuous when not realized in action."[64] Thus for Judaism, a disciplined life is a necessary condition for personal faith and a deep spiritual life.

The fundamental discipline nature of Judaism shines through

its liturgy. To be sure, the Jewish liturgy is a disciplined prayer service.[65] Liturgies are celebrated primarily in the synagogue and in the home.[66]

The liturgy in a synagogue is built around two major elements, namely the recitations of the *Shema* (proclamation of one universal eternal God) and the *Tephilla* (benediction and blessing). Upon these two central elements is constructed an elaborate disciplined prayer edifice of psalms, benedictions, doxologies, *piyyutim*, and ceremonies. The purpose of prayer in Judaism is to worship, praise, thank, and petition God. Prayer is a discipline (learning activity) which, because it is a discipline, confers upon the performer more pure learning of God and his law.

One of the most important Jewish liturgies celebrated in the home is Passover (*Pesach*). This joyful feast commemorates the most dramatic series of events in Jewish history, namely the Exodus from Egypt. The Passover liturgy is a fine example of the preeminence of discipline in Judaism, because its goal is to purposefully learn (*discere*) anew the saving grace of God given to his Chosen People and because its method of enactment is itself a discipline process. For all seven (or eight) days of the feast of Passover, leavened bread is forbidden in the home of a devout Jew; only unleavened bread (*matzah*) is permitted. On the first night of Passover, an elaborate ritualistic paschal meal, the *Seder* (meaning an ordered or disciplined banquet) takes place.[67] After some opening ceremonies the youngest person present asks the pivotal question: "Why is this night different from other nights?" There follow four specific set questions about the meaning of the paschal meal itself. So that all present will again learn (*discere*) to know and follow the Jewish way, the master of the house reads the main biblical narrative of the Exodus, thus fulfilling the biblical command to teach the children on *Seder* night (Ex. 13:8). After some further ritual ceremony, sweet and bitter herbs are mixed together symbolizing that genuine spiritual growth and learning (*discere*) necessarily involve sacrifice. Other ritual foods at *Seder* also bring the essential discipline character of this sacred meal to heightened salience. For example, salt water is present to symbolize the tears of the Jews in Exodus, and a roasted egg symbolizes the fruit of the Jews' discipline to God, namely the triumph of life over death. Then the main part of the meal is eaten, accompanied and followed by ritualistic activities.

Two other processes in Judaism throw further light on the centrality of discipline in this great religion. These two processes are the *bar mitzvah* and the dietary laws.

Bar mitzvah is the religious ritual in which a boy becomes a man. In Judaism the authentic sign of manhood is that one enjoys the liberating discipline of obedience to God's commandments (*bar mitzvah* means "son of the commandment").[68] The *bar mitzvah* takes place as soon as possible after the boy's thirteenth birthday. The central act and indeed principal symbol of the boy's attaining manhood is his being formally called up to read the *Torah* in the synagogue. The boy prepared for this event by a disciplined study of the *Torah* for several years. After the service, a festive ceremonial blessing (*kiddush*) is given, followed by an elaborate and often expensive banquet. Sometimes the newly inducted son of the commandment gives a Talmudic-type discourse during the banquet.

Jewish dietary laws, which are as complex as they are strict, represent another clear example of the axial place of discipline in Judaism. Devout Jews must discipline themselves not to eat a wide variety of foods formally declared to be unclean, including pork, hare, lobster, oyster, catfish, swordfish, and the like. Meat may not be consumed or even cooked together with milk or any other dairy product. Indeed, orthodox Jewish homes have two separate sets of dishes, one to be used for meat and the other for dairy items. Even meat from clean animals must be carefully koshered (that is, prepared and kept in a ritually clean manner) if it is to be eventually eaten.[69]

The history of biblical Judaism is one long saga of discipline.

Specifically, this is a history of how the Chosen People repeatedly strayed from God's appointed way and how they had to learn (*discere*) from God by being disciplined by God.

Throughout ancient, medieval, and much of modern history the Jews and their religion have been persecuted by others. In order to survive and walk faithfully in God's path, the Jews have relied heavily on learning (*discere*) in home, synagogue, and religious school. It is in these settings that the *Torah* is learned, that religious feasts are celebrated, and that the *halakhah* is integrated into daily life. All three—home, synagogue, and religious school—were and still are considered preeminently places for the disciplined learning of God's way.[70]

Because Judaism is so thoroughly imbued with discipline, there has always been a strong tendency among Jews to defer gratification, namely to make present sacrifices in order to attain later goals of value. The willingness to defer immediate gratification necessitates discipline since such postponement "implies the ordering [disciplining] of behaviors in terms of the relative importance of one's goals."[71] Empirical evidence suggests that it is largely because Jews tend to be disciplined in deferring immediate gratification that these persons tend to advance significantly within the social system.[72]

Christianity

Christianity is fundamentally a religion of discipline because Christianity is fundamentally a religion of the cross. The nature and effects of the cross stand at the center of Christianity. The cross is the touchstone of Christianity in that the cross is the standard against which everything in the Christian religion is ultimately measured. Even the central event in Christianity, namely, the resurrection of Jesus, receives much of its valence and meaning from the fact of the cross. The resurrection, as it were, stands in the shadow of the cross. Or put differently, the resurrection is the shadow thrown by the cross. To be sure, the cross and the resurrection are inseparable, and are two necessary and complementary dimensions of the same reality.

For Christians of every century, the cross is basically discipline because it is through accepting one's own daily crosses in union with the cross of Jesus that one comes to purposefully learn (*discere*) who God is, who one's own self is, and what life is. The cross is productive self-actualizing discipline because the cross is the kind of learning which necessitates personal sacrifice (*sacrum facere*, to make holy).

The worship services of virtually every branch of Christianity reflects the centrality of the cross with its objectification of discipline. In the Roman Catholic Church, for example, the divine liturgy or Mass may only be celebrated in the presence of a cross, and whenever possible the priest must wear a ceremonial outer garment featuring a cross prominently displayed on his back. Indeed, the Mass itself is considered by Catholics to be the existential sacrifice of Jesus on the cross, an unbloody sacrifice as real and as personal for Jesus as the original bloody sacrifice on Calvary.[73]

The founder of Christianity, Jesus, whom Christians also call the Christ, unequivocally made the cross and its discipline the indispensable requirement of those who wish to be his disciples (learners). Thus in a famous and pointed remark, Jesus states: "If anyone wants to be a follower of mine, let him renounce himself and take up his cross and follow me. For anyone who wants to save his life will lose it; but anyone who loses his life for my sake will find it."[74] Sometimes Jesus expresses the centrality of discipline in homey metaphors such as "I tell you, most solemnly, unless a wheat grain falls on the ground and dies, it remains only a single grain. But if it dies, it yields a rich harvest."[75] In Jesus' view, salvation is not attained by grand verbal expressions of loyalty to him or to his teachings, but rather by day-to-day nitty-gritty acts of submitting oneself to God's will through personal discipline. Thus Jesus forthrightly remarks: "Not everyone who calls me 'Lord, Lord' will enter the kingdom of heaven, but only those who do the will of my heavenly Father."[76]

In the writings of great Christian leaders since the time of Jesus, and in various practices of the church, the cross and its discipline (learning) have occupied a central place.

In the years immediately following the death of Jesus, the great apostle Paul traveled around the world "preaching Christ crucified."[77] Paul was typically straightforward and did not mince words about the centrality of discipline in Christianity: "You cannot belong to Christ Jesus unless you crucify all self-indulgent passions and desires."[78] Discipline is necessary in order to free oneself from those oppressive forces which hinder deeper self-actualization. In this vein, Paul notes that in order to be liberated from the slavery of sinful things which destroy the possibility for authentic self-actualization, one must crucify oneself with Christ so that in and through this crucifixion one might also be resurrected with him unto true life.[79] Paul the teacher did not exempt himself from the necessity of constant discipline: "I keep my body under subjection, lest possibly, after I have preached to others, I myself should become a castaway."[80] The result of the discipline of the cross in Paul's personal life was a new and eminently more fruitful existence for him, an existence in the liberating Jesus: "I have been crucified with Christ, so it is no longer I who live but now it is Christ who lives in me."[81] Like devout Christians in succeeding centuries, Paul believed that the preeminence and power of Christian discipline is found ultimately in Jesus. Jesus was quintessentially a person of discipline, and his human greatness and redeemership flow through this fact. It was in Jesus, Paul notes, that "God chose to reconcile the whole universe to himself, making peace through the shedding of his blood on the cross to reconcile all things, whether on earth or in heaven, through him alone."[82] In a glorious passage Paul states: "Though his state was divine, Jesus did not cling to his equality with God.

Rather, he emptied himself to assume the condition of a slave, being born in the likeness of men. He was even more humble than that in that he obediently accepted even death, death on a cross. Because of this, God greatly exalted him and bestowed on him the name which is above all other names so that at Jesus' name every knee must bend in the heavens, on earth, and under the earth, and every tongue acclaim Jesus Christ as Lord to the glory of God the Father."[83] Hence, if one is to become soaked with Jesus in one's own personal life, then one must become soaked with discipline also, the discipline (learning) of the cross day in and day out. Most persons regard discipline as ridiculous, preferring instead to do as they please. Paul recognizes this fact, and observes that discipline is one sign of holiness and wholeness: "The doctrine of the cross is sheer folly for those on the way to ruin, but to us who are on the way to salvation it is the power of God."[84] The discipline which Paul teaches is no legalism, no formalism, no rigorism. It is a discipline undertaken in the love of Jesus and through the love of one's own neighbor. In Paul's eyes, only love can preserve and authenticate discipline, because in the end there can be no genuine learning (*discere*) without love. For Paul, righteousness and salvation do not come from any law itself or from the law as a body, but rather from the way in which each person voluntarily dies in Christ by disciplining himself in such a way as to participate in the salvific reality of the cross of Jesus.[85]

The Fathers of the Christian church in the apostolic and sub-apostolic periods[86] continued the heavy stress on the cross and discipline begun by Jesus and carried on faithfully by Paul. The first known Father of the apostolic period, Clement of Rome, emphasizes that discipline is essential for genuine religious living. Clement regards discipline as constantly learning to imitate Jesus by incorporating into our personal and group lives the love of Jesus, a love which results in growth-producing order and harmony.[87] In his major work, Ignatius of Antioch states that the whole Christian life can be summed up in this fashion: one must become so positively disciplined that one dies to self so that one can thereby become a true disciple (learner) of Jesus.[88] The *Didachē* conceptualizes discipling as a way of life. This way of life as a whole is comprised of two complementary paths, each of which the Christian must follow if he wishes to learn (*discere*) Jesus. The first path is the path of life, and includes positive individual duties such as loving God and neighbor, as well as social duties like generosity to the poor and the education of children. The second path is the path of death, and centers on the extirpation from one's personal life of vices such as haughtiness, envy, avarice, and injustice.[89] The central theme of Hermas' important book is that the religious person is one who leads a disciplined life of ongoing repentance, a repentance which enables a person to be happy precisely because such a person eschews the hedonism of self-desire and instead practices virtue.[90] As expressed in his major work, Irenaeus' view of discipline runs directly counter to what he regards as the false and empty asceticism of the Christian Gnostics. Irenaeus holds that a person's human nature is essentially good, and that an individual can grow in grace only if he disciplines himself with the help of the Holy Spirit to do good and avoid evil. By disciplining one's passions, one can become free and attain full personhood. Discipline is positive because it is productive learning, because it is the achieving of a unified harmony of body, soul, and spirit.[91]

One of the greatest and most influential of all Christian heroes, Augustine of Hippo, led a highly disciplined monastic life for most of his years following baptism at the age of thirty-three. His writings and his life made discipline a focal point not only because he deeply regretted that he himself had morally fallen apart in his younger dissolute and undisciplined years, but also because he believed that productive discipline is absolutely necessary to be a disciple (learner) of Jesus. Augustine regards the essence of the Christian life as a constant discipleship undertaken by discipline. Discipline involves two principal elements: purging oneself of the basic pervasive vice of destructive self-love, and embracing the path of virtue by good thoughts and good desires and good deeds. Thus discipline accomplishes that which all significant learning is supposed to accomplish, namely to bring the person to wholeness by restoring in that individual the image and likeness of God, especially as embodied in acts of faith, hope, and love. Discipline is fundamental in life because when all is said and done, life is primarily a spiritual combat which one wages against evil influences from within and without.[92]

The great Christian thinkers and heroes of the Middle Ages were typically insistent on the necessity of productive discipline as essential for leading a Christian life. Anselm of Canterbury, Bernard of Clairvaux, Hugh of St. Victor, Francis of Assisi, Dominic, Bonaventure, Albert the Great, John Duns Scotus— each in his own way emphasizes the centrality of discipline in Christian living. The greatest of all the medieval Christian scholars, Thomas Aquinas, places discipline at the heart of the Christian life because in his view discipline is the major way in which a person comes to the touchstone of Christianity, namely love. Love is the measure of the Christian life because of all the virtues, only love can unite the person to God. Without love, there can be no true virtue, and the person who possesses the virtue of Christian love automatically possesses all other virtue. Discipline is thus pivotal in Aquinas' view because discipline is the way one purposefully learns to love and imitate Jesus. Since Aquinas' conception of discipline is intrinsically tied in with love, his view of discipline is highly positive. For Aquinas, everything involved in discipline (learning) begins from, flows through, and ends in love. Love entails both the daily renunciation of selfishness, and a progressive ongoing adherence to virtue. One acquires Christian perfection through discipline.[93]

All reformers, religious or political or social, place great store in discipline. One of the primary reasons reformers typically undertake reform is to restore to an institution or movement that pristine doctrinal and practical discipline which the reformers believe has been corrupted by time or circumstance. The restoration of what they believed to be pristine Christian discipline certainly underlay the efforts of the great Protestant reformers of the sixteenth century. Two of the most influential Protestant reformers were Martin Luther and John Calvin.

In Luther's view, discipline is the whole purposeful path a person travels to spiritual perfection. Therefore discipline is not a separate category of perfection. Rather, discipline pertains to all of Christian perfection. Discipline in a Christian sense does not consist in blind submission to law, but rather in open submission to the gospel. The gospel has two basic dimensions with respect to law: it has its own living fluid law, and it gives meaning and validity to the law. The gospel, then, justifies the person and the law. Discipline is the name we give to the continual struggle through repentance and reconciliation to attain spiritual life as given to us by God.[94]

For John Calvin, discipline is the entire process of the justified Christian life. Because of the Fall, the image of God in man, while not utterly destroyed, nonetheless is frightfully deformed. By God's saving power, a person is justified, not in a single act but in living a whole disciplined life in Jesus through mortification on the one hand and vivification of the Spirit on the other hand. Because the Christian life is itself discipline, a person has discipline by the grace of God. Thus the possession of discipline is an important sign of one's predestination to heaven. Conversely, the lack of discipline is an important sign of one's predestination to hell.[95]

Discipline has always been one of the basic and oft-repeated themes in the repertoire of virtually every great Christian preacher. In the eighteenth century, for example, John Wesley, the founder of Methodism, placed strong emphasis on discipline as the way in which a person concretely gives himself totally to

God. Discipline consists in giving oneself totally to God by dying to self. Discipline is not vague, but rather is practiced methodically by a variety of specific procedures, including fasting, meditation, the regulations of the worship service, and the performance of duties necessarily involved in one's particular state of life. For Wesley, the pivot of Christian existence is a personal experience of God's love. Such an experience brings with it new life. But this new life, in turn, must be preserved and cultivated through intellectual and moral discipline, that is to say, through unrelenting love of Jesus by repenting of one's sins and living according to the teachings of Jesus.[96]

Modern preachers are no less insistent on the centrality of discipline than the great preachers of old. Billy Graham and Fulton Sheen are representative examples of this fact. For Billy Graham, discipline means learning to be a good member of a family, a good member of a community, a good member of a church, and above all a good disciple of Jesus. Such discipline—discipleship—inevitably involves personal sacrifice. Salvation is free, declares Graham, but discipleship costs everything.[97] In Fulton Sheen's view, discipline consists in the entire process whereby a person becomes totally free to be himself by progressively liberating himself from evil and its possibilities. The attainment of this personal freedom involves an ongoing asceticism springing from a selfless love of God and permeated at every stage by this love—a love which shows us the Truth about God and the truth about ourselves.[98]

The many and varied religious practices engaged in by devout Christians down through the centuries illumine in a powerful manner the centrality of discipline in this great religion. The willingness of Christians to be martyred for their religion in ancient Rome and in modern missionary lands surely represents the supreme act of discipline. Existing side-by-side with these heroic acts of martyrdom is the sometimes more difficult discipline which Christian heroes and ordinary folk have endured in suffering with Jesus the difficulties of everyday life.[99] The devout Christian also seeks out additional discipline practices so that he can learn to imitate Jesus with a purer heart: the fasts of Lent and the other penitential seasons, mortification of divers kinds, spiritual exercises, retreats, and the like. Those Christians who seek a fuller discipline so as to learn Jesus more closely often seek out the monastic life, a life which centers around an all-embracing *regula* or discipline oriented toward liturgical worship and praise of God. Indeed, the founder of Christian monasticism in the West, Benedict of Nursia, regarded the monastery as basically a familial school for sanctity where the monks would learn through discipline and liturgical celebration how to follow Jesus more closely in their own personal lives.

Christian literature and liturgical celebrations have often used the image of the way or the path to depict the intrinsically developmental life of a Christian on earth. Thus a Christian is frequently described as a pilgrim on the path to eventual union with the divine. Almost always this path is depicted as an ascent, an ascent which is possible only through discipline. In classic Christianity, this ascent to God is said to occur in three progressively higher stages, namely the purgative way, the illuminative way, and the unitive way.[100] Each stage is permeated with discipline and achieved by discipline. Thus, for example, a famous study of Christian mysticism (the highest degree of the unitive way) concludes that all the great Christian mystical writers consider discipline with its beneficial purgative effects not as a goal but as a necessary dimension of the mystical life.[101]

Three Essential Religious and Moral Thrusts of Discipline

Because discipline is so basic and essential to both religion and morality, the fundamental thrusts of religion and morality are permeated with discipline. Three central religious and moral concerns illustrate this point: love, service, and ritual.

Love

Though love is emphasized far more by religious writers than by philosophers and psychologists specializing in morality,[102] nonetheless there is a strong accent placed on love by some philosophers and psychologists interested in morality. Erich Fromm, Carl Jung, and Walter Conn are representative examples.

In Erich Fromm's view, love is the fundamental answer to the problem of human existence. Love is also the route one must take to achieve personhood. Some individuals mistakenly believe that happiness and fulfillment consist in being loved; the truth of the matter is that happiness and fulfillment come from loving. Contemporary Western culture has transmogrified the human being from a person to a commodity. Even romance and falling in love have been debased into a situation in which an individual chooses a mate not on the basis of genuine love but on the basis of what his or her personal qualities are able to obtain in the social marketplace—a barter arrangement, as it were. While difficult to achieve in contemporary Western society, true love is still possible. In order to attain true love and to grow in the practice of true love, three concurrent conditions are necessary, namely discipline, concentration, and patience. Discipline enables the person to be free to love by helping that individual conquer the main obstacle to true love, namely narcissism. Discipline is the condition which enables one to learn how to love. Discipline and learning how to love are, in the end, of a piece. Love is an art which, like all other arts, must be learned and which, like all other arts, requires discipline at every turn.[103]

For Carl Jung, love of neighbor and love of all reality are directly dependent upon genuine love of self. Unless a person authentically accepts and loves himself, his attempts to love neighbor and world will be consumed in the fires either of narcissism on the one hand or of self-rejection on the other.[104]

Every human encounter, every moral act, depends on an inner connection to one's own being. Thus to be truly in touch with another person one must be in touch with the inmost recesses of one's own self. The main shadow of human relationships is love, and human relationship lies in the shadow of love.[105] Genuine love is "part of mankind's heavy toll of suffering, and nobody should be ashamed of having to pay his tribute."[106] Discipline is necessary to properly love oneself, to be genuinely in touch with oneself, to fruitfully endure the suffering involved in love. To be sure, discipline at bottom is learning (*discere*) these three primary sets of behaviors.

For Walter Conn, the ethicist, morality is ultimately grounded in personal fulfillment. In order to come to personal fulfillment, one must transcend oneself. Self-transcendence comes about through correct understanding (cognitive domain), responsible action (lifestyle domain), and most especially by genuine love (affective domain). Self-transcendence enables a person to become truly authentic because self-transcendence moves the individual to attain the possibilities of his real self. Being-in-love is the ground and goal of self-transcendence because the human being is most a person when his whole existence is grounded and bathed in love. The subjective drive for self-transcendence is conscience. Conscience involves all the individual's conscious and intentional operations insofar as these operations are practical, that is to say, heading toward decision and action within a context of love. It is love which is both the axis and context of conscience. It is love which enables conscience to flourish. It is love which enables conscience to authenticate the person in freedom. Self-transcendence and conscience require discipline at every turn—the discipline (learning) of becoming authentic to oneself through the self-transcending process, the discipline of refining and improving the correctness of one's understanding, the discipline of being self-critical so as to be true to one's conscience, the discipline of being responsible for one's actions, and above all the discipline of being genuine in one's love. Where there is no discipline there can be no creative personal growth, and where there is no creative personal growth there can be no genuine love and hence no conscience or self-transcendence.[107]

It is one of the supreme glories and inestimable strengths of the world's great religions that they ultimately make love the be-all and end-all. While cognition enables a person to have ideas about reality, it is love and only love which enables a person to be existentially united to a reality in all the dimensions of his humanity. Love, after all, is existential union in goodness, and the world's great religions all teach that union with God constitutes ultimate human fulfillment. The love which the world's great religions advocate is a highly disciplined love, a love characterized by self-surrender so that one can thereby be open to be united with God not on one's own terms but on God's terms.

At the everyday level, the surrender aspect of love reveals itself in the relationship which love has with rules. It is often thought that rules are solely the prescriptions of justice. But rules are also the prescriptions of love. Love instructs a person how he should behave, how he should treat others, even how he should utilize etiquette in social situations.[108] Love, and especially love permeated by religion, generates its own set of obligations.[109] Because love is so totally human and hence completely engulfs the self, it follows that love's prescriptions are more comprehensive and demanding than the prescriptions generated by other virtues or considerations. Love necessarily brings discipline with it because love can neither exist nor flower without discipline—the discipline to follow love's commands. Yet so great is the reality of love that these commands are sweet and joyous for the lover. Thus, in love the positive and fulfilling character of discipline clearly manifests itself.

One way in which love manifests itself in the concrete order is through commitment. Indeed, love is the hidden dimension and major power source for all genuine commitment. It is for this reason that commitment is so highly prized by all universal religions. Commitment is learning to love God more sincerely by dedicating oneself to whomever or whatever is the object of one's love. Discipline is one of the principle avenues on which commitment travels. It is impossible to be committed without discipline, since commitment is one's wholehearted journey toward a purposeful goal. Conversely, the exercise of commitment heightens one's discipline.[110] Discipline and commitment lead to a purity of heart, that is, the selfless pursuit of a worthwhile goal and rejection of any contaminating influence which might stand in the way of the realization of that goal.

Religion demands that we love others as we love ourselves. To love others in such a fashion takes discipline, especially when we do not like the other person.[111] This kind of love must be learned (*discere*), a learning which has to be renewed and revivified daily throughout a person's life. This kind of love is usually not a gush or a sudden warm feeling all over. This kind of love is discipline at its finest—a love which has learned and continues to learn that it is genuine only when we do things for others in a way which they themselves require rather than in a way which we want, or in a way designed to make us happy, or in a way which fulfills our unconscious needs.

World religions, and most especially Christianity, urge us to love what is not naturally lovable—lepers, criminals, ungrateful individuals, unruly students, and so forth.[112] Such selfless love is possible only in discipline, in purposefully learning to love no matter what the cost.

Christianity is a religion of love. The New Testament places love at the center.[113] Indeed, the apostle John defines God as love: "God is love, and the person who abides in love abides in God, and God in him."[114] Love reconciles and redeems—the essence of the Christian message.[115] The apostles John and Paul clearly teach that God's love was manifested not simply in the Incarnation, but also in the living out of the Incarnation as the atonement in Jesus' daily existence and ministry. The Incarnation, especially in its basic atonement characteristic, was discipline, a path which Jesus had to continually learn and tread. Those who would follow Jesus must also follow him in the atonement. Among the highest principles of the Christian life is that known as spiritual victimhood, a state in which the Christian, like his Lord before him, offers his life and works as a redemptive victim atoning for the sins of others. Spiritual victimhood is itself an extraordinarily high level of discipline, of learning how to imitate Jesus fully in the practical order.

Every level of Christian love from the simplest to the exalted spiritual victim necessitates discipline. Discipline in this case means learning and doing God's will. Discipline for the Christian means uniting oneself as closely as one can by uniting oneself to God's commandments. Discipline is often not easy. Love is often not easy. Great discipline is often very hard. Great love is often very hard. But great discipline makes great sacrifices sweet and fulfilling, just as great love makes great sacrifices sweet and fulfilling. As the apostle John puts it, "To love is to live according to God's commandments."[116]

The discipline axis of love as proposed by the world's great religions is beautifully summed up in a revealing passage written by a Hindu savant:

> Love is action.
> Devotion is practice.
> Surrender is experience.
>
> Love is realization.
> Devotion is revelation.
> Surrender is manifestation.[117]

Service

Service is the placing of one's resources at the disposal of others in order to help others in the realization of their own good.

Service and discipline go hand-in-hand. The essence of service lies in sacrificing personal advantage or desire for the good of others. Such personal sacrifice not only requires discipline but also is itself discipline because this kind of sacrifice necessarily involves goal-directed learning (*discere*) to fulfill oneself by helping others. Thus there is no service without discipline. Conversely, discipline is itself a form of service.

Service to one's neighbor and indeed to all humanity is a leitmotiv in both morality and religion.[118]

In the moral sphere, for example, John Dewey strongly asserts that discipline, like all education, must be directed not at correcting a learner's misbehavior but rather at forming both a general orientation to positive service and specific habits of such service.[119] For Dewey, a fundamental aim of authentic education is to serve society by helping to reconstruct it. Through this process of reconstructing society the learner himself becomes optimally reconstructed as a person. Such service to society cannot come about in the absence of discipline, a discipline illuminated and directed by critical intelligence.[120] Thus Dewey views discipline primarily as a moral trait because discipline simultaneously helps the person to productively expand the worth of his own activity and helps the person to give to society rather than just receive benefits from it.[121]

Service has always occupied a privileged and salient place in the world's great religions.

In both Jewish and Christian scripture, the true servant of God is one who teaches the will of God to the people, who ministers to the needs of the people, and who suffers on behalf of the people.[122] To be a servant in the Jewish and Christian traditions, then, is a great privilege and a great discipline.

Judaism is shot through and through with an emphasis on service—service to God, service to family, service to society. Such service is both material and spiritual. The material face of service in Judaism manifests itself in donations and philanthropy. Indeed, as a group, Jews are collectively the most philanthropic folk in America. This fact holds true for every socioeconomic stratum within American Jewry. The spiritual face of service is exemplified in this great religion's recognition that each Jew and also the religious house Israel is called to be the faithful servant of God, a fact which also teaches each Jew to engage in genuine service to his fellowman. The glorious passages in the later Isaiah luminously reveal the spiritual force of service in Judaism.[123] Hence the songs of the suffering servant depict the model servant of God, the perfect Jew, the person who is deeply consecrated to God's will even when he must endure great hardship for his service to God. Service in both its material and spiritual dimensions requires discipline, and indeed is itself discipline. To engage in God's service, a person must first be a disciple (learner) of God's word and way before that person can be of genuine service to others.[124]

Service is an indispensable and ever-present feature of Christianity.[125] Jesus became a servant of mankind[126] to reconcile human beings to God through this very service. There are many forms of religious service which the Christian can and ought to undertake.[127] Service, then, is not restricted to the clergy but is the duty and privilege of all Christians.[128] To worthily and effectively give service to God and to others, the Christian must discipline himself to be faithful to the gospel.[129] This discipline involves constant prayerful learning and relearning the gospel so that from this purposeful *discere* he can live out the gospel through his service.

Morality and religion both view parents and teachers as primarily service vocations. Parents and teachers are servants of their children since they place their own personal resources at the disposal of their children. Persons called to be parents and teachers fulfill themselves *as persons* by meeting their own individual needs and aspirations. But parents and teachers fulfill themselves *as parents and teachers* by helping children meet these children's needs and aspirations. The wonderful thing about the principle enunciated in the last sentence is that in helping children meet these children's needs and aspirations, parents and teachers thereby significantly contribute to meeting their own needs and aspirations.

Teaching and parenting mean that each teacher and each parent is primarily a person *for* others—a person *for* the children they serve. Put more clinically, teaching and parenting both are pure functions. Teaching and parenting as pure functions suggests that pedagogy and child-rearing are not entities in and for themselves but rather are activities organically related to something outside themselves, namely the facilitation of learning. Teaching and parenting as pure functions emphasizes that the teacher and the parent *in these roles* do not exist for themselves but rather for the children to whom they minister.[130]

To be a true servant is in a certain sense to be a redeemer. A person serves another so he can help the other attain some personal or sound objective on the other's own terms. Teaching and parenting in this perspective are redemptive processes. It is only through the discipline involved in successful servitude that teaching and parenting can keep their redemptive character. Without such discipline, teaching and parenting too easily can become alienating, competitive, and unilateral activities.[131]

In order to be an effective parent or teacher, a person must have discipline—the discipline involved in putting the child first, the discipline involved in sacrificing self-interest through putting one's resources not at the service of self but at the service of the child. Function connotes duty and responsibility; in the case of parenting and teaching, function implies that the person exercising this function is thereby charged with the duty and responsibility to make sure that the child acquires desired learning outcomes. One cannot be a function, one cannot be a person for others, if one lacks discipline. To be sure, it is discipline which constitutes the very process of learning how to serve effectively and truly.

Each teacher and each parent is a leader in his or her own right. But to be a real leader is to serve. This is a disciplined undertaking.[132]

Ritual

Ritual is the prescribed form of words and actions in a ceremonial structure. Ritual is necessary and indispensable for every viable secular and religious society. The proof of this last statement is immediately evident when one recalls that throughout the history of the world there has never been any lasting secular or religious society which did not possess considerable ritual.

Ritual is central both to civil and to religious societies. Indeed, most civil rituals have their direct counterparts in religious rituals, and vice versa. Civil society has its parades; religious society has its processions. Civil society has elaborate and elegant funeral ceremonies for its political and military leaders; religious society has moving and beautiful funeral ceremonies not only for its leaders but for ordinary believers as well. Civil society has a waking and a retiring ceremony (bugle, or such) for its personnel on a military installation; religious society has a waking and retiring ceremony (bell, or such) for its personnel in a monastery. Civil society in its schools has the pledge of allegiance ceremony to begin the day; religious society in its schools has the prayer ceremony to begin the day. Civil society follows a civic corporate life cycle of ceremonial feasts throughout the year such as New Year's, Presidents' Day, Memorial Day, Fourth of July, and so on, as well as a civic personal life cycle of ceremonial feasts throughout one's lifetime such as school graduations, civil marriage ceremonies, retirement parties, and so forth. Religious society follows an ecclesial corporate life cycle of ceremonial feasts throughout the year such as Advent, Christmas, Epiphany, Lent, Easter, Pentecost, and so on, as well as a religious personal life cycle of ceremonial feasts throughout one's lifetime such as baptism, confirmation, church marriage, church funeral rites, and the like.[133]

Ritual is central to civic and religious society for many reasons, one of the most important of which is identity. A society to remain a society needs ritual. Three principal functions of ritual are intimately related to identity, namely the restoration of identity, the reinforcement of identity, and the redirection of identity. A ritual enacts some basic axis or fundamental ontic characteristic of the society. This enactment serves to recommit to living operative memory these pivotal axes and characteristics, axes and characteristics which would have otherwise become occluded or weakened by time and circumstance. Furthermore, a ritual such as confession can restore a person's identity as a Christian-in-fellowship-with-Jesus, an identity lost by serious sin. A ritual reinforces identity by linking the past to the present, by repetitive rites within the ritual, and by a wide repertoire of affective and nonverbal forces which bond the essence of the ritual to the person in his humanity. A religious ritual redirects identity by sacralizing the participant's secular identity (or vice versa), and by enveloping stressful or major life-event situations with affective and behavioral support.[134]

Ritual is not a set of empty acts or vainglorious ceremonies.[135] Rather, ritual is an intense activity which possesses formidable pedagogical power in its own right. This fact is just as true for a street gang's initiation ceremony as it is for baptism or *bar mitzvah*.[136] The fact that ritual is highly disciplined (learning-full) in essence and action is one major factor accounting for its power.

Ritual is not a mere reflection or expression of religion. Rather, ritual is a vital dimension of religion itself, a deeply personalistic way of doing religion.[137]

Ritual and discipline are inseparable. By its very nature, ritual takes place in a prescribed controlled manner, that is to say in a disciplined manner. It is precisely because ritual is discipline in action that ritual is so heavily freighted with learning. Discipline, after all, is purposeful learning, and the greater the discipline, the greater the learning (*discere*).

Ritual is necessary for the survival and renewal of secular and religious society because productive learning (*discere*) is absolutely essential for the survival and renewal of every kind of society.

Ritual calls religion back to its roots, to its primal sources of strength. Such, too, is the function of discipline, namely to call persons and societies back to their life-giving roots and primal sources. A person or a society without civic ritual is without roots, cut off from the vital sources. So also a person or a society without religious ritual is without roots, severed from the vital sources.

Ritual reveals the festive and positive face of discipline. Ritual is a basic way in which discipline rejoices in joyful moments, weeps in sorrowful moments. For these reasons, ritual and other forms of productive discipline are eminently human.

Ritual is a form of discipline which lays bare three essential functions of discipline, namely restoration of personal/societal identity, reinforcement of personal/societal identity, and redirection of personal/societal identity. As a person or a society grows in discipline, so too does that person or society deepen his/its sense of identity. Conversely, as a person or a society decreases in discipline, so too does that person or society diminish his/its sense of identity. Much of the personal and societal identity crisis facing current American society can be directly traced to this society's growing loss of discipline.

Ritual teems with discipline in that it causes a role reversal which rewires and restructures a person's everyday system of order. The greater the role reversal, the greater the possibilities for learning. In everyday life, a person often loses touch with his existential roots, severs the main wires as it were. Ritual restores and strengthens the principal wires connecting the person with those primal personal, community, and cosmic realities which give his life meaning, dignity, and worth.[138]

Christianity has always recognized the ritual dimension of discipline. To be sure, the earliest Christian documents suggest two principal types of ritual in the Church, namely a ritual for instruction (catechumenate) and a ritual for worship (liturgy). Both rituals prescribe certain types of dress, conduct, prayers, order of activities, and so forth.[139] On closer inspection it will be found that both forms of ritual are primarily educative in nature and intent. The ritual of instruction and the ritual of worship are complementary forms of discipline and hence complementary forms of learning. The liturgy teaches a person to be truly religious as much if not more than more conventional forms of religion teaching. The liturgy, after all, is primarily a learning event, an event in which a person existentially learns in the concrete how to holistically know, love, and serve God.

The teacher or parent wishing to enhance the discipline of the child he or she serves might do well to introduce more ritual into the life of the child. Ritual in everyday life, as well as enhanced rituals of special civic and religious events, will go a long way in helping the child learn (*discere*) his own identity, the meaning of life, and his place in the scheme of things.

Pivots of Discipline

The Law of Nature

From Plato and Aristotle onward, philosophers and other serious thinkers have held that there is a fundamental guiding law of nature innate in each person and indigenous to each society. Though adherence to the reality of the law of nature substantially ebbed in the first sixty years of the twentieth century, it has now begun to make something of a comeback, though in a more expansive and sophisticated form. In bygone centuries, the natural law tended to be conceptualized as highly specific absolutized imperatives emanating almost mechanistically from the nature of a reality. The new view is that the natural law is "a definite course of growth and development which tends to ensue from the inherent structure and flow of a particular reality as this reality interacts with other realities. Natural law thus describes the basic structure and progressive unfolding of a particular reality according to the dynamics of that reality's own exigencies and interactive functioning."[140] There is a generalized law of nature which individuals and societies must follow if they are to fulfill their own potential.

One of the principal uses of discipline relates directly to the law of nature. It is discipline which enables the person and the society to live according to the natural law. Phrased more accurately, it is discipline which constitutes the positive and progressively upward axis of that maturational and developmental journey which a human being or a society makes in personal or corporate fulfillment. Thus a person or a society characterized by a high degree of discipline will be "on axis" with respect to that person's or society's own fulfillment. Conversely, a person or a society characterized by a low degree of discipline will be "off axis" with respect to that person's or society's own fulfillment. Consequently, discipline and fulfillment are inseparable from one another. In a sense, they are different faces of the same reality.

Discipline is the process of enabling the conditions of the natural law to be realized in a person or in a society. Discipline is also the medial and end product which results when these natural law conditions are realized.

The Natural Law and Individual Growth

The natural law provides an inner axis which helps enable the individual to become what that person is capable of becoming.

Furthermore, the natural law provides a general description of the basic structure and progressive unfolding of personal self-actualization. Such a description provides an especially helpful guideline to an individual in making those decisions which will be of singular help to him in his journey in self-fulfillment.

It is of the essence of morality that a person become fully that which he is authentically capable of becoming. Thus the natural law underlying personal self-fulfillment is extremely important from the standpoint of morality. One of the most important bases and justifications of morality is that it directly leads to holistic self-fulfillment. Conversely, immorality is immorality because it directly leads to the disintegration and even to the ruination of the person as a person. Discipline is crucial in the moral scheme of things because (1) discipline enables the person to learn (*discere*) conceptually what the natural law says to him about the contours of his humanity, and (2) discipline enables the person to learn (*discere*) morality in practice by actually doing morality in his own daily life.

Self-fulfillment is also central to religion. Religion looks at self-fulfillment not only from the eyes of man but also from the eyes of God. Thus the natural law is precious to religion for two basic reasons. First, the natural law is of indispensable help to the person in the fulfillment of his own humanity. Second, the natural law is the terrestrial footprint of the more cosmic law of God. The law of God is imaged to a certain degree in the law of nature, since religions universally teach that nature was created by God and is indwelt by God. While encompassing the law of nature in its entirety, the law of God goes beyond the law of nature. This "going beyond" in no way suspends or violates the law of nature. Rather, this "going beyond" completes what is incomplete in the law of nature. This "going beyond" addresses itself to the Godlike or "human plus" or superhuman dimensions of one's personality. This "going beyond" calls a person to the highest level of humanity, namely holiness, by calling that person to a far greater degree of sacrifice than is generally demanded by the law of nature. (Sacrifice, as was shown earlier in this chapter, comes from two Latin words, *sacrum* and *facere*, meaning to make holy.) Discipline is crucial in the religious scheme of things because (1) discipline enables the person to learn (*discere*) what the law of nature and the law of God say to him about the contours of his humanity, and (2) discipline enables the person to learn (*discere*) religion in practice by actually doing religion in his own daily life.

The law of God as interpreted by virtually every universal religion teaches the believer to reject cheap grace.[141] Cheap grace refers to that tendency in religion for a person to think that he can dispense with obedience to rightful authority (including the natural law) and do whatever he wants because of a mistaken notion that, no matter what he fails to do, God will automatically give him the grace which saves. In other words, to believe in cheap grace is to believe that personal sacrifice is unnecessary for a person who accepts God in faith. In the practical order, a person rejects the false reality of cheap grace not so much by conceptually repudiating it as by disciplining himself in his daily life to make those sacrifices necessary to live in and through the salvific law of God.

In Christianity, the law of God is quite direct—a person must lose his life so that he may thereby find it.[142] This requires sacrifices. These sacrifices are rarely heroic, occasionally great, usually the small sacrifices involved in living the law of God in the nitty-gritty of one's everyday life. Much as following the law of nature redeems one unto one's natural self, so too does following the law of God redeem one unto one's Godlike self. Jesus redeemed each person; but each person must cooperate in this redemption by dying on his own everyday cross. This is discipline, and through this discipline one learns truly about himself and about others and about Jesus.[143] Discipline is purposeful, channeled learning; without the discipline of embracing one's everyday crosses no matter how distasteful they might be, there is no genuine learning about oneself, about others, or about Jesus.

The Natural Law and Societal Growth

The law of nature indicates the general path and parameters which a society must heed if that society is to grow and prosper. History provides ample evidence that those societies which frequently violate the law of nature soon decay and disintegrate as a result.

In his brilliant and world-famous analysis of the rise and fall of civilizations throughout history, Pitirim Sorokin asserts that contemporary American and European society is undergoing a convulsive crisis. Europe and America have embraced a sensate culture, namely a culture whose goal is sensuous pleasure, whose axis is wholly temporal, whose truth is relativistic, and whose values are nihilistic. Sorokin maintains that the tragic debilitating consequences of contemporary overripe sensate culture are palpably evident: tragic dualism, chaotic syncretism, quantitative colossalism, and diminishing creativeness. Tragic dualism is the double-faced Janus—a culture which incorporates mutually destructive opposites such as the glorification of the human person and the degradation of the human person. Chaotic syncretism is the attempted integration of totally incompatible opposites, a sham integration which inevitably leads to a huge cultural stomach ache and thus to cultural vomit—religions based on drugs, television blaring out violent, wanton killing on one channel and heroic moral self-denial on another channel, public schools attempting to teach morality to students hell-bent on making the school a setting for their immoral tendencies. Quantitative colossalism is the belief that enormity necessarily equals quality, that mass equals class, that riches equal virtue, that a big reality, however vulgar, automatically excels a smaller reality, however exquisite. Diminishing creativeness is rife—cheap mystery thrillers for relaxation have replaced great classics for enrichment, sculptures made from twisted automobile tail-pipes and other assorted junk have replaced Michelangelo marbles, electronic music has replaced Mozart, hastily scribbled sentences have replaced carefully-crafted prose, and so on. In short, the imminent fall of contemporary Western culture is being brought about by the flagrant rejection of the natural law. Fraud and force have supplanted morality and law. Sorokin believes that only by purifying itself of its present destructive sensate culture and returning to an adherence of the law of nature can contemporary society achieve that kind of beneficial catharsis necessary to produce a noble and moral world.[144] In such a view, discipline is essential—the discipline of learning and living the law of nature. If sensate culture has all but ruined contemporary American society, then it is only through positive discipline that the healing and growth-producing law of nature can be restored.

Modern European and American society has its own special kind of cheap grace, namely the notion that a person can do whatever he wants because sooner or later the government will automatically give him the resources necessary for secular salvation. Thus, for example, a person will not budget his money in the expectation that the government will bail him out of debt. Or again, a student will not work diligently in school in the expectation that the government will automatically give or provide him with a good job no matter how unskilled he might be. Quite frequently, modern government not only is itself undisciplined, but it also promotes a lack of personal and corporate discipline in the citizenry.

One sector in which American society's embrace of cheap grace is most easily seen is that of work. In the frame of cheap grace, work is a distasteful chore to be avoided whenever possible. One major consequence of this cheap-grace frame has been the unfortunate radical split between work and humanity. Attendant upon this radical split between work and humanity has been the progressive loss of discipline which has increasingly debilitated American society in the second half of the twentieth century. Work, after all, is impossible without discipline; indeed, work can be viewed as "the disciplined organization of activities toward the accomplishment of designated tasks."[145] While all work necessitates discipline, nonetheless it would be erroneous to regard discipline as nothing more than work. Discipline may or may not involve work, hard work, or distasteful activities. There are times in which discipline is pleasant, not at all difficult, and devoid of distasteful realities. Indeed, the exclusive identification of discipline with hard work and distasteful realities has led to a negative view of discipline, a view that discipline is something which must be endured rather than embraced. Unfortunately, some parents and teachers holding this negative and erroneous conception of discipline have used discipline to cover up their own pedagogical inadequacies, lack of preparation, and just downright laziness. These parents and teachers make learning distasteful to children by telling them that "application for the sake of application, for the sake of training, is alone disciplinary. This is more likely to occur if the subject matter presented is uncongenial, for then there is no motive (so it is supposed) except the acknowledgment of duty or the value of discipline. The logical result is expressed with literal truth in the words of an American humorist: 'It makes no difference what you teach a boy so long as he doesn't like it.'"[146] It is small wonder, then, that so many persons have failed to properly identify discipline with goal-directed learning.

Religion, incorporating as it does the law of God, indicates the general path and parameters which secular and religious societies must follow if those two fundamental human groupings are to grow and flourish.

In order to confer upon individuals those corporate benefits which necessarily flow from an exemplary society, religion typically establishes its own society. Each great universal religion has a special name and a special theory for its religious society. In Christianity, the special name and special theory is church. The church, or *ecclesia*, is the corporate body of believers and contains within itself as one aspect, but only one aspect, an institutional dimension and organization called the *ecclesiasticum*. The church, the *ecclesia*, is the worshiping and praying and fellowshiping community. The *ecclesiasticum* is a denomination's institutional face and political apparatus. The *ecclesia*, therefore, cannot be considered equal or identical to the *ecclesiasticum*. The church, then, is an ecclesial reality, a corporate body, a religious society which exists to continually provide its members with enriched opportunities for experiencing religion and for clarifying their religious experiences. Through worship, prayer, and instruction the church educates its members so that their souls might become open to religious experiences of the deepest kind. [147] The church is the mystical body of Jesus, the sacrament of salvation. [148]

The two most essential characteristics of the church, then, are that it is salvational and that it is educational. For these two reasons, the church is permeated through and through with discipline because there can be neither salvation nor education in the absence of discipline. As a corporate body, as the communion of saints, the church requires love of neighbor. This love necessitates discipline—yet in and through such discipline one learns (*discere*) how to properly love not only one's neighbor but oneself as well. [149] As the *ecclesia*, Christian religious society necessitates the discipline of learning and living its precepts—a discipline which not only educates but sanctifies. Without personal or corporate discipline, then, there is no true education or sanctification in the *ecclesia*. Consequently, when discipline is strong the church is strong, and when discipline is weak the church is weak.

Developmentalism

Development is the consequence of the ongoing interaction between the growing organism and the environment. The human being, therefore, is an interactive emergent, a person whose self emerges or comes into being by virtue of the processive interaction between his organism and his environment. In developmentalism, the environment does not simply modify the organism in a minor or partial manner, channeling or deflecting its inner dynamic trajectory toward immediate fulfillment. Rather, developmentalists regard the environment as interacting so totally and so pervasively with the organism that it actively merges with that organism to produce not a simple modification of the organism but a new reality, namely the here-and-now person. Developmentalism has great import for the way in which a parent or teacher conceptualizes and implements discipline.

In the twentieth century there has been a growing number of important moral philosophers and religious scholars who maintain that development constitutes the basic nature and thrust of the human person. These moral and religious scholars are often, though not always, grouped under the heading of process thinkers. The positions of two of these thinkers are especially germane to the notion of developmental discipline. These two thinkers are John Dewey in the moral sphere and Pierre Teilhard de Chardin in the religious realm.

John Dewey views development as both the process and the goal of life. Indeed, states Dewey, life is fundamentally development and growth. Since education and life-experiences are ultimately the same, the educational process does not have any goal outside itself. Rather, the educational process is its own goal. Thus the basic purpose of education is not to acquire some sort of product learning "out there." Instead, the basic purpose of education is to come to increasingly higher stages of personal development. Put in terms of morality, the basic purpose of education is not to help the person achieve some moral goal independent of himself but instead to keep on growing as a moral person. With respect to discipline, all the parent or teacher can do is arrange environmental conditions in such a way that these conditions will interact productively with the learner's organism. Discipline, then, can never come from outside the learner, since discipline is the controlled goal-directed course of the learner's own development, a development which takes place not on the extrinsic educator's terms but exclusively on the terms of the intrinsic developmental process of interactive emergence itself. For Dewey, then, discipline is the dynamic fusion of the organism and the environment in such a fruitful way that the learner thereby achieves control of himself for the attainment of his own processive goals. In Dewey's view, discipline is not something which one person does to another but rather constitutes the balanced self-involvement which a person has with his environment.[150]

Pierre Teilhard de Chardin, more than any other religious thinker in this century or perhaps in any other century, possesses a truly cosmic vision of reality.[151] For Teilhard, all development is necessarily processive, necessarily evolutionary. The evolution of the cosmos, and the evolution of each person as well, is an ascent toward consciousness.[152] The world was, still is, and always will be necessarily a-building. "The world should be likened not to a bundle of elements artificially held together but rather to some organic system animated by a broad movement of development which is proper to itself."[153] The inexorable course of cosmic development is directed toward what Teilhard terms hominization, namely the progressive personalization of the universe. Hominization achieves its highest point in the developing consciousness of the human being, a consciousness which in turn reverberates throughout the entire cosmos.[154] The apex of the cosmos—an apex which is simultaneously the peak of fulfillment and the ground through which this fulfillment comes about—is what Teilhard calls Omega. Omega is the incarnate Jesus. The limitless power and pervasiveness of Omega in cosmic development stems directly from the limitless power and pervasiveness of the Incarnation. Teilhard views the Incarnation in its cosmic developmental dimensionality. "Since Christ is Omega, the universe is physically impregnated to the very core of its matter by the influence of his super-human nature. The presence of the Incarnate Word penetrates everything, as a universal element. It shines at the common heart of things, as a center that is infinitely intimate to them and at the same time (since it coincides with universal fulfillment) intimately distant."[155] Indeed, "by its structure Omega, in its ultimate principle, can only be a distinct Center radiating at the core of a system of centers."[156] Omega is origin, power, axis, and endpoint of all cosmic development. Omega ultimately incorporates all realities integrally in itself.[157] Development, then, is the interactive convergence of all reality toward and in Point Omega. This developmental convergence produces greater and greater organic synthesis of the cosmos. Synthesis brings with it union, a union which heals divisions and binds all reality into an organic whole. Such union is necessary not only for the ultimate harmonious integration of the cosmos but also for the basic preservation of the authentic distinctiveness of each reality. "In any domain— whether it be the cells of a body, the members of a society, or the elements of a spiritual synthesis—union differentiates. In every organized whole, the parts perfect themselves and fulfill themselves."[158] (Such a position is, of course, contrary to Hinduism with its belief that in union, the parts are totally submerged and lose their identity.) Point Omega, the center and goal of cosmic development, is "at once one and complex, in which, bound together by the person of Christ, may be seen enclosed one within the other (one might say) three progressively deeper centers: on the outside, the immanent ('natural') apex of the humano-cosmic cone; further in, at the middle, the immanent ('supernatural') apex of the 'ecclesial' or Christic cone; and finally, at the inmost heart, the transcendent, triune, and divine center: the complete Pleroma coming together under the mediating action of Christ-Omega."[159] The Omega is so powerful and embracing that it enables the human being to be liberated from the destruction which would otherwise accompany death. Thus death itself is hominized.[160]

For Teilhard, the basic purpose of life and of education is not to acquire some sort of product learning "out there." Instead the basic purpose of education is to come to increasingly higher states of development by plunging oneself into the dynamic core of all personal and cosmic existence, namely Omega. For each and every person Omega is at once the basic process of education and the basic goal of education. In this conceptualization of education, discipline is the way in which a person takes hold of his own Omega-soaked development so as to most effectively share in the progressive building of oneself and the progressive building of the cosmos.[161] Discipline is the way in which a person best learns (*discere*) to actively cooperate in the Christification of himself and the cosmos.[162] "It is through the medium of education that there ensues, directly and indirectly, the gradual incorporation of the World in the Word Incarnate."[163] Discipline is the royal road to hominization, to progressively higher levels of consciousness and personhood. Like all evolutionary processes, discipline takes place in a rhythmic, oscillating cycle of attachment and detachment. The person attaches himself to the cosmos so as to dialectically discover himself through the richness which his interaction with the Omega-impregnated cosmos offers him. Then the person detaches himself from the cosmos so as to dialectically discover himself in his creative Omega-filled solitude as pointed out by Jesus who in the gospel commands his disciples to leave everything to follow him. Then the person enters again the attachment phase, and the developmental cycle continues.[164] Through the developmental discipline (learning) of attachment and detachment, the person is enabled to ascend to higher and higher levels of development and in this way to become progressively more hominized. Attachment and detachment give to the learner what all positive discipline gives, namely purity. In Teilhard's theory, this purity is purity to fully embrace the universe,[165] purity to see physical matter in its proper light as universal Host,[166] purity to appreciate how God is All in all,[167] and purity to throw oneself without reserve into the ongoing developmental flow of the world toward the Pleroma, that is toward the fullness of consummation in God.[168] In Teilhard's view, the key to all discipline, the key to real purity, is love, because love is the energy underlying and flowing through all developmental convergence. "Love in all its subtleties is nothing more, and nothing less, than the more or less direct trace marked on the heart of the element by the psychical convergence of the universe upon itself."[169]

Interest

The etymology of the word interest at once unlocks the basic meaning of this word and shows the intimate connection which necessarily exists between interest and discipline. The present English word interest is a later variation of the older English word interess,[170] which in turn came directly from the Latin verb *interesse*. This Latin word means to be between, to be concerned, to be of importance, to share in.

Interest, then, is that force or involvement which joins two realities which otherwise would be separated or distant from each other. In terms of learning, interest is the force or involvement which joins the learner to some subject matter or other reality which otherwise would be remote or foreign to him.

The enormous strength of interest in the learning process lies in the fact that interest bonds and unifies the person with the reality in which he is involved. Thus the previous separation or distance between a person and the other reality is overcome. In interest, the other reality dynamically enters the individual's immediate world. As a result, this other reality no longer is "other," but is transformed into a dimension of self. Interest, then, does not lead a person to become absorbed or engaged in some reality; interest is the absorption or engagement itself. This absorption accounts for the fact that genuine interest is not fleeting but lasts for a relatively long period of time. After all, when a person is engrossed in a reality, he needs to abide with that reality in order to maintain that self-fulfilling activity which is perforce necessitated by this absorption.[171]

There is always purpose and power in interest—the purpose of developing and fulfilling oneself through a reality which is intimately related to one's own needs or personality thrusts, and the power automatically generated by any activity which is perceived to contribute directly to one's personal development and fulfillment.

The intimate and intrinsically necessary relationship between interest and discipline can be summed up as follows. Discipline is the educational process whereby interest is rendered optimally learning-full. Discipline is the educational process in which the learning inherent in all interest is released and directed.

The close and in some ways inseparable linkage between discipline and interest is natural. Discipline and interest are correlative dimensions of the same basic phenomenon, namely learning. Interest is the involvement dimension of learning. Discipline is the direction dimension of learning. Interest is that dimension of learning whereby an individual becomes so involved, so absorbed, so at one with an object or idea that significant learning automatically ensues. Discipline is that dimension of learning whereby an individual so productively harnesses and directs the enormous energy and inclusiveness of interest that what ensues is highly relevant and purposeful learning. Discipline mobilizes interest. Discipline brings the forces of interest under control for the sake of making interest optimally purposeful and productive. Discipline helps the individual recognize and accomplish the purposes inherent in interest, purposes which otherwise might well go unrecognized and unaccomplished. Discipline functions as a gyroscope for interest. Discipline brings about the synaptic junction between interest and action. Discipline brings interest to fruition.

In one respect, authentic discipline is impossible without interest. If discipline is severed from interest, then in all probability discipline will become dry and needlessly burdensome. The end result of such a sorry state of affairs is that discipline will cease to be discipline. After all, discipline is productive and fruitful personal learning (*discere*).

An almost surefire pedagogical principle for promoting and maintaining authentic discipline is this: wherever possible, insert discipline into the context of personal and social interest. Sometimes such personal and social interest might already be there. At other times, the teacher or parent needs to work with the learner either to enhance somewhat dormant interests or to develop genuine new interests. In any case, the more that discipline is intertwined with interest, the greater likelihood there is that discipline will be positive and developmental.

Most employers are well aware of the intimate relationship of discipline and interest. One of the most important qualities an employer looks for in an employee is personal interest in that with which the job deals. If the employee has no real interest in the requirements of the job, but only in the salary or working conditions or prestige attendant upon the job, then such a person probably never will develop the discipline necessary to perform well in that job. Recently an executive director of a scholarly book publishing company told me that she had hired an administrator to run the day-to-day operations of the company. The new employee was highly intelligent, had glowing references from previous employers, and in general was a very talented individual. But the new employee made countless mistakes every day, mistakes due to a severe lack of discipline. It shortly transpired that the new administrator had no genuine interest in the duties and nitty-gritty activities necessarily entailed by the job. This lack of interest resulted in the poor discipline which in turn precipitated the torrent of mistakes. Several weeks after taking the job, the employee resigned.

To link discipline with the constellation of the learner's genuine personal or social interests is not soft pedagogy. To link discipline with the learner's interests is not abdication of "proven" worthwhile learning procedures or outcomes to the whims and caprices of the learner's interests. First of all, interests by definition are not whimsical or capricious. Interests are relatively long-lasting and are deeply rooted in the soil of the learner's personality. Second, far from being soft pedagogy, the personal effort involved in linking discipline to the learner's interests is hard work for both the learner and the teacher. Effecting a linkage between discipline and one's own interests is difficult for a learner because now he must harness and mobilize not some reality which is incidental or marginal to him, but a reality which is precious and close to him. Accomplishing a linkage between discipline and the learner's interests is difficult for a teacher because now the teacher cannot simply rattle off his prepared or prepackaged lesson, but instead must work hard in emptying himself in such a manner that he puts the learner in first place and that he devises creative pedagogical procedures designed to promote learning on the learner's own terms, on the terms of the learner's own interests.

John Dewey was a person who was very sensitive to charges that interest-based education is tantamount to soft pedagogy. The fact of the matter is that John Dewey was one of the most implacable twentiety-century foes of soft pedagogy. Indeed, one of Dewey's major indictments of both traditional subject-centered teaching and the child study movement was that both represented soft pedagogy.[172] Dewey's advocacy of interest-based education was done explicitly and unequivocally for the sake of tough pedagogy. Dewey was a thoroughgoing rationalist who believed that unremitting use of critical intelligence is the key to everything worthwhile in the world. Dewey's advocacy of interest was rooted in his conviction that critical intelligence develops and flourishes best when it flows with the waterfall of interest, a waterfall whose power is effectively harnessed for productive use by the turbines and irrigation ditches of discipline.

The Sage of Morningside, as Dewey was sometimes called, despised the pedagogical malpractice of using interest as a lure or bait for learning. Such a sordid teaching gimmick debases interest to the state of personal pleasure or pain. To use interest as a lure, writes Dewey, "means to attach some feature of seductiveness to material otherwise indifferent; to secure attention and effort by offering a bribe of pleasure. This procedure is properly stigmatized as 'soft pedagogy'; as a 'soup-kitchen' theory of education."[173] At a deeper level, Dewey castigated the use of interest to lure learners as an abject failure to adequately understand and deal with interest. In Dewey's view, the misguided attempt at "making" something interesting implies an intrinsic separation between the learner and what has to be learned, a separation which is itself antithetical to the very concept and reality of interest. After all, interest destroys separation. Indeed, the very word interest directly implies that no separation exists. Dewey trenchantly asserts that "when things have to be *made* interesting, it is because interest itself is wanting. Moreover, the phrase is a misnomer. The thing, the object, is no more interesting than it was before. The appeal is simply made to the child's love of something else. He is excited in a given direction, with the hope that somehow or other during this excitation he will assimilate something otherwise repulsive."[174] On this same point, Dewey writes: "When material has to be made interesting, it signifies that, as presented, it lacks connection with purposes and present power: or that if the connection be there, it is not perceived."[175] In other words, when interest is employed as a lure or bait, then such pedagogical malpractice proves that the material is irrelevant, useless, and inherently uninteresting. After all, if the material were relevant, useful, and inherently interesting, then why is it necessary for the parent or teacher to use some extrinsic pleasurable activity as a bait to lure the learner into dealing with the material?

Self-Control

Though discipline and self-control are intimately related to each other, they are not identical.

Discipline is purposeful learning (*discere*). Self-control is power. Discipline is that kind of optimal learning brought about through the efficient marshalling and harnessing of the psycho-physiological and environmental resources at one's command. Self-control is that kind of power brought about by effective regulation of one's impulses, needs, desires, and wishes.

All discipline involves a measure of self-control. But not all self-control is discipline.

Though in no way identical to self-control, discipline is impossible of attainment without self-control. Self-control is often necessary to empower an individual to begin an activity, to continue an activity, or to see an activity to its conclusion. This holds true even for an activity in which a person has an interest. Self-control is necessary if a person is to choose to pursue a particular worthwhile interest when several other worthwhile interests are also available. Self-control is necessary if a person is to continue pursuing an interest in the face of competing interests and in the face of possible hard work which the pursuit of the initially-chosen interest requires.

The power of discipline stems from two sources, namely the demands placed on the person by his involvement in the learning activity itself, and the demands placed on the person by self-control. Because discipline is learning (*discere*), it follows the contours and pathways necessitated by whatever particular learning activity the individual is pursuing. All learning proceeds according to an intrinsic order necessarily presented by the learning task, an order in which the exigencies of the objective task involved are blended into the learner's psychological functioning. Learning (*discere*) becomes possible and operational when the self so effectually merges with the objective learning task that what results is a harmonious and fruitful ordering of all the elements involved. In addition to the power accruing to discipline by virtue of the "internal" ordering which results from the learner's psychological identification with the objective task, there is also a vital power accruing to discipline by virtue of the "external" ordering brought about by self-control. Self-control is that personal regulation of one's own activities which does not directly flow from the identification of self with an objective activity but rather from a regulation stemming from an even more personological function of the self, as for example, the will. Self-control is especially helpful and necessary when for some psychological or environmental reason one's interest falters, when obstacles arise which render completion of the task especially difficult, when persons or institutions or other forces endeavor to compel an individual to discontinue the learning task, and so on.

Self-control is not identical to discipline because self-control denotes only a power to learn and not the learning itself (*discere*). Thus if self-control is directed solely toward producing greater self-control, the result will be neither discipline nor learning. This principle is important for parents and teachers. If self-control is to yield results in terms of positive learning and discipline, it must be targeted to some reality outside itself. Self-control for the sake of self-control will typically produce miseducative results—a neurotic person, an uptight individual, a martinet, and so forth. One reason why some otherwise moral and religious persons are so authoritarian and narrow-minded is that these individuals mistakenly equate morality and religion with self-control instead of with discipline. Self-control yields only power. Power tends to corrupt, and absolute power, especially when affixed to morality and religion, tends to corrupt absolutely. It is precisely for this reason that many of the great Christian saints and spiritual masters have strongly cautioned against the prideful results which rootless self-control often breeds in some susceptible individuals. A person who has self-control without discipline will tend to consider himself superior to those wretches who are deficient in self-control. Such a haughty attitude soon leads to a kind of idolatry of the self, a situation in which a person acquires an inordinate or twisted love of self, looks down on others, and considers the basic source of his power to be himself rather than God—all sins of pride in the Christian tradition. Healthy Christian self-control, especially as practiced in mortification and asceticism, can never be done for itself, but must always be inserted into the wider contexts of discipline and general religious learning.

If self-control is not identical to discipline, neither is other-control the same as discipline.[176] When one person attempts to control the other, the direct result is not discipline but coercion. Whatever discipline might happen to result from other-control is accidental and incidental. To command or boss another person is not to teach him; rather to command or boss another individual is simply to command or boss him.[177] Other-control is aimed directly at forcing an individual to do what the other wants him to do; other-control is not aimed at learning per se. Parents and teachers who substitute other-control for discipline are substituting force for discipline, and eventually will probably end up with children not only who are undisciplined but also who have learned in the process to flout all other-control, even in its legitimate forms. If other-control is to become discipline it must be done in such a way as to disappear as soon as possible and be replaced by the more gentle environmental forces which will interact with the person in such a fruitful way as to bring about worthwhile learning.

Punishment

Though at times discipline might include punishment, nonetheless discipline ought never to be equated in whole or in part with punishment.

Discipline is learning (*discere*). Punishment is a painful penalty inflicted on an individual by another person, by oneself, or by some environmental condition. Discipline is positive; it is geared to enable an individual to learn some new worthwhile cognitive, affective, or lifestyle behavior. Punishment is negative; it is designed to enable an individual to remove or otherwise unlearn some unwanted cognitive, affective, or lifestyle behavior. Discipline, then, is positive because it is aimed at inducing a person to behave. Punishment, for its part, is negative because it is aimed at inducing a person *not* to behave.

Punishment is negative because it tells a person what *not* to do. Punishment does not tell a person what course of action to undertake. Punishment says: "Stop that behavior!" Punishment never says: "Begin such and such a behavior!"

Punishment brings to a halt the continuance of a particular cognitive, affective, or lifestyle behavior. But punishment does not necessarily reverse the person's preference for either that particular behavior or for the class of behaviors to which that particular behavior belongs.

Punishment eradicates a surface behavior, but may well leave unaffected the larger cluster of motives, tendencies, impulses, and drives which gave rise to the surface behavior.[178]

One review of the pertinent theoretical and empirical research literature concludes that this selfsame research has not satisfactorily ascertained whether punishment actually eliminates responses or merely suppresses them.[179] This conclusion is particularly germane to parents and teachers since an important effect of punishment might well be to place the unwanted behavior into a potentially more harmful form (the unconscious) or to unwittingly provide a mechanism whereby the unwanted behavior emerges in some different, more powerful observable form such as another unwanted behavior.

Punishment becomes effective in changing behavior in the direction of positive learning when it is deliberately used within the wider affirmative context of discipline. When properly employed, punishment, like any other form of chastisement, comprises one and only one discretionary phase of discipline. The fundamental utility of punishment in the totality of the discipline process is to eradicate those obstacles which might prevent the benefits of discipline from being accomplished. Eliminating behaviors which obstruct discipline is sometimes necessary before a person can acquire worthwhile learnings. But in no case should punishment ever be mistaken for discipline. Punishment becomes disciplinary only when it is incorporated into the overall context of that positive and productive learning process called discipline.

The irrefutable fact that punishment of itself does not yield positive learning is supported by countless examples. One of the best-known of these examples is the American prison system. The prison system is an environment of punishment without discipline. Despite the best intentions of certain high-minded penal officials and social reformers, American prisons are punishing environments. The prisoner is punished by just being there. Furthermore, the isolation from family, the cells, the regimen, the type of work, the food, the attitude of the armed guards—all these are directly and unmistakably punitive. This set of facts accounts for the incredible recidivism rate among released prisoners. Nearly 80 percent of all prisoners who have been released from jail subsequently commit new crimes and are sent back to jail. Punishment, whether in prison or in any other situation, is negative, and by itself yields only negative effects. If punishment is to yield positive effects, it must necessarily be inserted into the context of discipline, namely the context of positive goal-directed learning.

Except when it is self-inflicted, punishment is a form of other-control. As such, punishment in and of itself is not discipline but coercion. Other-control is aimed directly at forcing the learner to do what the other person wants him to do; other-control is not aimed at learning per se. There are legitimate pedagogical moments when forms of other-control like punishment are necessary and even desirable. However, the parent or teacher who uses the other-control mechanism of punishment must bear in mind that if she is to educate rather than simply coerce, she must insert the punishment into the broader and positive context of discipline. Other-control devices such as punishment do not of themselves bring about self-control in the person being punished. Rather, other-control devices simply breed a liking or a disliking of other-control on the part of the individual being punished. This principle largely accounts for the fact that heightened rebelliousness is a firstfruit of any form of punishment which is not placed within the wider and positive envelope of discipline.

Before pinpointing some of the side effects of punishment, it might be well to briefly consider the scope of punishment. Punishment may be physical, psychological, spiritual, or verbal. Thus punishment might consist in slapping a child, in ridiculing him, in depriving him of a spiritual desire, or in verbal reproof. Punishment consists in administering an unpleasant stimulus to a learner or in removing a pleasant stimulus. Thus, punishment might include publicly chastising a child, or removing some positive stimulus such as praise or food.

One of the most frequent side effects of punishment is aggression. This fact has been demonstrated over and over again with animals as well as with human beings.[180] Summarizing some of the pertinent empirical research, one social scientist concludes that a painful stimulus such as punishment tends to elicit an aggressive reaction which is then affixed to the most convenient target for attack.[181] The reaction to be aggressive toward the punisher, and to attack him in some way, is almost instinctive in human beings and animals. The more severe the punishment, the more severe the aggression or attacking behavior tends to be.[182] Sometimes the individual suppresses his natural aggressive reactions toward the punisher out of fear of receiving further punishment for such aggression; more often than not, however, such an individual will vent his aggression on some other, relatively innocent person or circumstance.

Another common side effect of punishment is the forging of defense mechanisms to ward off or avoid the psychological pain which punishment normally inflicts. Such defense mechanisms may or may not accompany overt or suppressed acts of aggression directed toward the punisher. Some of the defense mechanisms erected against punishment are healthy, while others are neurotic in nature. Avoidance strategies used by individuals to psychologically defend themselves against punishment include deliberate deception and concealment.[183]

Some psychologists contend that personal and social inhibitions stem primarily from a conditioned fear of punishment.[184] It is surely difficult for a person to be spontaneous and open in an atmosphere where punishment lurks in the foreground or background.

There are some children in whom punishment seems to give rise to the curious side effect of making them happy. In the case of some of these children, punishment provides them with the attention they crave. In other cases, punishment appears to make the children happy because it meets their basic needs for security, for limits, and for unambiguity.[185]

When considering the side effects of punishment, it is well to remember that punishment of every kind is a form of violence. Thus violence is an irradicable process content of punishment.[186] Consequently the use of punishment tends to teach the learner either to react in some sort of violent way to the parent's/

teacher's violence or to seek avoidance of this violence. For example, a child who is punished for aggression at home or school will tend to suppress his aggressive behavior in these settings for fear of retaliation. However, that child will most probably imitate the punitive and aggressive behavior of the parent or teacher in another environment where the punitive consequences of his aggressive behavior are not feared.[187] A celebrated research study reveals that pupils who have punitive teachers "manifest more aggression in their misconducts, are more unsettled and conflicted about their misconduct in school, and are less concerned with learning and school-unique values" than pupils who have nonpunitive teachers.[188]

Despite the foregoing important caveats about punishment, it is well to recall that the available research suggests that even though there are undesirable side effects from punishment, nonetheless these unfortunate side effects are not as detrimental as some people have suggested. When used judiciously, punishment can be quite effective in suppressing unwanted behaviors without adversely affecting desirable behaviors. This general principle excludes the following forms of punishment: that which is extremely severe; that which is administered randomly so that the contingencies are unclear to the recipient; and that which is administered by a hostile, cruel, or rejecting individual.[189] The best way to elevate punishment to educational worth is to insert it into a broader context of discipline, a context whose positive and learning orientation will bring out the productive potential of punishment.

Elsewhere,[190] I enunciate twenty basic principles governing the educational and discipline use of punishment. These twenty principles are given below, in slightly revised form.

First, punishment should be used only as the last resort. Only when alternatives to punishment have failed should punishment be used. *Second*, punishment should at all times be corrective, and never of a vengeful, penal, or deterrent type. *Third*, punishment should be such that its process and product outcomes are directly linked to positive and desirable behavior. *Fourth*, the form and type of punishment should be psychologically appropriate to the learner. *Fifth*, the learner should both know and accept the purpose of the punishment. *Sixth*, the learner should realize that he is being punished. *Seventh*, punishment should be true punishment, namely something unpleasant to the learner. Thus, for example, detaining a pupil after school might not really be punishment in those neighborhoods in which detention will gain considerable peer prestige for that pupil. Of course punishment can be true punishment yet not be harsh. *Eighth*, punishment should not be of the superfluous variety, as for example the type whose purpose is "to make sure they keep in line." There is no real educational or discipline value in such punishment. *Ninth*, if punishment must be administered, the parent or teacher should act firmly and decisively. *Tenth*, once punishment has been opted by the parent or teacher, he should punish the learner as soon as possible after the misbehavior. Delaying punishment seriously weakens its effectiveness, because the aversive reinforcement is not immediate. *Eleventh*, punishment should be short and simple. Prolonged punishments either lose their effectiveness or seriously damage a learner emotionally. *Twelfth*, the punishment should be commensurate with the seriousness of the misbehavior. *Thirteenth*, the punishment should normally be administered in such a way that it does not publicly embarrass or humiliate the learner. Very occasionally, public punishment is advantageous from the point of view of group pressure on the offender, but even in these rare instances great caution should be exercised. *Fourteenth*, while administering punishment, the parent or teacher should not continually refer to the learner's past offenses. *Fifteenth*, the punishment should always be just and administered fairly. *Sixteenth*, the group should never be punished for the offenses of one individual. A parent or teacher should not inflict reprisals on all the children in order to force an undisclosed or covert culprit to reveal his identity. *Seventeenth*, punishment should always be administered in a manner which manifests a conscious liking for and acceptance of the person being punished. *Eighteenth*, when punishment is necessary, the parent or teacher should not threaten; he should act. Punishment in the present is more effective than a threat of future punishment. Furthermore, the parent or teacher should not make threats which he cannot or will not carry out. *Nineteenth*, punishment should never be administered in anger or in a spirit of rancor. *Twentieth*, after the punishment has been administered, the parent or teacher should "let bygones by bygones" and restore a normal relationship with the learner.

Inserting punishment into the wider and more embracing context of discipline enables punishment to eventually yield beneficial educational results primarily because the discipline context provides that positive learning and goal-direction inherently lacking in punishment. One pedagogical procedure which a parent or teacher can use as an entry point in the overall process of inserting punishment into the wider context of discipline (learning) is this: always make sure that an act of punishment is immediately followed by a positive and goal-directed stimulus or activity. This positive and goal-directed stimulus or activity should be such that it either is or directly leads to that kind of worthwhile behavior of which the punished behavior is the opposite. For example, if a parent slaps the hand of a child because the child is eating in the wrong way, the parent should immediately follow this punishment by directly assisting the child to eat in the desired manner.

Because punishment is inherently negative and often produces undesirable consequences, it should be avoided whenever possible. Furthermore, there are educational procedures which in many cases are far more effective than punishment in producing discipline. For lack of a better term, these educational procedures are generically called alternatives to punishment. Unfortunately, many parents and teachers resort more to the methods of punishment than to procedural alternatives to punishment. There are many causes for this sorry state of affairs. One primary cause is that in their younger days many parents and teachers in their own education experienced negative punishment more frequently than positive procedural alternatives to punishment. A person tends to teach in the manner in which he himself has been taught. Another major reason why educators administer punishment instead of alternatives to punishment is that devising positive alternatives to punishment frequently requires more personal exertion and more pedagogical creativity than simply administering punishment. Many parents and teachers simply do not wish to expend the effort in fashioning constructive alternatives to punishment. These parents and teachers take the easy way out and just administer straightforward punishment. Such a situation is ironic, since by role-definition the parent or teacher is required above all to be a master of pedagogical procedure.

The most effective pedagogical strategy[191] for implementing positive alternatives to punishment is that of the structured learning situation. In the structured-learning-situation strategy, not just one or two but rather all the available variables in the learning environment are deliberatively arranged so that they productively interact with each other in such a way that desired learning outcomes are thereby facilitated.[192] By virtue of its position within the broader pedagogical ecology of the structured learning situation, a particular pedagogical method or technique thereby takes on added educational potency and enhanced possibilities for success. Consequently, if the following pedagogical procedures for alternatives to punishment are to be optimally effective, they should be placed within the broader ecology of a structured learning situation.

One pedagogical alternative to punishment is that of changing the environment in some way. From a developmentalist point of view, learning is the concomitant and the consequence of an individual's interaction with his environment. Hence a change in environment will manifest itself in a change in how and what one learns. If a child is disruptive, then the parent or teacher should seek out and alter those features of the environment which interact with the child in such a way as to produce the disruption. Indeed, it might be the whole environment which produces the disruptive behavior. If a child refuses to play basketball in the school gymnasium, for example, the teacher might wish to alter the basic environment or some of its features so as to make basketball-playing attractive to the child. If the parent or teacher first locates the learner's cluster of interests, he will then be in a favored position to select or highlight those features of an environment which are most resonant with the learner's basic personality configuration.

Another pedagogical alternative to punishment is that of avoiding the kind of environment in which an undesirable or unwanted behavior is likely to occur. If a boy tends to become violent after watching a violent television program, a parent would do well to remove the television set from the home, to restrict television viewing to nonviolent programs, or to engage in an even more enjoyable activity in the same time frame that the violent program is being aired, rather than punishing the boy for becoming violent after watching a violent program.

Prompts and cues have proven to be effective alternatives to punishment. Prompts and cues are positive stimuli which provide a direct or indirect impetus for performing a desired behavior. A prompt may be verbal or nonverbal. It may take many forms, including a suggestion, a persuasive gesture, prefeeding, and modeling. Prefeeding is an effective prompt when used skillfully. Prefeeding is the process in which a person is given a small portion of a desirable or pleasant feature of an activity before he engages fully in that activity, such as giving a person a small sum of money before he performs a task with the larger balance to be delivered after the task has been successfully completed. Setting a concrete example, or modeling, is frequently an effective prompt, especially with small children. Many persons, particularly the younger ones, seem to be highly motivated to imitate the behavior of significant others.

By positively reinforcing an object, idea, or activity other than the undesirable reality, the parent or teacher can effectively direct the learner away from the unwanted reality and thus eliminate the occasion of punishment. For example, if a child wishes to play instead of studying, the parent or teacher can attach a progressively wider and more intense repertoire of positive reinforcements to the conditions surrounding the activity of studying. Such conditions will induce the child away from play and toward the studying. The more that such positive reinforcers are directly connected with the nature and texture of the desired activity, the more these reinforcers will become genuinely educational and disciplinary.

One of the most successful of all alternatives to punishment is nonreinforcement. In technical language, nonreinforcement consists of no linked stimulus-response pleasant or unpleasant consequence accruing to an individual for making a particular behavioral response. Phrased more simply and more popularly, nonreinforcement means that nothing happens as a result of an individual's initial response. A parent or teacher uses nonreinforcement when she ignores a child's disruptive behavior. The advantages of using nonreinforcement procedures are many. For example, the pertinent empirical research suggests that nonreinforcement is more powerful than punishment in eliminating unwanted behaviors.[193] (Indeed, punishment may well serve to reinforce a child's undesirable behavior since the act of punishment itself dramatically shows the child that his behavior gets a rise out of the parent or teacher.) Also, nonreinforcement seems to be free of the objectionable by-products associated with punishment.[194]

In the moral and religious sphere, punishment should be used very sparingly, if at all. To be sure, the function of morality and religion is to bring out the finest qualities in a person, to elevate the individual to the highest possible state of human existence. Viewed in this perspective, morality or religion cannot be forced on a person. Conversely, a person who is punished for infractions of morality or religion will not become more moral or more religious by being punished; rather, all that punishment (and nonreinforcement) can do at best is to prevent the person from repeating a particular immoral or irreligious behavior. But even here the ripple effects of punishment for an immoral or irreligious act often are more detrimental than the immoral or irreligious act itself. Quite a few formerly moral and religious persons have been turned away from morality and religion because these individuals were punished in one way or another for an immoral/irreligious behavior by a moral parent or by a religious teacher. Children and adults expect understanding, compassion, mercy, love, and reconciliation from persons espousing morality and religion for the simple reason that these ultrahuman qualities are precisely those which morality and religion claim to have in abundance. When parents or teachers who profess to teach morality and religion use pedagogical procedures in which these qualities are lacking, then learners naturally come to seriously doubt whether morality and religion really possess these special qualities after all.

The sun and the wind argued between themselves which was the stronger. To settle the issue, it was agreed that each in turn would attempt to force a man who was walking along a city street to remove his overcoat. Mustering its harshest force, the wind blew, and blew, and blew, but the harder it blew, the more the man bundled his overcoat around himself. Then the sun tried. It shone clear and warm, and soon the man, seeing that it had become such a fine day, took off his overcoat, stretched his arms, and said to himself: "How wonderful is life!"

"God is love," writes the apostle John in his First Epistle.

The lessons are clear. The parent or teacher who wishes to promote constructive discipline will usually attain far greater positive results by warmth and kindness than by harshness or punishment. Further, the parent or teacher who wishes to follow in the footsteps of God can do it best by constantly showing his pupils love.

The parent or teacher who uses the sword of punishment incurs a risk in doing so, "for all those who take up the sword will perish by the sword."[195]

Reconstruction and Transformation

Authentic discipline empowers an individual to grow as a person. Authentic discipline empowers an individual to fruitfully integrate his own powers with the forces of the universe. Authentic discipline empowers the individual to reconstruct and transform both himself and society. For all these reasons, discipline is a creative activity and not a ruinous one.

The essential reconstructive and transformative nature of discipline ultimately derives from the fact that discipline is learning—purposive, channeled, goal-directed learning. In its most basic operation, every learning activity is fundamentally one of reconstruction and transformation. After all, learning consists in that basic reconstruction and transformation of a person's way of thinking, way of feeling, or way of acting. When a person learns new cognitive material, the way he thinks is thereby reconstructed and transformed. When a person learns new affects, the way he feels is thereby reconstructed and transformed. When a person learns new lifestyle behaviors, the way he comports himself is thereby reconstructed and transformed. Where there is no personal reconstruction and transformation there is no learning. The greater the personal reconstruction and transformation, the greater and more significant the learning.[196]

A moral educationist who takes the central reconstructive and transformative axis of education and discipline very seriously is John Dewey. One of Dewey's most fundamental and most pervasive principles is that in and of itself "the educational process is one of continual reorganizing, reconstructing, transforming."[197] In Dewey's view, then, the goal of human growth and development can only be attained when the process of education is recognized for what it is, namely a constant reorganizing and reconstructing of experience. Such reorganization and reconstruction of experience is essentially transformational in that it adds to the meaning of experience and increases one's ability to direct the course of subsequent experience.[198]

Though Dewey's view of education embraces both individual and social reconstruction, it remained for two of his later followers, George Counts and Theodore Brameld, to place especially heavy stress on education as social reconstruction.

George Counts contends that the role of education and of its principal institutional agent, the school, is not to mirror society but to reconstruct it. Counts notes that there is no such thing as purely individual education; all education necessarily takes place in an interactive social context. Since education by its very nature transforms an individual, it must therefore transform society in order to be true education. If education is to be really effective, it must be the rallying point for building a new civilization rather than simply contemplating past or present civilizations. As spearheads of educational endeavor, schools have a very heavy obligation to advance social interests. Such advancement should not occur by promoting particular political reforms but by offering students expanding social possibilities for the future. Every element in the school—teacher, curricula, architecture, pedagogical procedures—should focus on the reconstruction and transformation of society. Counts recognizes that the reconstructive role of education in transforming society requires a great deal of personal learning, that is to say a great deal of discipline. Thus Counts writes: "Any individual or group that would aspire to lead society must be ready to pay the costs of leadership: to accept responsibility, to suffer calumny, to surrender security, to risk both reputation and fortune. If this price, or some important part of it, is not being paid, then the chances are that the claim to leadership is fraudulent. Society is never redeemed without effort, struggle, and sacrifice. Authentic leaders are never found breathing that rarefied atmosphere lying above the dust and smoke of battle."[199]

Theodore Brameld is so thoroughly convinced that the axis and goal of education is personal and social reconstruction that he has pioneered a new philosophy of education called reconstructionism.[200] As formulated by Brameld, reconstructionism regards education as the primary process and major vehicle for building a new and better world. The orientation of reconstructionism is toward the future, toward deliberately fashioning a finer, more democratic world. Education is primarily a revolutionary force, a force whose means and ends are constantly directed toward effecting cataclysmic as well as minor changes in the world. Though reconstructionism eschews all religious reality and objective value systems, nonetheless reconstructionism is basically a moral philosophy which seeks to bring about a more humanistic personal and social existence. A primary goal of reconstructionist education is to produce persons of action, for it is only through persons of action that genuine individual and social reconstruction can occur. Reconstructionism produces disciplined individuals. By virtue of their discipline, reconstructed individuals listen to the voices of present and potential culture, and then unselfishly place their resources at the disposal of the democratic imperative. Healing the false division between means and ends, reconstructed individuals work tirelessly to transform the world by hastening the convergence of world cultures for increasingly creative individual/social democratic living.[201]

The basic texture of developmentalism is reconstruction and transformation. As noted earlier in this chapter, developmentalism is a philosophical and psychological position which holds that a person is essentially an interactive emergent, namely one whose personhood is forged in the dynamic interaction between the organism and its environment. Developmentalism thus asserts that personal identity and personal growth come about through the transformational effects wrought by the reconstructional interaction between organism and environment.

A recurring refrain in Lawrence Kohlberg's symphony of moral reasoning and moral education is that of reconstruction. Kohlberg's research suggests that moral judgment is the process of personal reconstruction as one interacts with one's environment. Moral development involves the emergence of new, progressively higher, qualitatively different structures of personal response. These progressively higher structures occur in a series of irreversible stages. Each stage represents a significantly different personal construction of morality from the previous stage. If a parent or teacher wishes to help the learner attain the next higher stage of moral judgment, then such a parent or teacher must structure the learning situation in a manner that the learner will be enabled to break out of his old structure and reconstruct a new orientation to morality. [202]

The central purpose of all moral and religious discipline, regardless of the specific form it takes, is the total transformation of the person. [203]

Many psychologists and psychotherapists interested in religion assert that self-transformation is the key to both religious experience and personal wholeness. Self-transformation in this context does not imply barren self-annihilation, but rather the recentering and reconstruction of the self around a transcendental reality which points to God or is suffused with God. [204]

Every major religion contains important and cherished myths. A myth is a narrative or poetic description which employs image-full stories, poems, allegories, symbols, and the like to reveal the basic origin, spirit, meaning, and transcendence of human action and cosmic reality. A myth may or may not be literally true. However, a myth is always existentially and transcendentally true, especially to its adherents. A religion or moral system typically enjoins its members to live and learn (*discere*) that system's major myths. A myth is a form of discipline, the discipline of viewing reality from a certain perspective and the discipline of living life in a certain way. In the informed opinion of a foremost scholar in comparative religion, the primary purpose of major myths is to renew and reconstruct each new generation's basic moral and religious system. At the deepest existential level, the vestiges and husks of the old moral or religious cycle must be destroyed in order that the true living spirit of morality or religion might be reborn into the realities of the present age. Only when temporally-specific objectifications of morality or religion are plowed under can the new buds of an authentic moral or religious springtime appear. The function of myth, then, is to assist a moral or religious system to remain ever fresh by remaining ever authentic to its ultimate foundations and wellsprings. In short, the function of myth is discipline—the discipline of keeping a moral or religious system on track.[205]

Reconstruction and transformation are fundamental processes and basic objectives for every universal religion. Reconstruction and transformation are among the most enduring blessings of discipline.

A major objective of Islam is "the reformation and the reconstruction of society on the eternal and all-embracing principles set forth in the *Qur'an* and the life example of the last Apostle of God."[206] Such reformation and reconstruction can only come about by Islam, by surrender, by complete discipline (learning) of God on God's own terms.

The overriding discipline of the Christian life is to do whatever is necessary and helpful to restore all reality in Jesus. The New Testament speaks over and over again about personal transformation and societal reconstruction, a transformation and reconstruction which can only come about by the discipline of dying to self unto Jesus. In his second letter to the *ecclesia* at Corinth, the great apostle Paul writes: "If any person lives in Christ, he is thereby a wholly new creation. And indeed, the older order has then passed away, and the new order has arrived."[207] Writing to the Christian community in Ephesus, Paul urges the faithful to "put on the new self which has been created according to God's image in the goodness and holiness of truth."[208] Paul makes it very clear how a person can achieve essential reconstruction and transformation when he boldly writes to the churches in Galatia: "I have been crucified with Christ, and so it is no longer I who live but now it is Christ who lives in me."[209] The ideal of the Christian life has always been a person's total abandonment to God as one lives in one's own here-and-now daily life. Abandonment of self to God is not easy, and entails much discipline and sacrifice.[210] It is in the discipline of learning God through self-abandonment that one is able to transform oneself and reconstruct society. In the beautiful words of Pierre Teilhard de Chardin, it is by discipline to God that each religious person "must *construct*—starting from the most natural zone of his own self—a work, an *opus*, into which something enters from all the elements of the earth. He *makes his own soul* throughout all his earthly days; and at the same time he collaborates in another work in another *opus*, which infinitely transcends, while at the same time it narrowly determines, the perspectives of his individual achievement: the completion of the world."[211]

Conclusion

Discipline is the process of goal-directed, purposive, channeled, energetic learning. Discipline is thus the royal road *of* learning. Perhaps the most important single thing which a parent or teacher can do in teaching discipline is to help the learner to place his trust in the process of discipline. When a person trusts the discipline process, he is already learning to a significantly high degree. When a person trusts the process of discipline, he is already transforming himself and ransoming the world.

Notes

1. This essay represents a further development and refinement of my previous essay on discipline which appeared in James Michael Lee, *Principles and Methods of Secondary Education* (New York: McGraw-Hill, 1963), pp. 542–577. In this present essay I am sharpening the entire focus of my previous discussion of discipline, and am also fleshing out the moral and religious thrust of discipline.

2. *Discere* is the infinitive and means to learn. For the sake of simplicity and ease of understanding, I make use of the infinitive *discere* throughout this essay when referring to the English word learning, regardless of the grammatical form of this English word.

3. A few Latin examples will briefly illustrate this point. *Cognoscere* means to learn cognitively by investigation or inquiry. *Noscere* means to acquire a cognitive knowledge of some reality. *Percipere* means to perceive or to understand. *Scire* means to know.

4. *"Eademne erat haec disciplina tibi, quum tu adolescens eras?"* ("Did you receive the same kind of character training when you were a youth?"), in Titus Maccius Plautus, *Bacchides*, III.3.17. Translation mine.

5. *"Imitari, Castor, potius avi mores disciplinamque debebas . . ."* ("Castor, you should have patterned yourself after the principles and conduct of your grandfather . . ."), in Marcus Tullius Cicero, *Pro regio Deiotaro*, X. Translation mine.

6. "Discipline," in *A New Dictionary on Historical Principles . . .*, volume III, part 1D (Oxford, England: Clarendon, 1897), p. 415.

7. Robert T. Hall and John V. Davis, *Moral Education in Theory and Practice* (Buffalo, N.Y.: Prometheus, 1975), pp. 13–26.

8. For a fine discussion of rule theory and act theory, see Brenda Munsey, "Cognitive-Developmental Theory of Moral Development: Metaethical Issues," in Brenda Munsey, editor, *Moral Development, Moral Education, and Kohlberg* (Birmingham, Ala.: Religious Education Press, 1980), pp. 161–181.

9. Richard S. Peters, "Concrete Principles and the Rational Passions," in Nancy F. Sizer and Theodore R. Sizer, editors, *Moral Education* (Cambridge, Mass.: Harvard University Press, 1970), pp. 29–54.

10. John Dewey, *Experience and Education* (New York: Macmillan, 1958) pp. 23–85.

11. John Dewey, *Moral Principles in Education* (New York: Greenwood, 1959), pp. 26–32.

12. Jean Piaget, *The Moral Judgment of the Child*, translated by Marjorie Gabain (New York: Free Press, 1965), pp. 1–103.

13. Piaget discovered that in learning to practice rules, a child goes through four successive stages on a continuum: purely motor and individual; egocentric imitation of other persons' use of codified rules; incipient cooperation to mutually control and unify rules; codification of mandatory rules known to self and to everyone else. Piaget found three progressive stages in how a child comes to think about rules: seeing rules as noncoercive and nonobligatory because of the child's almost exclusive motor functioning; regarding rules as sacred and untouchable and everlasting because they emanate from adults; viewing rules as laws flowing both from the nature of things and from mutual consent. Ibid., pp. 16–19.

14. Ibid., pp. 355–375. Piaget's critical views of the teacher's authority as derived by divine right rather than by democratic consent are sometimes overlooked by religious personages commenting on the Swiss genetic epistemologist. See, for example, Frank W. Lewis, "What the Value/Moral Educator Can Learn from Piaget," in Thomas C. Hennessy, editor, *Value/Moral Education: The Schools and the Teachers* (New York: Paulist, 1979), pp. 167–191.

15. James Michael Lee, "Christian Religious Education and Moral Development," in Munsey, editor, *Moral Development, Moral Education, and Kohlberg*, p. 328.

16. These six stages occur within three discrete hierarchical levels, namely preconventional, conventional, and postconventional. At the preconventional level there are the punishment and obedience orientation (stage 1), and the instrumental relativist orientation (stage 2). At the conventional level there are the interpersonal concordance or "good boy—nice girl" orientation (stage 3), and the "law and order" orientation (stage 4). At the postconventional level there are the social-contract legalistic orientation (stage 5), and the universal ethical-principle orientation (stage 6). At times, Kohlberg has postulated a metaphoric stage 7 which is intimately tied in with religion, or at least with a kind of

religion. See Lawrence Kohlberg, "Stages of Moral Development as a Basis for Moral Education," in C. M. Beck, B. S. Crittenden, and E. V. Sullivan, editors, *Moral Education: Interdisciplinary Approaches* (Toronto: University of Toronto Press, 1971), pp. 23–92; Lawrence Kohlberg and Clark Power, "Moral Development, Religious Thinking, and the Question of a Seventh Stage," in *Zygon* XVI (September, 1981), pp. 203–259.

17. For Kohlberg, justice is a universal principle and value and not a relative one. Ten subsidiary universal moral values flowing from justice are as follows: laws and rules, conscience, personal roles of affection, authority, civil rights, contract and trust, punishment, property rights, and truth. See Richard H. Hersh, Diana Pritchard Paolitto, and Joseph Reimer, *Promoting Moral Growth* (New York: Longman, 1979), pp. 83–86.

18. Bill Puka, "Kohlbergian Forms and Deweyan Acts: A Response," in Munsey, editor, *Moral Development, Moral Education, and Kohlberg*, pp. 449–453.

19. Jack Braeden Arbuthnot and David Faust, *Teaching Moral Reasoning: Theory and Practice* (New York: Harper & Row, 1981), pp. 139–185.

20. I think it is safe to say that this pedagogical procedure is ultimately based on Leon Festinger's celebrated theory of cognitive dissonance. See Leon Festinger, *A Theory of Cognitive Dissonance* (Stanford, Calif.: Stanford University Press, 1957).

21. Peter Scharf, *Moral Education* (Davis, Calif.: Responsible Action, 1978), pp. 198–209; Elsa Wasserman, "An Alternative High School Based on Kohlberg's Just Community Approach to Education," in Ralph L. Mosher, editor, *Moral Education: A First Generation of Research and Development* (New York: Praeger, 1980), pp. 265–280.

22. Salvation, which for Hinduism is the ultimate liberation, "is found, in fact, by a mental discipline, in which one traces everything back to its source." A. C. Bouquet, *Hinduism* (London: Hutchinson University Library, 1962), p. 62.

23. The Brahman is at once totally transcendent and totally immanent with respect to the world. See Jitendra Nath Banerjea, "The Hindu Concept of God," in Kenneth W. Morgan, editor, *The Religion of the Hindus* (New York: Ronald, 1953), pp. 48–50.

24. Benjamin Walker, *The Hindu World: An Encyclopedic Survey of Hinduism*, volume II (New York: Praeger, 1968), pp. 530–535.

25. See *The Ten Principal Upanishads*, translated by Purdhit and

W. B. Yeats (New York: Macmillan, 1965), pp. 85–117 (*Chhāndôgya-Upanishad*).

26. K. M. Sen, *Hinduism* (Baltimore: Penguin, 1961), pp. 39–40.

27. Rammurti S. Mishra, *Fundamentals of Yoga* (New York: Julian, 1959), p. 7.

28. Karel Werner, *Yoga and Indian Philosophy* (Delhi: Motilal Banarsidass, 1977), pp. 71–92; Mircea Eliade, *Yoga: Immortality and Freedom*, translated by Willard R. Trask (New York: Pantheon, 1958), pp. 3–46.

29. Harvey Day, *About Yoga: The Complete Philosophy* (London: Thorsons, 1951), pp. 33–36.

30. Justin O'Brien, "Yoga and the Western Consciousness," in Matthew Fox, editor, *Western Spirituality: Historical Roots, Ecumenical Routes* (Notre Dame, Ind.: Fides/Claretian, 1979), pp. 369–385.

31. Consider, for example, some illustrative aphorisms of Pātañjali: "Yoga is the control of the ideas in the mind" (Section I, #2). "When there is control of that also, the seedless Contemplation arrives, because there is now the control of all" (Section I, #51). "Yoga in active life consists of Body-conditioning, Self-study and Attentiveness to God. . . . From Body-conditioning, with the decline of impurity, come the powers of the body and the senses. From Self-study arises contact with the desired divinity. From Attentiveness to God comes the power of Contemplation" (Section II, #s 1, 42–45). Pātañjali, *Yoga Aphorisms*, translated by Ernest E. Wood, in Ernest E. Wood, *Practical Yoga* (North Hollywood, Calif.: Wilshire, 1976), pp. 231, 234, 237.

32. Chinmoy, *The Inner Promise* (New York: Simon and Schuster, 1974), pp. 99–101.

33. Zen appears to have originated in India. It was carried to China around 520 A.D. where it was, and still is, called *Ch'an*. In the twelfth century, *Ch'an* was transplanted to Japan. In modern times, Japanese Zen is better known and more extensively practiced worldwide than Chinese *Ch'an*.

34. T. P. Kasulis, *Zen Action / Zen Person* (Honolulu: University Press of Hawaii, 1981), pp. 116–124.

35. D. T. Suzuki, *Living by Zen*, edited by Christmas Humphreys (London: Rider, 1972), pp. 26–33.

36. Alan W. Watts, *The Spirit of Zen* (New York: Grove, 1958), p. 21.

37. Paul Wienpahl, *The Matter of Zen: A Brief Account of Zazen* (New York: New York University Press, 1964), pp. 31–32.

38. H. M. Enomiya Lassale, *Zen Meditations for Christians*, translated by John C. Maraldo (La Salle, Ill.: Open Court, 1974), p. 18.

39. Nonrationality should not be equated with irrationality. Irrationality is an act which is contrary to reason. Nonrationality is an act which lies outside the parameters of reason. Irrationality is governed by the canons of reason, while nonrationality is not so governed. Irrationality is a corruption of reason. Nonrationality is another way of cognition, a way which many Western and Eastern philosophers and psychologists claim is superior to reason.

40. Christmas Humphreys, *Zen: A Way of Life* (New York: Emerson, 1962), pp. 149–150.

41. D. T. Suzuki, *Zen Buddhism: Selected Writings*, edited by William Barrett (Garden City, N.Y.: Doubleday Anchor, 1965), p. 144.

42. D. T. Suzuki, *The Training of the Zen Buddhist Monk* (Kyoto: Eastern Buddhist Society, 1934).

43. Idries Shah, *The Elephant in the Dark* (London: Octagon, 1974) pp. 57–58.

44. Muhammad Zafrulla Khan, *Islam* (London: Routledge and Kegan Paul, 1962), pp. 100–111.

45. See K. Wagtendonk, *Fasting in the Koran* (Leiden, The Netherlands: Brill, 1968). Wagtendonk notes that "at the root of the fast of Ramadān is the fast of the Jewish Day of Atonement" (p. 141).

46. David Edwin Long, *The Hajj Today* (Albany, N.Y.: State University of New York Press, 1979), pp. 3–23.

47. As the pilgrim approaches Mecca, he puts on two seamless garments and refrains from shaving for the duration of the *hajj*. He first visits the *Ka'bah* and kisses the black stone. Then he walks around the stone seven times, ascends two mountains, journeys to Minā, hears a sermon at Arafāt, spends the night at Muzdalifah, and offers sacrifice on the last day.

48. John Alden Williams, *Islam* (New York: Braziler, 1961), pp. 92–135.

49. Asaf A. A. Fyzee, *Outlines of Muhammadan Law*, 2d edition (London: Oxford University Press. 1955), pp. 13–21.

50. Mohamad Jawad Chirri, *Inquiries About Islam* (Beirut: n.p., 1965), pp. 158–165.

51. Ignaz Goldziher, *Introduction to Islamic Theology and Law*, translated by Andras Hamori and Ruth Hamori (Princeton, N.J.: Princeton University Press, 1981), pp. 116–166.

52. Thus Seyyed Hossein Nasr quotes the well-known definition of Sufism given by Junayd: "Sufism is that God makes thee die to thyself and become resurrected in Him." Seyyed Hossein Nars, *Sufi Essays* (Albany, N.Y.: State University of New York Press, 1971), p. 69.

53. Williams, *Islam*, pp. 137–173.

54. Arthur Hertzberg, editor, *Judaism* (New York: Brazurler, 1962), pp. 71–79, 185–195.

55. Hayim Halevy Donin, *To Be a Jew* (New York: Basic Books, 1972), pp. 24–27; Robert M. Seltzer, *Jewish People, Jewish Thought: The Jewish Experience in History* (New York: Macmillan, 1980), pp. 66–77.

56. Will Herberg, *Judaism and Modern Man* (New York: Meridian, 1951), pp. 286–294.

57. Louis Finkelstein, "The Jewish Religion: Its Beliefs and Practices," in Louis Finkelstein, editor, *The Jews: Their History, Culture, and Religion*, volume II, 3rd edition (New York: Harper & Row, 1960), p. 1740. Finkelstein goes on to write that failure to accept the beliefs of Judaism or to follow its prescriptions do not themselves serve to excommunicate a Jew. Rather, such failure simply renders the person a less-than-devout Jew, to put it euphemistically.

58. Adin Steinsaltz writes: "If the Bible is the cornerstone of Judaism, then the Talmud is the central pillar, soaring up from the foundation and supporting the entire spiritual and intellectual edifice." Adin Steinsaltz, *The Essential Talmud*, translated by Chaya Galai (New York: Basic, 1976), p. 3; see also Isaac Unterman, *The Talmud* (New York: Bloch, 1952).

59. The two great talmudic fonts are the Babylonian *Talmud* and the Jerusalem *Talmud*. The former is the more authoritative.

60. Samson Raphael Hirsch, *Judaism Eternal*, volume II, translated by I. Grunfeld (London: Socino, 1956), pp. 157–160.

61. *Halakhot* is a collection or codification of such laws.

62. Finkelstein, "The Jewish Religion: Its Beliefs and Practices," p. 1739.

63. Donin, *To Be a Jew*, p. 30.

64. Abraham Joshua Heschel, *Between Man and God: An Interpretation of Judaism*, edited by Fritz A. Rothschild (New York: Harper & Row, 1959), p. 177.

65. Eugene B. Borowitz, *How Can a Jew Speak of Faith Toady?* (Philadelphia: Westminster, 1969), pp. 108–129.

66. Before the destruction of the Temple in Jerusalem by the Ro-

mans in the year 70 of the Christian era, the central Jewish liturgy was the sacrifice(s) conducted in the Temple. Strictly speaking, the synagogue is a house of public prayer while the Temple is (or more precisely, was) the house of priestly sacrifice.

67. Joseph Kalir, *Introduction to Judaism* (Washington, D.C.: University Press of America, 1980), pp. 19–24.

68. In relatively recent times some Jewish congregations have begun to celebrate what they call a *bat mitzvah* ("daughter of the commandment") for girls. When celebrated, the *bat mitzvah* often is more of a birthday celebration than a religious affair.

69. Samuel Dresner, *The Jewish Dietary Laws* (New York: Burning Bush, 1959).

70. Simon Greenberg, "Jewish Educational Institutions," in Louis Finkelstein, editor, *The Jews: Their History, Culture, and Religion*, volume II, pp. 1254–1260.

71. James Michael Lee and Nathaniel J. Pallone, *Guidance and Counseling in Schools* (New York: McGraw-Hill, 1966), p. 345.

72. Bernard Berelson and Gary A. Steiner, *Human Behavior: An Inventory of Scientific Findings* (New York: Harcourt, Brace, and Jovanovich, 1964), pp. 469–470.

73. Joseph A. Jungmann, *The Mass of the Roman Rite*, translated by Francis A. Brunner, and revised by Charles K. Riepe (New York: Benziger, 1959), pp. 133–147.

74. Matthew 16:24–25.

75. John 12:24.

76. Matthew 7:21.

77. 1 Corinthians 1:23.

78. Galatians 5:24.

79. Romans 6:16.

80. 1 Corinthians 9:27.

81. Galatians 2:20.

82. Colossians 1:20.

83. Philippians 2:6–11.

84. 1 Corinthians 1:18.

85. Galatians 2:21.

86. The apostolic period is that era in which the Fathers were taught directly or indirectly by the original apostles. Most patrologists hold that the apostolic period came to an end around the middle of the second century of the Christian era. The sub-apostolic period began at that time and lasted until the middle of the fourth century.

87. Clement of Rome, *Letter to the Corinthians*, IV-XXIII, XLV-LVII. This letter was probably written sometime between 90–99 A.D.

88. Ignatius of Antioch, *Letter to the Romans*. This beautiful letter was written around 110 A.D.

89. *Didachē*, I-VI. The *Didachē* was most probably written sometime between 120–180 A.D.

90. Hermas, *The Shepherd*, II. This work was written sometime around the year A.D. 150.

91. Irenaeus, *Against the Heresies* IV, 37–41. This important piece of early Christian literature was written about the year A.D. 185.

92. Augustine, *The Trinity*, XII, XIV; Augustine, *The Christian Combat*, I-XIII; Augustine, *Christian Doctrine*, I, 10–17; III, 10; Augustine, *The Magnitude of the Soul*, XXXIII. These works were written between 390–430 A.D.

93. Thomas Aquinas, *Summa Theologica* I-II, q. 23, a. 6–7; I-II, q. 65, a. 2, 4, 5; I-II, q. 66, a. 6; II-II, q. 184, a. 1–2. This monumental work was composed during the second half of the thirteenth century.

94. For a good summary of Luther's position on this point, as elucidated in a variety of the great reformer's writings, see Paul Althaus, *The Theology of Martin Luther*, translated by Robert C. Schultz (Philadelphia: Fortress, 1966), pp. 251–273.

95. John Calvin, *Institutes of the Christian Religion*, I, 15, 4; II, 3, 13; III, 3, 5; III, 11, 2; III, 11, 10; III, 17, 5.

96. For a good comprehensive drawing together of Wesley's diverse writings and sermons on this subject, see Robert W. Burtner and Robert E. Chiles, editors, *A Compend of Wesley's Theology* (Nashville, Tenn.: Abingdon, 1954), pp. 195–236.

97. Billy Graham, *Billy Graham Speaks*, compiled and edited by Cort R. Flint et al. (New York: Grosset and Dunlap, 1968), pp. 41–42.

98. Fulton J. Sheen, *Lift Up Your Heart* (New York: McGraw-Hill, 1950), pp. 118–149; Fulton J. Sheen, *Thinking Life Through* (New York: McGraw-Hill, 1955), pp. 129–139.

99. For a fine overview of the lives of Christian heroes and the discipline which characterized their lives, see Elliott Wright, *Holy Company* (New York: Macmillan, 1980).

100. Adolphe Tanquerey, *The Spiritual Life*, 2d edition, translated by Herman Branderis (Westminster, Md.: Newman, 1930), pp. 297–699.

101. Evelyn Underhill, *Mysticism*, 12th edition (New York: Dutton, 1930), pp. 128–231.

102. Most religionists make love the basis and goal of religion. Such is generally not the case with philosophers and psychologists of morality. Lawrence Kohlberg, for example, makes justice rather than love the basis and goal of morality.

103. Erich Fromm, *The Art of Loving* (New York: Harper & Row, 1956), pp. 1–35, 83–88, 107–115.

104. C. G. Jung, *Psychological Reflections*, edited by Jolande Jacobi (New York: Harper & Row, 1953), pp. 87–88.

105. James Hillman, *Insearch* (New York: Scribner's, 1967), pp. 35–39, 125. Hillman is a leading interpreter of Jung's thought.

106. C. G. Jung, *The Development of Personality*, translated by R. F. C. Hull (Princeton, N.J.: Princeton University Press, 1954), p. 125.

107. Walter E. Conn, *Conscience: Development and Self-Transcendence* (Birmingham, Ala.: Religious Education Press, 1981), pp. 3–12, 202–215.

108. In 1 Cor. 13:4–7 the apostle Paul provides some well-known rules of conduct prescribed by love. See also Robert E. Fitch, *Of Love and Suffering* (Philadelphia: Westminster, 1970), pp. 82–86.

109. Gérard Gilleman, *The Primacy of Charity in Moral Theology*, translated by William F. Ryan and André Vachon (Westminster, Md.: Newman, 1959), pp. 253–279.

110. See Howard Thurman, *Disciplines of the Spirit* (New York: Harper & Row, 1963), pp. 13–37.

111. G. Ernest Thomas, *Disciplines of the Spiritual Life* (Nashville, Tenn.: Abingdon, 1963), pp. 61–70.

112. C. S. Lewis, *The Four Loves* (New York: Harcourt, Brace, and Jovanovich, 1960), pp. 176–180.

113. Viktor Warnach, *Agape: Die Liebe als Grundmotiv der neutestamentlichen Theologie* (Düsseldorf: Patmos, 1951), p. 472.

114. 1 John 4:16.

115. James Michael Lee, "The Authentic Source of Religious Instruction," in Norma H. Thompson, editor, *Religious Education and Theology* (Birmingham, Ala.: Religious Education Press, 1982), pp. 104–105.

116. 2 John:6.

117. Chinmoy, *Songs of the Soul* (New York: Herder and Herder, 1971), p. 39.

118. Edward Schillebeeckx, *Ministry*, translated by John Bowden (New York: Crossroads, 1981), pp. 5–74.

119. Dewey, *Moral Principles in Education*, pp. 15–16.

120. Anent this point, Dewey adds: "There is no discipline in the world so severe as the discipline of experience subjected to the tests of intelligent development and direction." Dewey, *Experience and Education*, p. 114.

121. John Dewey, *Democracy and Education* (New York: Macmillan, 1916), p. 417.

122. Albert McClellan, "Equipping in Servanthood," in John Hendrix and Lloyd Householder, editors, *The Equipping of Disciples* (Nashville, Tenn.: Broadman, 1977), pp. 150–151.

123. Isaiah 42–55.

124. Isaiah 50:4–5.

125. Schillebeeckx, *Ministry*, p. 70.

126. John 13:12–17.

127. 1 Corinthians 12:4–11.

128. Senvice is of the essence of the clergy. The higher the rank, the more the cleric is supposed to be of service. In Roman Catholicism, one of the pope's most important titles is "the servant of the servants of God." "All offices and ministries [of the Church] are for the sake of service, never for domination." Richard P. McBrien, *Catholicism*, volume II (Minneapolis, Minn.: Winston, 1980), p. 23, italics deleted.

129. André Lemaire, *Ministry in the Chruch*, translated by C. W. Danes (London: SPCK, 1974), pp. 3–41.

130. For a further development of this point, see James Michael Lee, *The Flow of Religious Instruction* (Birmingham, Ala.: Religious Education Press, 1973), pp. 225–229.

131. Henri J. M. Nouwen, *Creative Ministry* (Garden City, N.Y.: Doubleday, 1971), pp. 2–20.

132. Robert K. Greenleaf, *Teacher as Servant* (New York: Paulist, 1979), pp. 15–16, 206–207.

133. For an analysis of ritual in secular society, see Algernon D. Black, *Without Burnt Offerings: Ceremonies of Humanism* (New York: Viking, 1974).

134. Hans Moll, *Identity and the Sacred* (New York: Free Press, 1976), pp. 244–245.

135. E. H. Erikson, "Ontogeny of Ritualization in Man," in *Philosophical Transactions of the Royal Society of London*, series B, volume CCLI, 1966, pp. 337–350.

136. Roger Grainger, *The Language of the Rite* (London: Darton, Longman, and Todd, 1974), pp. 4–5.

137. Victor Turner, "Religion in Current Cultural Anthropology,"

in Mircea Eliade and David Tracy, editors, *What is Religion?* (New York: Seabury, 1980), pp. 68–71.

138. Writing of key rituals in the life of the Zinacantans of Mexico, Vogt states: "Rituals of reversal not only serve to express the society's concept of calendar time, but to 'rewire' the crucial connections in the social structure by providing symbolic statements of traditional social imperatives and basic imperatives of the Zinacantan worldview." For the entire article, see Evon Z. Vogt, "Rituals of Reversal as a Means of Rewiring Social Structure," in Agehananda Bharati, editor, *The Realm of the Extra-Human* (The Hague: Mouton, 1976), pp. 201–211.

139. Theodor Klauser, *A Short History of the Western Liturgy*, translated by John Halliburton (London: Oxford University Press, 1969), pp. 5–44.

140. Lee, "The Authentic Source of Religious Instruction," p. 196.

141. The term cheap grace was made famous by a Protestant theologian, Dietrich Bonhoeffer, who defined it as "the justification of sin without the justification of the sinner. Grace alone does everything . . . and so everything can remain as it was before." Dietrich Bonhoeffer, *The Cost of Discipleship*, 2d edition, translated by Reginald H. Fuller (New York: Macmillan, 1963), p. 35.

142. On this point, see John S. Dunne, *The Reasons of the Heart* (Notre Dame, Ind.: University of Notre Dame Press, 1978), pp. 93–129.

143. Georgia Harkness, *Disciplines of the Christian Life* (Richmond, Va.: Knox, 1967), pp. 31–36.

144. Pitirim A. Sorokin, *The Crisis of Our Age* (New York: Dutton, 1941).

145. Neil J. Smelser, "Vicissitudes of Work and Love in Anglo-American Society," in Neil J. Smelser and Erik H. Erikson, editors, *Themes of Work and Love in Adulthood* (Cambridge, Mass.: Harvard University Press, 1980), p. 105.

146. Dewey, *Democracy and Education*, p. 157.

147. Urban T. Holmes, *Ministry and Imagination* (New York: Seabury, 1976), p. 76.

148. 1 Corinthians 12:1–27. See also Friederich Jürgenmeier, *The Mystical Body of Christ as the Basic Principle of the Spiritual Life*, translated by Harriet G. Strauss (New York: Sheed and Ward, 1954), p. 27.

149. Max Thurian, *Modern Man and the Spiritual Life* (New York: Association, 1963), pp. 36–39.

150. Dewey, *Democracy and Education*, pp. 14–22, 28–34, 55–62.

151. Loren Eiseley characterizes the contributions of Teilhard in this way: "A soaring mind capable of reading in the stony hieroglyphs of nature a spiritual message denied to lesser men."

152. Pierre Teilhard de Chardin, *The Phenomenon of Man*, translated by Bernard Wall et al. (New York: Harper & Row, 1959), p. 258.

153. Pierre Teilhard de Chardin, *Hymn of the Universe*, translated by Gerald Vann (New York: Harper & Row, 1965), p. 93.

154. Teilhard de Chardin, *The Phenomenon of Man*, pp. 164–180.

155. Pierre Teilhard de Chardin, "My Universe," in Ewert Cousins, editor, *Process Theology* (New York: Newman, 1971), pp. 252–253.

156. Teilhard de Chardin, *The Phenomenon of Man*, p. 262, italics deleted, spelling Americanized.

157. Ibid., p. 259.

158. Ibid., p. 262, italics deleted, comma added, spelling Americanized.

159. Pierre Teilhard de Chardin, *Activation of Energy*, translated by René Hague (London: Collins, 1963), p. 149, italics deleted, spelling Americanized, one upper case rendered into lower case.

160. Teilhard de Chardin, *The Phenomenon of Man*, p. 272.

161. Teilhard de Chardin, *Hymn of the Universe*, pp. 113–114.

162. Pierre Teilhard de Chardin, *The Divine Milieu*, translated by Bernard Wall (New York: Harper & Row, 1969), pp. 101–102.

163. Pierre Teilhard de Chardin, *The Future of Man*, translated by Norman Denny (New York: Harper & Row, 1964), p. 35.

164. Teilhard de Chardin, *The Divine Milieu*, pp. 69–76.

165. Teilhard de Chardin, *Hymn of the Universe*, p. 70.

166. Teilhard de Chardin, *The Divine Milieu*, p. 36.

167. Teilhard de Chardin, *The Phenomenon of Man*, p. 310.

168. Teilhard de Chardin, *The Divine Milieu*, p. 25.

169. Teilhard de Chardin, *The Phenomenon of Man*, p. 265.

170. "Interest," in *A New Dictionary on Historical Principles* . . . , volume V, part II, pp. 392–394.

171. John Dewey, *Interest and Effort in Education* (Boston: Houghton Mifflin, 1913), p. 14.

172. Dewey, *Experience and Education*, pp. 19–20; John Dewey, "Criticisms, Wise and Otherwise, on Modern Child Study," in *National Education Association, Addresses and Proceedings* (Washington, D.C.: The Association, 1897), pp. 867–868.

173. Dewey, *Democracy and Education*, pp. 148–149.

174. Dewey, *Interest and Effort in Education*, pp. 11–12.

175. Dewey, *Democracy and Education*, p. 150.

176. When treating of other-control, and in the following section, I am restricting my analysis to that aversive kind of control deliberately exercised by another individual. I am excluding the countless unintentional activities of control engaged in by other persons. I am also excluding the control features which B. F. Skinner properly contends are inherent characteristics of every interactive environment. See B. F. Skinner, *Beyond Freedom and Dignity* (New York: Knopf, 1971), pp. 18–43; B. F. Skinner, *About Behaviorism* (New York: Vantage, 1974), pp. 208–227.

177. P. S. Wilson, *Interest and Discipline in Education* (London: Routledge and Kegan Paul, 1971), pp. 77–80.

178. George R. Wesley, *Spare the Rod* (Washington, D.C.: University Press of America, 1979), p. 16.

179. Gary C. Walters and Joan E. Grusec, *Punishment* (San Francisco, Calif.: Freeman, 1977), p. 13.

180. See, for example, R. R. Hutchinson, "By-Products of Aversive Control," in Werner Honig and J. E. R. Staddon, editors, *Handbook of Operant Behavior* (Englewood Cliffs, N.J.: Prentice-Hall, 1977), pp. 415–431.

181. Knud S. Larsen, *Aggression: Myths and Models* (Chicago: Nelson-Hall, 1976), pp. 4–7.

182. B. F. Skinner, *Science and Human Behavior* (New York: Free Press, 1953), p. 190.

183. O. Hobart Mowrer, "Psychoneurotic Defenses (Including Deception) as Punishment-Avoidance Strategies," in Byron A. Campbell and Russell M. Church, editors, *Punishment and Aversive Behavior* (New York: Appleton-Century-Crofts, 1969), pp. 449–466.

184. Paul Brown and Rogers Elliott, "Control of Aggression in a Nursery School Class," in Edwin I. Megarge and Jack E. Hokanson, editors, *The Dynamics of Aggression* (New York: Harper & Row, 1970), p. 101.

185. Wilson, *Interest and Discipline in Education*, p. 95.

186. For a short treatment of process as content, see James Michael Lee, "Process Content in Religious Instruction," in Iris V. Cully and Kendig Brubaker Cully, editors, *Process and Relationship* (Birmingham, Ala.: Religious Education Press, 1978), pp. 22–30.

187. Walters and Grusec, *Punishment*, p. 176.

188. Jacob S. Kounin and Paul V. Gump, "The Comparative Influences of Punitive and Nonpunitive Teachers upon Children's Conceptions of Misconduct," in *Journal of Educational Psychology* LII (February, 1961), p. 49.

189. Walters and Grusec, *Punishment*, pp. 176–177.

190. Lee, *Principles and Methods of Secondary Education*, pp. 566–568.

191. In *The Flow of Religious Instruction* I develop a basic and comprehensive taxonomy of the teaching act. Ranging from the most general to the most specific, the elements of this taxonomy are as follows: approach, style, strategy, method, technique, and step. *Approach* is the primary, fundamental orientation of the teaching-learning act, e.g., social-science approach, philosophical approach. *Style* is the basic overall pattern or mode which serves as the indicator of the specific direction which the activities of the teaching-learning act will take, e.g., teacher-centered versus learner-centered. *Strategy* is the comprehensive, systematized, concrete scaffolding on, around, and through which are placed the more specific methods and techniques of the teaching-learning act, e.g., transmission strategy, discovery strategy, structured-learning-situation strategy. *Method* is the internally ordered set of pedagogical procedures which are arranged in discrete generalized bodies or classes, e.g., problem-solving, individualized teaching. *Technique* is the concrete, tangible, and specific way in which a pedagogical event is structured in a given teaching-learning situation, e.g., lecturing, role-playing, project. *Step* is the highly specific behavior unit or behavior sequence through which the here-and-now instructional practice is enacted, e.g., giving praise, smiling. I contend that teaching of all kinds can only be effective when there is internal consistency and harmony of all six elements in the taxonomy of the instructional process. For example, the technique of role-playing will not be really effective if it is conjoined to a teacher-centered style or a transmission strategy. See Lee, *The Flow of Religious Instruction*, pp. 28–38.

192. For an advocacy of the structured-learning-situation strategy, see ibid., pp. 201–202, 207–208, 234–237, 243–247; also James Michael Lee, "The *Teaching* of Religion," in James Michael Lee and Patrick C. Rooney, editors, *Toward a Future for Religious Education* (Dayton, Ohio: Pflaum, 1970), pp. 59–64.

193. Lee, *The Flow of Religious Instruction*, p. 81.

194. Skinner, *Science and Human Behavior*, p. 192.

195. Matthew 26:52.

196. For a treatment of significant learning, see Carl R. Rogers, *Freedom to Learn* (Columbus, Ohio: Merrill, 1969), pp. 158–159.

197. Dewey, *Democracy and Education*, p. 59.

198. Ibid., pp. 89–90.

199. George S. Counts, *Dare the School Build a New Social Order?* (New York: Day, 1932), p. 4. Sources for the other ideas used in this treatment of Counts come from this same book, specifically, in order, pp. 15–16, 37, 29–30, 19.

200. Some philosophers of education contend that reconstructionism is not so much a formally new philosophy of education as a variant of progressivism.

201. Theodore Brameld, *Patterns of Educational Philosophy* (New York: Holt, Rinehart, and Winston, 1971), pp. 346–563; Theodore Brameld, *Education as Power* (New York: Holt, Rinehart, and Winston, 1965), pp. 31–40.

202. James Loder criticizes both Lawrence Kohlberg and James Fowler for their alleged exclusion of negation in their respective maps of moral development and faith development. James E. Loder, "Negation and Transformation: A Study in Theology and Human Development," in Christianne Brusselmanns and James A. O'Donohoe, convenors, *Toward Moral and Religious Maturity* (Morristown, N.J.: Silver Burdett, 1980), p. 189.

203. Richard J. Foster, *Celebration of Discipline* (New York: Harper & Row, 1978), pp. 54–55.

204. Loder, "Negation and Transformation: A Study in Theology and Human Development," pp. 178–180.

205. Mircea Eliade, *Myth and Reality*, translated by Willard R. Trask (New York: Harper & Row, 1963), pp. 39–53.

206. Aisha Bawany Wakf, *Islam: An Introduction* (Karachi: n.p., n.d.), p. 2.

207. 2 Corinthians 5:17.

208. Ephesians 4:24.

209. Galatians 2:20.

210. The uphill struggle to attain total self-abandonment to God is detailed in such classics of spirituality as J. P. De Gaussade, *Self-Abandonment to Divine Providence*, translated by Algar Thorold (Springfield, Ill.: Templegate, 1959).

211. Teilhard de Chardin, *The Divine Milieu*, p. 29.

CHAPTER 8

Discipline Into Tomorrow:

A Concluding Statement

The end result of the discipline process for the children and youth who will inherit the American culture is the development within them of a social conscience. In essence then, the moral foundation of the culture must be transmitted to its inheritors during their developing years in such a way as to insure that they become productive, contributing members of a democratic society. Furthermore, it has been our contention that the discipline process described in detail will develop the moral aspects of (1) a work ethic, (2) perseverance, (3) constructive self-criticism, (4) cooperation, and (5) responsibility toward family. In the final analysis, the social order itself and the individual's quality of conduct are equally important. When a culture shows an over-dramatization of either the importance of the individual or of the group, the end result is the degeneration of both the culture and the individual.

Parents and teachers have the responsibility to prepare youth by assisting them in becoming worthy members of society; therefore discipline should be in harmony with natural development and must be designed and enacted to sustain and further the moral traits of the culture and a social efficiency within the developing youth. A productive, fulfilling, moral life results from being fully and adequately what one is capable of becoming by means of living and working with others. When this responsibil-

243

ity is not fulfilled and youth do not acquire their rightful social inheritance, the necessary balance of contributing to as well as receiving from life with others cannot exist. Thus, there results the identity extremes of pessimistic individualism or pervasive materialism. In either case, the widening and deepening of a conscious social life and the true realization of meanings that come from a conscious social life are lost.

Social problems such as dropping productivity, increasing welfare rolls, disrespect for others, and increasing crime rates are the end result of an educational framework (formal and informal, school and home) which has failed to develop people for their culture. When these symptoms emerge, too often an idealized past becomes the solace and hope for a better tomorrow. However, longing for a reminiscent social spirit by attempting the re-enactment of a former social order inevitably fails to solve present-day concerns.

Failure in the preparation for life can rarely be overcome by success in life, for the moral or immoral foundations by which one lives are formed too soundly. Today's preparation of the young calls for a process to deal with today's social realities. Discipline of the young provides parents and teachers with the opportunity to improve society, and it is the means by which the American culture can prepare its inheritors for greatness in the twenty-first century.

Appendix*

The experimental studies of Lawrence Kohlberg, based on earlier work of Dewey, Durkheim, and Piaget, suggest that in all cultures the development of moral judgment passes through three levels which include six invariantly sequenced stages:

Preconventional Level

At this level the child is responsive to such rules and labels as good or bad and right or wrong. He interprets these labels in purely physical or hedonistic terms: If he is bad, he is punished; if he is good, he is rewarded. He also interprets the labels in terms of the physical power of those who enunciate them—parents, teachers, and other adults. The level comprises the following two stages:

Stage 1: Punishment and Obedience Orientation. The physical consequences of action determine its goodness or badness regard-

Reference Note: A wealth of information exists which deals with Lawrence Kohlberg's moral-developmental theory. The condensation used above has been extensively employed since Kohlberg first summarized his moral-developmental stages in "The Claim to Moral Adequacy of a Highest Stage of Moral Judgment," which appeared in *Journal of Philosophy* LXX (October 25, 1973), pp. 630–646.

less of the human meaning or value of these consequences. Avoidance of punishment and unquestioning deference to power are valued in their own right, not in terms of respect for an underlying moral order supported by punishment and authority, the latter being stage 4.

Stage 2: Instrumental Relativist Orientation. Right action consists of that which instrumentally satisfies one's own needs and occasionally the needs of others. Human relations are viewed in terms similar to those of the marketplace. Elements of fairness, of reciprocity and equal sharing are present, but they are always interpreted in a pragmatic way. Reciprocity is a matter of "you scratch my back and I'll scratch yours," not of loyalty, gratitude, or justice.

Conventional Level

At this level, maintaining the expectations of the individual's family, group, or nation is perceived as valuable in its own right, regardless of immediate and obvious consequences. The attitude is one not only of conformity to the social order but of loyalty to it, of actively maintaining, supporting, and justifying the order, and of identifying with the persons or group involved in it. This level comprises the following two stages:

Stage 3: Interpersonal Concordance or "Good boy—Nice girl" Orientation. Good behavior is that which pleases or helps others and is approved by them. There is much conformity to stereotypical images of what is majority or "natural" behavior. Behavior is frequently judged by intention: "He means well" becomes important, and one earns approval by "being nice."

Stage 4: "Law and Order" Orientation. Authority, fixed rules and the maintenance of the social order are valued. Right behavior consists of doing one's duty, showing respect for authority, and maintaining the social order for its own sake.

Postconventional Level

At this level there is a clear effort to reach a personal definition of moral values—to define principles that have validity and application apart from the authority of groups or persons and apart from the individual's own identification with these groups. This level also has two stages:

Stage 5: Social-Contract Legalistic Orientation. Generally, this stage has utilitarian overtones. Right action tends to be defined in terms of general individual rights and in terms of standards that have been critically examined and agreed upon by the whole society. There is a clear awareness of the importance of personal values and opinions and a corresponding emphasis on procedural rules for reaching consensus. Other than that which is constitutionally and democratically agreed upon, right is a matter of personal values and opinion. The result is an emphasis both upon the "legal point of view" and upon the possibility of making rationally and socially desirable changes in the law, rather than freezing it as in the "law and order" stage 4. Outside the legal realm, free argument is the binding element of obligation. This is the "official" morality of the U.S. government and the Constitution.

Stage 6: Universal Ethical Principle Orientation. Right is defined by the conscience in accord with self-chosen ethical principles, which in turn are based on logical comprehensiveness, universality, and consistency. . . . At heart, these are universal principles of justice, of the reciprocity and equality of human rights, and/or respect for the dignity of human beings as individual persons.

Passage through these stages can be accelerated, slowed, or even brought to a halt, depending on the interaction of the individual's ways of mediating or structuring his experience and the structural features of the environment itself. It also depends upon a reorganization of cognitive-affective elements which can be achieved only by the individual. This reorganization can be stimulated by external agents, but it cannot be controlled by them. Passage from lower to higher levels allows the individual to achieve a more stable equilibrium and to use his moral judgments to control his behavior and thus handle moral problems in a more efficient and consistent manner.

Index of Names

Index of Subjects

Other Important Books from Religious Education Press

MORAL DEVELOPMENT, MORAL EDUCATION, AND KOHLBERG
edited by *Brenda Munsey*

A seminal volume on the interrelated topics of moral development, moral education, and religious education. An interdisciplinary treatment from the perspectives of religious education, philosophy, psychology, and general education. These original essays bring together some of the most important scholars in North America, Europe, and Israel. ISBN 0-89135-020-9

CONSCIENCE: DEVELOPMENT AND SELF-TRANSCENDENCE
by *Walter E. Conn*

A pioneering new look at the structure and growth of conscience from the interdisciplinary perspectives of theology, ethics, and psychology. Major themes include conscience as the basic form which personal authenticity takes, and conscience as flourishing in self-giving love. ISBN 0-89135-025-X

THE RELIGIOUS EDUCATION OF PRESCHOOL CHILDREN
by *Lucie W. Barber*

A holistic approach embracing all areas of the child's religious life—cognitive, affective, and lifestyle. The most significant work to date on the religious education of preschool children in home and church. ISBN 0-89135-026-8

RELIGIOUS EDUCATION MINISTRY WITH YOUTH
edited by *D. Campbell Wyckoff and Don Richter*

This multifaceted volume provides the religious educator of youth with solid empirical data on the psychological and religious development of youth together with the necessary theoretical information. ISBN 0-89135-030-6

CELEBRATING THE SECOND YEAR OF LIFE:
A PARENT'S GUIDE FOR A HAPPY CHILD
by *Lucie W. Barber*

A practical guide for religious parenting and educating. This book is organized around psychologically-proven ways in which parents and members of the helping professions can successfully develop five basic capacities in the child *and* in themselves: trust and faith; a positive self-image; self-confidence and independence; a joy for learning; the ability to associate with others happily.
ISBN 0-89135-015-2

THE SHAPE OF RELIGIOUS EDUCATION
by *James Michael Lee*

No one can discuss contemporary religious education meaningfully unless he or she has read this book. Widely acclaimed as a classic in the field. ISBN 0-89135-000-4

THE FLOW OF RELIGIOUS EDUCATION
by *James Michael Lee*

A serious in-depth look at the nature and structure of the religion teaching process. This volume provides that kind of solid and systematic framework so necessary for the effective *teaching* of religion. A major work. ISBN 0-89135-001-2

THE BIG LITTLE SCHOOL, second edition revised and enlarged
by *Robert W. Lynn and Elliott Wright*

This classic history of the American Sunday School in a revised and updated form. A superb and delightful analysis of how the American Protestant Church perceived its educational mission throughout the years, and how it actually went about bringing religion to the hearts and minds of the taught as well as the teachers.
ISBN 0-89135-021-7

CAN CHRISTIANS BE EDUCATED?
by *Morton Kelsey*

An examination from the standpoint of depth psychology some of the most critical concerns in contemporary religious education, including education for love, education for spiritual wholeness, and education for positive emotional values. This volume integrates religious education with growth in the religion teacher's own personal spirituality. ISBN 0-89135-008-X

RELIGIOUS EDUCATION IN A PSYCHOLOGICAL KEY
by *John H. Peatling*
A perceptive look at religious education from a psychological perspective. This volume shows how psychology can empower religious education to enrich the spiritual lives of learners. A major feature of this book is the penetrating way in which it reveals the religious dimension of psychology and the psychological dimension of religion. ISBN 0-89135-027-6

CREATIVE CONFLICT IN RELIGIOUS EDUCATION AND CHURCH ADMINISTRATION
by *Donald E. Bossart*
A stimulating volume centering around two major themes: the myriad possibilities for growth inherent in all conflict, and the specific procedures which can be used in religious settings to bring out the productive potential in conflict. This interdisciplinary volume deals with the theological dynamics, psychological dynamics, sociological dynamics, and educational dynamics of conflict. ISBN 0-89135-048-9

IMPROVING CHURCH EDUCATION
by *H. W. Byrne*
A bible-centered approach to effective Christian education ministry. Written from an evangelical Protestant perspective, this comprehensive book explains practical and workable models for successful total church education, including models for grouping people for effective teaching and learning, models for improved instructional space, models for enriched teaching, and models for improved staffing. ISBN 0-89135-017-9

RELIGIOUS EDUCATION AND THEOLOGY
edited by *Norma H. Thompson*
Provides a wide spectrum of contrasting views on the intrinsic connection of religious education with theology. ISBN 0-89135-029-2